AF519588

A POST-COPYRIGHT WORLD

A POST-COPYRIGHT WORLD

NANDITA SAIKIA

SERIALS PUBLICATIONS
NEW DELHI (INDIA)

© Nandita Saikia

First Published – 2009

ISBN: 978-81-8387-290-4

All rights reserved with the Publisher, including the right to translate or reproduce this book or parts there of except for brief quotations in critical articles or reviews.

Published by

SERIALS PUBLICATIONS
4800/24, 1st Floor, Ansari Road
Darya Ganj, New Delhi-110002 (India)
Phone : 23245225. Fax : 91-11-23272135
E-mail: serials@satyam.net.in

CONTENTS

Introduction *vii*

PART I
The Evolution of Copyright

1. Back in the Day 1
2. Copyright as a Natural Right 10
3. The Indian Story 15

PART II
Snapshots of the Law

4. The Indian Copyright Act, 1957 30
5. Contracts 81

PART III
The Law at Work

6. Regulation by Fear 88
7. Copyrightability 94
8. Literary Squabbles 104
9. Academia and Education 113
10. Perpetual Youth and Perpetual Copyright 117
11. The Supremacy of the Written Word 120

12. Comments on Blogs 123
13. Advertisements 131
14. Online Privacy 136
15. What You Wear 140
16. Hardly Music to the Ears 145

PART IV
Beyond Copyright

17. Copyright and Access to the Law 151
18. The Permission Culture 180
19. New Business Models 189
20. The Reality and the Rhetoric 197

References 207

Appendix 208

INTRODUCTION

This is a quasi-legal book which tries to explore the idea of copyright as a concept (as opposed to copyright as a law). It isn't a standard text on copyright which explicates the intricacies of the law and claims to be authoritative. Instead, focusing on the idea that traditional copyright laws as we know them are not particularly well suited to the world in which we live, all this book does is touch on the basic principles of copyright law from an Indian perspective.

> The characterization of the statutory
> copyright as an author's copyright, however, is one
> of the great canards of history.
> — Lyman Ray Patterson

A few years ago, IBM ran a series of advertisements with the blurb: *The Future is Open*. That assertion albeit perhaps not in exactly the same context as IBM meant it could well prove to be prophetic. We live in a world which has been placing more and more importance on such things as access to information, openness, transparency, and sharing. Copyright law does very little to help any of those things.

In fact, looked at from a historical perspective, copyright law has much less to do with protecting the creators of artistic works than it has to do with protecting traders who sell those works. It isn't so much a system based on lofty moral ideals than the foundation of a business model which helps distributors, printers and others of their ilk make money.

As far as that goes, one can't argue against the right of copyright-dependent industries to make money — that's a right which everyone has assuming they do it legally. However, with the arrival of the Internet and changing social values, there will probably come a time when a large fraction of the world's people do not see 'piracy' as a mortal sin. Copyright will not disappear but it will become less important and less enforceable, in all probability to the great disgruntlement of the publishing and recording industry.

Once this happens — and it has already begun to happen — there will necessarily have to be new business models brought into existence which enable artists to be remunerated without the aid of middlemen (otherwise known as publishers and distributors). This book tries to look at what a post-copyright world would look like keeping in mind that even in such a world, copyright is unlikely to immediately become irrelevant.

Any part of the text of this book may be freely used and modified by anyone provided it is attributed and shared under the same terms. In writing this book, I have included some material from *LawMatters.in* as well as material written by Karl Fogel, President of QuestionCopyright.org on the history of copyright, new business models, and the rhetoric of the copyright industry, and by James Grimmelmann, Associate Professor at the New York Law School on access to the law. I am very grateful to both James and Karl for having made their work available.

The content of this book, as is probably evident by now, is not impartial: it leans away from copyright. However, although it questions copyright, it should not be construed as encouraging or suggesting that the copyright in any work be violated. It is not legal advice and it should not, under any circumstances, be considered to be such. The information is provided on an as-is basis and may not be complete, accurate or up-to-date. No action should be taken or omitted on the basis of its contents. And if such action is taken or omitted, those who have been involved in writing or publishing this book will not be responsible or liable.

Nandita Saikia

PART I

The Evolution of Copyright

1

BACK IN THE DAY

In recent years, the most commonly seen manifestation of copyright one has tended to come across is of the recording industry suing randomly chosen file sharers and, if one lives in a country like India, of copyright being infringed ad infinitum with a plethora of 'pirated' CDs, VCDs, DVDs and books available at every random street corner. Although much of the world has been disgusted and shocked by the way in which the recording industry has gone about protecting its copyrights, it sympathizes with the stereotypical impoverished artist whom copyright supposedly protects. There is one group of people not shocked by the record industry's policy of suing randomly chosen file sharers though: historians of copyright, as Karl Fogel[1] points out.

Karl is the President of QuestionCopyright.org, an organization which, as its name suggests, focuses on questioning the idea that copyright is necessary to promote creative expression. Historians of copyright, he says, already know what everyone else is slowly finding out: that copyright was never about paying artists for their work, and that far from being designed to support creators, copyright was designed by and for distributors — that is, publishers, which today includes record companies. A close look at history shows that copyright has never been a major factor in allowing creativity to flourish. Copyright is an outgrowth of the privatization of government censorship in sixteenth-century England. There was no uprising of authors suddenly demanding the right to prevent other people from copying their works; far from viewing copying as theft, authors generally regarded it as flattery. The bulk of creative work has always depended, then and now, on a diversity of funding sources such as commissions, teaching jobs, grants or stipends, and patronage. The introduction of copyright did not change this situation. What it did was allow a particular business model — mass pressings with centralized distribution — to make a few lucky works available to a wider audience, at considerable profit to the distributors.

The first copyright law was a censorship law. It had nothing to do with protecting the rights of authors, or encouraging them to produce new works. Authors' rights were in no danger in sixteenth-century England, and the recent arrival of the printing press (the world's first copying machine) was, if anything, energizing to writers. So energizing, in fact, was it that the English government grew concerned about too many works being produced, not too few. The new technology was making seditious reading material widely available for the first time, and the government urgently needed to control the flood of printed matter, censorship being as legitimate an administrative function then as building roads.

The method the government chose was to establish a guild of private-sector censors, the London Company of Stationers, whose profits would depend on how well they performed their function. The Stationers were granted a royal monopoly over all printing in England, over old works as well as new, in return for keeping a strict eye on what was printed. Their charter gave them not only exclusive right to print, but also the right to search out and confiscate unauthorized presses and books, and even to burn illegally printed books. No book could be printed until it was entered in the Company's Register, and no work could be added to the Register until it had passed the Crown's censor, or had been self-censored by the Stationers. The Company of Stationers became, in effect, the government's private, for-profit information police force. [2]

The system was quite openly designed to serve booksellers and the government, not authors. New books were entered in the Company's Register under a Company member's name, not the author's name. By convention, the member who registered the entry held the 'copyright', the exclusive right to publish that book, over other members of the Company, and the Company's Court of Assistants resolved infringement disputes. [3]

This was not simply the latest manifestation of some pre-existing form of copyright. It was not as though authors had formerly had copyrights, which were then taken away and given to the Stationers. The Stationers' right was a new right, though one based on a long tradition of granting monopolies to guilds as a means of control. Before this moment, copyright — that is, a privately held, generic right to prevent others from copying — did not exist. People routinely printed works they admired when they had the chance, an activity which was responsible for the survival of many of those works to the present day. One could, of course, be enjoined from distributing a specific document because of its potentially libelous effect, or because it was a private communication, or because the government considered it dangerous and seditious. But those were all reasons that had to do with public safety or damage to reputation, not with the ownership of property. There had also been, in some cases, special privileges (then called 'patents') allowing exclusive printing of certain types of books. But until the Company of Stationers came into existence, there had not been a blanket injunction against printing in general, nor a conception of copyright as a legal property that could be owned by a private party.

For about a century and a third, this partnership worked well for the government and for the Stationers. The Stationers profited from their monopoly, and through the Stationers, the government exercised control over the spread of information. The English Civil War, however, considerably changed the political landscape of the country and around the end of the seventeenth century, owing to large political changes, the government relaxed its censorship policies, and allowed the

Stationers' monopoly to expire. This meant that printing would return to its former anarchical state, and was of course a direct economic threat to the members of the Company of Stationers, accustomed as they were to having exclusive license to manufacture books. Dissolution of the monopoly might have been good news for long-suppressed authors and independent printers, but it spelled disaster for the Stationers, and they quickly crafted a strategy to retain their position in the newly liberal political climate.

The Stationers based their strategy on a crucial realization, one that has stayed with publishing conglomerates ever since: authors do not have the means to distribute their own works. Writing a book requires only pen, paper, and time. But distributing a book requires printing presses, transportation networks, and an up-front investment in materials and typesetting. Thus, the Stationers reasoned, people who write would always need a publisher's cooperation to make their work generally available. Their strategy used this fact to maximum advantage. They went before Parliament and offered the then-novel argument that authors had a natural and inherent right of ownership in what they wrote, and that furthermore, such ownership could be transferred to other parties by contract, like any other form of property.

Their argument succeeded in persuading Parliament. The Stationers had managed to avoid the odium of censorship, as the new copyrights would originate with the author, but they knew that authors would have little choice but to sign those rights back over to a publisher for distribution. There was some judicial and political wrangling over the details, but in the end both halves of the Stationers' argument survived essentially intact, and became part of English statutory law. The first recognizably modern copyright, the Statute of Anne, was passed in 1709 and took effect in 1710.

The Statute of Anne — which conferred copyright protection for twenty-one years after the first publication of a work — is often held up by champions of copyright as the moment when authors were finally given the protection they had long deserved. Even today, it continues to be referenced both in legal arguments and in press releases from the publishing industry. But to interpret the enactment of the statute as an authors' victory flies in the face of both common sense and historical fact. Authors, having never had copyright, saw no reason to suddenly demand the rather paradoxical power to prevent the spread of their own works, and did not do so. The only people threatened by the dissolution of the Stationers' monopoly were the Stationers themselves, and the Statute of Anne was the direct result of their lobbying and campaigning. In the memorable words of the contemporary Lord Camden, the Stationers ". . . came up to Parliament in the form of petitioners, with tears in their eyes, hopeless and forlorn; they brought with them their wives and children to excite compassion, and induce Parliament to grant them a statutory security."[4] To make their argument more palatable, they had proposed that copyright would originate with the author, as a form of property that could be sold to anyone — anticipating, correctly, that it would most often be sold to a printer.

This proposal was a shrewd tactical move, because one of Parliament's concerns was to prevent the re-establishment of a centralized monopoly in the book trade, with its attendant potential for a renewal of censorship by the Crown. Benjamin Kaplan, Professor of Law emeritus at Harvard University and a respected copyright scholar, describes the Stationers position succinctly:

". . . . The stationers made the case that they could not produce the fragile commodities called books, and thus encourage learned men to write them, without protection against piracy. . . There is an apparent tracing of rights to an ultimate source in the fact of authorship, but before attaching large importance to this we have to note that if printing as a trade was not to be put back into the hands of a few as subject of monopoly — if the statute was indeed to be a kind of 'universal patent' — a [legal] draftsman would naturally be led to express himself in terms of rights in books and hence to initial rights in authors. A draftsman would anyway be aware that rights would usually pass immediately to publishers by assignment, that is, by purchase of the manuscripts as in the past. . . . I think it nearer the truth to say that publishers saw the tactical advantage of putting forward authors' interests together with their own, and this tactic produced some effect on the tone of the statute."[5]

The Statute of Anne, taken in historical context, is the smoking gun of copyright law. In it, we can see the entire apparatus of modern copyright, but in still-undisguised form. There is the notion of copyright as property, yet the property is really intended for publishers, not authors. There is the notion of benefiting society, by encouraging people to write books, but no evidence was offered to show that they would not write books without copyright. Rather, the Stationers' argument was that publishers could not afford to print books without protection from competition, and furthermore that printers could not be depended to reproduce works faithfully if given unfettered freedom to print. The corollary, they implied, was that without the prospect of reliable distribution, authors would produce fewer new works.

Their argument was not unreasonable, given the technology of the time. Making a perfect copy of a printed work required access to the original press and compositor, anyway; if reliable reproduction were to be encouraged, then a single-holder copyright system had a certain logic to it. And the publishers would now be effectively forced to pay authors in return for exclusive printing rights (although in fact the Stationers had sometimes paid authors even before, simply to guarantee the completion and delivery of a work). The authors who succeeded in selling this new right to printers had no particular motivation to complain — and naturally, we don't hear very much about the authors not so favoured. The consolidation of author's copyright probably contributed to the decline of patronage as a source of income for writers,[6] and even allowed some authors, though always a small minority, to support themselves solely from the royalties their publishers shared with them. The fact that a given copyright could only be held by one party at a time also helped prevent the proliferation of divergent variations, a problem that had vexed authors perhaps even more than plagiarism.

But the overall historical record is clear: copyright was designed by distributors, to subsidize distributors, not creators.

This is the secret that today's copyright lobby never dares say aloud, for once it is admitted, the true purpose of subsequent copyright legislation becomes embarrassingly clear. The Statute of Anne was just the beginning. Having granted the premise that copyrights should exist at all, the English government found themselves under pressure to extend copyright terms further and further. In the long legal saga that ensued, what's important is not the particular sequence of laws and verdicts, but the identity of the plaintiffs: they were just the sort of stable, settled business interest capable of sustaining litigation and lobbying over a period of decades — that is, they were publishers, not authors. They had proposed the author's copyright out of economic interest, and only after the crutch of a censorship-based monopoly had been taken away from them. When it became clear that the tactic worked, they lobbied to strengthen copyright.

And this is still the pattern today. Whenever the copyright terms are extended or powers increased, it is the result of pressure from the publishing industry. The lobbyists will sometimes trot out a superstar author or musician as an exhibit, a human face for what is essentially an industry effort, but it's always quite clear what's really going on. All you have to do is look at who's paying the lawyers' fees and lobbyists' bills, and whose names appear in the court dockets — those of publishers.

FOOTNOTES

1. This chapter on the history of copyright has been written by Karl Fogel.
2. These events can be read in any history of copyright. A good online resource regarding their legal implications is 'Copyright And 'The Exclusive Right' Of Authors'
<lawsch. uga. edu/jipl/old/vol1/patterson. html> Journal of Intellectual Property, Vol. 1, No. 1, Fall 1993, by Professor Lyman Ray Patterson, Pope Brock Professor of Law at the University of Georgia and a noted copyright scholar. His description of this earliest copyright is concise and revealing:
The event in the history of Anglo-American copyright that led to the shaping events of the seventeenth and eighteenth centuries was the

Charter of the Stationers' Company granted in 1556 by Philip and Mary. . . . The Charter gave the stationers the power to make 'ordinances, provisions, and statutes' for the governance of 'the art or mistery of [s]tationery,' as well as the power to search out illegal presses and books and things with the power of 'seizing, taking, or burning the foresaid books or things, or any of them printed or to be printed contrary to the form of any statute, act, or proclamation. . . ."

The power to burn offending books was a benefit to the sovereign (a weapon against unlawful publications), and a boon to the stationers (a weapon against competition). The book-burning power thus shows the real motivation for the Charter, to secure the allegiance of the stationers as policemen of the press for the sovereign in an uncertain world.

3. Benjamin Kaplan, 'An Unhurried View of Copyright', Columbia University Press, 1967, pp. 4-5.
4. Kaplan, p. 6.
5. Kaplan, pp.7-9.
6. Steinberg, S H; Five Hundred Years of Printing; Penguin Books, 1955, revised 1961; pp. 218-230

2

COPYRIGHT AS A NATURAL RIGHT

Having once got their rights protected by the Statute of Anne, printers attempted to continue to have their rights protected beyond the term of copyright stipulated by the statute by claiming that copyright — a right which no one had heard of before 1709 — was a natural right; an inherent and inalienable right.

They did successfully manage to argue that a perpetual common law copyright existed in the 1769 case of Millar v. Taylor.[7] It was a case which had nothing to do with the 'starving artist' (in this case, a poet) and, not too surprisingly, involved competition between two printers instead. One of them — Millar — had purchased the publishing rights for 'The Seasons' by James Thomson. After the copyright expired, another printer, Robert Taylor, used Thomson's work in his own publication. Millar went to Court claiming that there existed a perpetual common law copyright, and that that right could be assigned by an author to a printer (which is what he claimed had happened). This meant that after the completion of the term of copyright, the work in which copyright subsisted would not fall into the public domain and that copyright would effectively last for all eternity. Copyright, at this time though, did not include the rights of translation or abridgment.

The Scots, however, did not agree and said so in the case of Hinton v. Donaldson. And later, in the 1774 case of Donaldson v. Beckett,[8] the House of Lords agreed with the Scots and rejected the existence of a perpetual common law copyright. Lord Camden said, "The arguments attempted to be maintained on the side of the respondents, were founded on patents, privileges, Star Chamber decrees, and the bye [sic] laws of the Stationers' Company; all of them the effects of the grossest tyranny and usurpation; the very last places in which I should have dreamt of finding the least trace of the common law of this kingdom; and yet, by a variety of subtle reasoning and metaphysical refinements, have they endeavoured to squeeze out the spirit of the common law from premises in which it could not possibly have existence."[9]

Nonetheless, the idea of 'copyright as a natural right' did not die and has in our times made its way into the Universal Declaration of Human Rights. This means that although copyright, is, without a doubt, the creation of statute, it has been accorded the status of a natural human right in international law — the International Covenant on Economic, Social and Cultural Rights also speaks of authors' rights to the protection of not only the moral but also material i.e. economic interest in their works. Considering that the UDHR and the ICESCR treat copyright as a human right to an extent, one can only suppose that if all else fails in some copyright litigation, one could always say, "My Lord, I further contend that my client has a fundamental, inherent, and inalienable human right as has been recognized by the UDHR and the ICESCR to have his copyright enforced so as not to defeat the ends of justice, equity and good conscience."

Article 27 of the Universal Declaration of Human Rights says that everyone has the right freely to participate in the cultural life of the community, to enjoy the arts and to share in scientific advancement and its benefits. It then goes on to say that everyone has the right to the protection of the moral and material interests resulting from any scientific, literary or artistic production of which he is the author.

The International Covenant on Economic, Social and Cultural Rights is more elaborate. In Article 15, it says that the States recognize the right of everyone to take part in cultural life, to enjoy the benefits of scientific progress and its applications, and, most importantly to the present discussion, to benefit from the protection of the moral and material interests resulting from any scientific, literary or artistic production of which he is the author. The steps to be taken by the States to achieve the full realization of this right are required to include those necessary for the conservation, the development and the diffusion of science and culture. The covenant goes on to say that States undertake to respect the freedom indispensable for scientific research and creative activity, and recognize the benefits to be derived from the encouragement and development of international contacts and co-operation in the scientific and cultural fields.

This is one of the most disturbing rights in the Universal Declaration of Human Rights. The 'right' is in direct conflict with the right to share information freely, and to build on the work of others (that is, to create derivative works, such as translations or abridgements). The latter rights come across as being much more convincing as natural rights! [10]

It's unlikely that anyone would complain if this right was used to protect the moral rights of the individual author but one would probably begrudge corporations seeking to protect their profits the banner of human rights.

Speaking specifically of material rights, there is no way, in a property-based system, to restrict copyrights to individual authors (even if that were a desirable thing, which it probably would not be — it is no better for an individual to tell a person that he cannot make a translation of his book than for a corporation to say so). If copyrights are to have value as property, then they must be saleable; if they are saleable, then they will inevitably accumulate in the hands of organizations that specialize in such accumulation.[11]

It's also hugely unclear how things would operate if an individual author had assigned his copyright. The human rights conventions apply to human beings and not to companies but that doesn't answer what would happen if a company argued that the human's right to the protection of the material interests of his work as an author depended on the application of the covenant to the work even if the human being had assigned some or all of his rights in it.[12]

The problem is in the UDHR's recognition of some alleged natural human right to restrict other people from sharing and using information. This clause probably got in there via an appeal to sympathy for poor, downtrodden authors and other artists, and was viewed more as a non-controversial protection from exploitation than as anything else. And if it merely protected attribution, that's exactly what it would be: protection from exploitation. But by including material as well as moral interests, it does not simply prevent exploitation. By protecting 'material' interests in purely non-material goods, it stops protecting human rights and starts protecting corporate interests.

The right has so far not been brought up in copyright litigation in India and it's doubtful whether it'd be recognized. In the Jolly George case, the Supreme Court held that the signing of a treaty ignites legislative action at home but does not automatically make it a part of the corpus juris of the country.

The Jolly George ruling is no longer strictly followed but the change has been seen in cases which involve non-debatable and far more straightforward human rights such as the payment of compensation to a victim of police brutality and the formulation of guidelines to curb sexual harassment in the workplace. Also, in both these cases, there were no Indian laws which could have been applied so the treaties didn't do much apart from fill lacunae in municipal law.

Another concern about the intellectual property clause in the UDHR is its propaganda value even in countries unaccustomed to taking any UN document seriously. It means that companies based on information monopolies can (and do) point to the UDHR in countries such as the US and say: 'See, the rights we're arguing for are so uncontroversial that they're even in the Universal Declaration of Human Rights!'[13]

India, however, doesn't have a strong tendency to disregard international law (although it really doesn't do too well at the implementation stage) so there might conceivably be legal consequences if one were to stretch one's imagination. The UDHR probably couldn't be used for propaganda though:

to the uneducated, neither one of the terms (UDHR or human rights) would mean anything and to the educated, it would be difficult to reconcile corporate profits with human rights especially since Indians usually think of human rights in terms of the right not to be subjected to such things as violence and discrimination. It'd take a lawyer to be able to do such things as apply a human right to a company without flinching which is why one can only suspect that anti-copyright infringement campaigns in India have focused on saying: 'Piracy is against the law. Kill piracy.'

FOOTNOTES

7. Burr 2303; 98 Eng Rep 201 (1769)
8. 17 Hansard, Parl Hist 990
9. <nationmaster. com/encyclopedia/History-of-copyright-law>
10. This paragraph is an edited comment by Karl Fogel.
11. This paragraph is an edited comment by Karl Fogel.
12. Appeals to Human Rights: The Next Battlefield?: <williampatry. blogspot. com/2008/01/appeals-to-human-rights-next. html>
13. This paragraph is an edited comment by Karl Fogel.

3

THE INDIAN STORY

PRE-BRITISH INDIA

Coming to India,[14] contemporary copyright law has developed gradually over the course of more than a hundred and fifty years. Artists in ancient India, like artists in the rest of the ancient (and, for that matter, medieval world), had no notion of copyright in the contemporary sense of the word. Works were freely shared and if one artist were to copy the work of another, that other artist would in all likelihood have been flattered. At any rate, he would certainly not have rushed to a lawyer to sue for copyright infringement.

Some books in Medieval Europe contained book curses which the pro-copyright lobby now usually point to when they attempt to demonstrate that copyright existed long before the 1709 Statute of Anne. A book curse was a passage in a book which cursed book thieves usually with excommunication, anathema, or damnation. Excommunication was a mild curse since it was reversible in the Middle Ages, anathema involved removing the thief from the sight of both God and the Church, and damnation damned thieves to hell (possibly permanently). Other book curses warned thieves that they would be sentenced to death if they stole a book: they would be sent 'up the ladder and down the rope'. The curses were, however, not about preventing the content in books from being copied: they were about preventing the books themselves from being stolen, or borrowed and not returned.

In the Middle Ages, both in Europe and in the rest of the world, books and scrolls were usually notoriously expensive products: they were copied by hand often on expensive material and illuminated with gold, silver and the powders made of precious stones. Book curses protected not so much the intellectual effort which had gone into writing the text of the book but the book itself as a tangible product.

As far as India is concerned, it isn't easy to speak of copyright in the country during pre-British times simply because no such concept existed in the way in which it is understood today. Indian artists relied on patronage, and some patrons sometimes exacted a form of copyright. Shah Jahan, for example, may well have created his own form of exclusivity contract. He reportedly cut off the thumbs of some of the artisans who worked on the Taj Mahal to ensure that they couldn't produce any other similar work.

The arts in India were, as a general rule, supported by royalty and the aristocracy as well as by other members of the elite. The way in which they were supported varied a great deal and could range from communities contributing to pay artists to do such things as build places of worship to a family being retained from generation to generation by another family to create some form of work such as the biographies of successive kings of a particular dynasty. In addition to this, there were individuals such as the nine gems of the Court of the Mughal Emperor Akbar who were patronised for their exceptional talents. And perhaps, far more commonly, artists were not retained throughout their lives but were commissioned to execute specific pieces of work such as creating a painting or a sculpture.

If at all any form of copyright existed, it certainly wasn't something that was widely prevalent.

THE COMPANY PERIOD

The British first introduced copyright in British India through national legislation in 1847. Prior to that, an imperial copyright enactment, the Literary Copyright Act, had been passed by the British in 1842. However, the 1842 legislation was thought to be inadequate for India, so the 1847 Act was promulgated in India as Act XX of 1847 with the aim of encouraging learning in India.

Under this 1842 Act, books first published in the Great Britain by authors who were residents of British possessions were protected by copyright throughout the British dominions. And copyright was infringed if 'any bookseller or printer, or other person whatsoever, in any part of the United Kingdom of Great Britain and Ireland, in the Isles of Man, Jersey or Guernsey, or in any other part of the British dominions' printed, reprinted or imported a protected book. And under the Indian 1847 Act which had been passed by the Governor General in Council books first published in India were protected by copyright. Under both the Acts of 1842 and 1847, copyright allowed its owners to print and reprint the books it protected.

The 1847 Indian Act was passed a good 137 years after the first copyright law, the Statute of Anne, came into effect in England. One of the interesting features of Indian Copyright Law as a result of this is that it was introduced in India as a mature law. There were no debates in India about whether authors should be granted a copyright at all or about what nature of work copyright should protect. By the time the British introduced copyright law to India, they had already answered those questions, presumably to their own satisfaction.

There was, at this time, the International Copyright Act of 1838 which was later superseded by the Law Relating to International Copyright of 1844 also in existence. The 1844 Act (which protected both books and works of art) did not initially provide for a right of translation. In fact, in Section 18, it categorically said: 'Provided always and be it enacted, That nothing in this act contained shall be construed to prevent the printing, Publication, or Sale of any Translation of any Book the author whereof and his Assigns may be entitled to the Benefit of this Act.' It was later amended in 1852 to provide for a five-year translation right with reference to certain foreign works (specified by Order in Council) following a copyright agreement between France and England.

The copyright law introduced by the British in 1847 was extremely different from that which is seen in India today. Indian copyright law has been amended several times and contemporary law is obviously a result of all those amendments. For one thing, the 1847 copyright law had a much shorter copyright term: under it, copyright was to subsist during the lifetime of the author in addition to subsisting for seven years after his death but in no case could it exist for more than a sum total of forty-two years. The length of time for which copyright protection subsisted was then, across the board, much less than what it is today. And initially, copyright protection did not extend to a variety of works. For example, in its earliest avatar, copyright law did not protect engravings. However, after a campaign in which William Hogarth — famous for such works as 'The Marriage Contract' — was closely involved, engravers were brought within the ambit of copyright protection in 1735.[15] The law gave engravings protection for a term of fourteen years from their first publication. Interestingly, this campaign had much to do with ensuring that printers did not keep all the profits from engravings to themselves causing the starving artists whose rights they supposedly championed to actually starve.

In contemporary Indian copyright law, the seven-year posthumous term was extended to sixty years in the 1990s. By and large, this was due to extensive lobbying by the publishing industry. In some countries, such as the US, copyright terms have even been extended for old works so that works from the 1920s which had come into the public domain in the 1980s are now back to being protected by copyright. There is no conceivable reason why this should be the case: artists who created their works in the 1920s are no longer alive to enjoy royalties. The only persons who can benefit by such extensions of the term of copyright are, by and large, companies and artists' descendents who now own the copyrights concerned. And the much-touted justification for copyright protection is that it is required to sustain artists, not to sustain corporate houses or the grandchildren of artists.

Coming back to the 1847 copyright enactment in India though, the Act recognized copyright infringement in similar terms as modern law. To infringe a copyright, one had to print a work which was protected by copyright for the purposes of sale, hire or exportation. It was enough if an attempt was made to sell, hire or export an unauthorized copy, or if the unauthorized copy was exposed for sale, hire or exportation for the person to be guilty of infringement. A suit was to be instituted not in a District Court but in the 'highest local court exercising original civil jurisdiction', and infringing copies were deemed to belong to the owner of the copyright.

The Act had a provision that is comparable to Section 17 of the Indian Copyright Act, 1957. It said that if works were created for 'any encyclopaedia, review, magazine, periodical work or work published in a series of books or parts' under a contract of service, their copyright would be owned by the 'proprietor, projector, publisher or conductor'. However, unlike in modern law, the creator himself appears to have no stake in the copyright at all — in modern law, the proprietor is the first owner of the copyright in the work only insofar as the copyright relates to the publication of the work in any newspaper, magazine or similar periodical, and even this is subject to contract.

One of the most striking differences though between the copyright law of the 1840s and modern law was that copyright, like a trade mark in today's law, had to be registered with the Home Office to enjoy the benefit of protection against infringement granted by the Act. However, even if it was not registered with the Home Office, the author could sue under laws other than the 1847 Copyright Act.

BRITISH INDIA

The next major wave of change in copyright law in India came in 1914. By this time, it was the British Government and not the East India Company which formed the government in India. There had been discussions[16] for many years before 1914 about the need for copyright reform but nothing was done to reform copyright. The Indian Councils Act of 1861 prohibited the provinces from promulgating local laws on the subject of copyright and at the national level, there were three different systems at play.

The first was the International Copyright regime. The second was British Imperial Law which applied to the Empire and the third was Indian National Law. The three regimes in some ways stifled each other. The British representatives at the international level had limited powers to agree to copyright reforms, and National Law could not be amended till the British had reformed their own domestic law with which Indian law was required to be compatible. Also, unlike various self-governing dominions such as Wales, domestic law not only had to be consistent with British law but also had to meet with the approval of the Secretary of State who had power over the decisions of the Governor-General and the Legislative Council. Nonetheless, the systems didn't create too many problems in terms of application and operation. They either acted independently or cumulatively as the need arose.

The British finally amended their own copyright law in 1911. In the 1911 Act, the term of copyright was life plus fifty years. There was a full translation right and the Act became operative from July 1, 1912. The Act was applicable to the Colonies which had some powers to modify it under Section 27, and it recognized the existence of copyright in every original literary, dramatic, musical and artistic work subject to certain restrictions regarding the place of publication of published works and the nationality of the authors of unpublished work. It defined copyright as the sole right to produce or reproduce a work or any substantial part of it in any material form whatsoever, and the copyright in a work was deemed to be infringed when any person did anything which the owner of the copyright had the sole right to do without his consent.

Copyright was recognized to be a statutory right, and Section 31 of the 1911 Act said that no person was entitled to copyright or any other similar right in any published or unpublished literary, dramatic, musical, or artistic work except under and in accordance with the 1911 Act itself, or any other statutory enactment for the time being in force. However, the Section went on to say that nothing in it was to be construed as abrogating any right or jurisdiction to restrain a breach of trust or confidence.

Following this, Indian copyright law was overhauled in 1914. The 1914 Act did very little more than extend the provisions of 1911 Act to India. It only applied to works first published in British India and comprised a sum total of fifteen sections; today's Indian Copyright Act contains over seventy-nine.

One of the important features of the 1914 Indian law was that the right to translate work into other languages was extremely wide. Section 4 of the Act said: "In the case of works first published in British India, copyright shall be subject to the limitation that the sole right to produce, reproduce, perform or publish a translation of the work shall subsist only for a period of ten years from the date of first publication of the work; provided that if within the said period the author, or any person to whom he has granted permission to do so, publishes a translation of any such work in any language, copyright in such work as regards the sole right to produce, reproduce, perform or publish a translation in that language shall not be subject to the limitation prescribed in this sub-section."

Basically, this meant that once a work was published, for a period of ten years after publication, the author was the only person who had the right to translate it or get it translated. After ten years, anyone could translate it even though the work would still be protected by copyright. However, if during those ten years, the author himself were to translate the work into another language, or get someone else to do so, then even after the ten-year period, no one would be able to translate the work into the language(s) in which it had already been translated by the author or the person he had allowed to translate it.

This can be explained in two ways. One goes back to Macaulay, his infamous 1835 minute on Education and his saying that all the literature of India and Arabia is worth less than a bookshelf of good European literature. Considering that the 'White Mughals'[17] had all but disappeared by 1835, he, and many other Englishmen, may well have believed this at the time. However, it could equally well have been that by 1914, choosing to continue to believe that the Occident was superior to the Orient, implanting the idea that European (and in particular, English) learning was better than Indian learning, and obliquely fortifying the two in legislation was in itself an insidious act of imperialism. This explanation, however, doesn't hold much water since the vast majority of the books expected to have been translated would probably have been works first published in Indian languages and not in English.

The second explanation is far more charitable to the English and is basically that the English truly believed in the White Man's Burden, that they believed that they had a duty to spread learning and educated the 'natives', and that they did what they could to facilitate the educational progress of the country. To this end, through the law, they encouraged as many books as possible to be translated, especially into vernacular languages, so that learning would be as widely disseminated as possible. Considering the history of the translation right in India, this is entirely possible. The 1886 Berne Convention did not confer a full translation right and Indian courts held that among the monopolies conferred by copyright on its owners, a right of translation did not exist under British imperial law.[18] In 1890, the Bombay High Court held that a translation was not a copy because skill, time and labour were employed in creating it and also noted that they were for the use of 'a different class or race of readers' in Munshi Shaik Abdurruhma'n v. Mirza Maomed Shira'zi.[19] Five years later, in the 1895 case of MacMillan v. Shamsul Ulama M Zaka,[20] while hearing a case where the alleged infringement by translation had taken place in Delhi, the Bombay High Court said that it had no jurisdiction to hear the case but that did not stop it from deciding that that translations were not copies. Saying that it was a question of what the law actually said and not what it should have said, Farran J commented, "There is here a conflict of rights and interest; a conflict between the intellectual interests of the persons for whom the translations are intended, and the caprice or possible pecuniary interest of the proprietor of the copyright, if he shall not, or shall, intend to translate the work himself, or cause it to be translated. There is no hardship on him; he can always protect himself by being first in the field with a translation...".

Macmillan was less than amused and approached Clarendon and Oxford University Press for financial help to pursue litigation by filing a suit in Delhi and later, possibly by appealing to the Privy Council. Although OUP was not willing help Macmillan pay legal bills, it did agree to lobby for legislative change. Cambridge University Press joined in the effort too. Obviously, the publishers did not say that they were worried about their profits. Instead, as Markby of OUP put it, OUP's main concern was that it would 'under existing law, be unable to prevent works published in England being translated by incompetent persons'. The practice at the time though, at least as far as some of OUP's publications were concerned, was for would-be translators to ask for permission to translate OUP's books. This permission — although presumably not even necessary — would be readily granted without the payment of licence fees with the requirement that the translations be 'accurate and ungarbled' and that they acknowledge OUP's having granted permission on their title pages. Three copies of the translation were also required to be sent to OUP on publication. So, in effect, the problem of possible incompetence had already been dealt with by allowing for the publication of 'authorized translations'.[21] What had not been dealt with was enabling publishers such as OUP to make money by allowing translations to be made.

Ultimately, the Secretary of State sought a change on behalf of British publishers. However, the Government of India refused to change Indian law on the subject of translations. And when, in 1908, Britain agreed to the inclusion of a full translation right in the revised version of the Berne Convention,[22] which was reflected in the 1911 English Copyright Act, the Government of India circumvented the provision in the 1914 Indian Copyright Act by allowing only a limited translation right for works which were first published in India. It did this by exploiting Section 27 of the 1911 English Copyright Act which allowed it a minimal amount of leeway which it used to avoid recognizing a full translation right.

Whatever the rationale behind allowing only a limited translation right in India for works first published in India may have been, it didn't work too well for authors. In 1956, when the Joint Select Committee of the Indian Parliament recommended that the translation provision be continued, R D Sinha argued that the provision had 'worked to the utter detriment of the authors' and supported his argument by saying:

"Most of the novels by Sarat Chandra Chatterjee were translated in Hindi, while the author was yet alive. The author's novels, in translation sold thousand of copies, but the author did not get a pie out of the sale-proceeds. Something like this happened in the case of Gurudeva (Tagore). Publishers in Hindi and other languages were making good money out of the translations of his works, but the poet, revered by the nation, was in his extremely old age touring the country for money to support the Shanti-Niketan."[23]

The other major change wrought by the 1914 Act was that it introduced criminal sanctions for copyright infringement.[24] This change is far more easily explained in terms of India's colonial legacy and the policies followed by the British in India.

Broadly speaking, the British brought a number of Indian practices such as Sati and widow remarriage within the framework of the legal system they introduced in the country. However, being far more interested in enriching the Empire and not antagonizing Indians by interfering in local socio-religious beliefs than in anything else, they also created a legal chasm between the public and private spheres of life which simply did not exist earlier.[25] An analysis of their laws in India shows that for the most part, the laws were designed to operate in the public sphere and deal with matters such as trade and commerce. They place far more emphasis on property than on freedom, on curtailing violence than on minimizing factors which lead to violence. Seen in this context, it is difficult to be surprised that the 1914 Act treated copyright infringement as a criminal offence.

The 1914 Act was amended more than once before India attained independence in 1947. Nonetheless, it continued to remain in force till the Copyright Act of 1957 came into force on January 24, 1958.

INDEPENDENT INDIA

The 1914 Act did not lay down the best possible copyright regime for India, even according to those who believed in copyright, and there is little evidence that there were many detractors then. In addition to this, it was incompatible with the 1948 Brussels Act of the Berne Convention and the 1952 Universal Copyright Convention. After independence in 1947, India therefore drafted a new copyright law which came into force about ten years after independence.

The 1957 law was far more comprehensive that the 1914 law but being rather shortsighted, it has not really stood the test of time. This has resulted in its being amended several times over the years to do such things as allow for performers' rights and make provisions for advances in technology. It has also been subject to the interpretation of courts which have not always agreed with each other. For example, in the case of Maganlal Savani v. Rupam Pictures (P) Ltd.,[26] the Bombay High Court held that 'exploitation' of copyright includes exploitation by all scientific and technological devices that may be invented in future. The Madras High Court though appeared to have a diametrically opposite opinion when a similar issue had earlier come up before it in Raj Video Vision v. K Mohanakrishnan.[27]

Although the 1957 Indian Act relies heavily on the 1956 English Copyright Act, it "was not in any sense a replication of the English legislative proposals. In this sense, the 1957 Act was the first truly Indian legislation after well over two centuries of the subjection to the 'imperial' law," as Upendra Baxi has observed. The problem was that it was "drafted in ways which make it meaningful only to judges and lawyers and sometimes not even to them. But the fact remains that the country had its own law of copyright for the first time in contemporary history; and, for weal or woe, it represented the law-policy choices made by its independent legislature."[28]

This new Indian law which was formulated with the aid of the Joint Select Committee contained two major changes in Indian copyright law. Firstly, the need to register a copyright to be able to sue for copyright infringement was done away with. Secondly, and probably even more importantly, no provision was made in the new copyright law for the 'gratuitous' supply of books to designated libraries. Instead, the requirement to deliver free copies of published books to national libraries was made into law in a separate statute: the 1954 Delivery of Books and Newspapers (Public Libraries) Act. While this in itself may not seem important, it was the first time when the issues of access to information and the commodification of information were separated in such unequivocal terms. Also, by removing the registration requirement, commodification was, in a way, enhanced since the impediments to suing for the unauthorized use of intellectual property were decreased. Simultaneously, access to information through the provisions of copyright law was decreased.

The commodification of information was further solidified through subsequent amendments to the law. For example, in 1992, the law was changed so that the term for which works were protected by copyright increased by ten years: earlier the term was life plus fifty years after the death of the author of the work; it is now life plus sixty years. Also, infringement of copyright may involve communication of the work whose copyright has been infringed to the public. In 1994, the law was amended so that communication to the public for the purpose of determining whether or not infringement had occurred did not require any member of the public to have actually seen or heard the work communicated. What that effectively meant was that the infringement of a work protected by copyright now requires not communication of the work to the public but the mere transmission of the work to the public. Considering that one of the aims of copyright law is presumably not the recreation of the English language, the term communication in the statute is misleading. It is, however, possibly indicative of a larger propaganda issue.

The terminology used in the arena of copyright is often designed to have a feel-good effect: copyright keeps artists from starving, and a moral 'sanction': if copyright is violated, those violating it will be responsible for having artists starve.

In 2002, Geofrey Yu, the Assistant Director General in charge of copyright at WIPO suggested that the economic and business aspects of copyright be downplayed when he spoke of the public's awareness of copyright saying:

"...Unfortunately, we cannot turn the clock back and find a new term in place of 'copyright' be we can at least downplay the term 'rights'. ... Within the copyright community such as we are today in this room, it is fine to refer to artists, composers, performers and enterprises as 'rights holders'. But it is poor public relations to employ the same terms when speaking to politicians, consumers, users, and the public. With them, we must use the terms devoid of legal jargon, terms, which are at least neutral or better still, inclusive, conveying meanings with which the public can identify. So 'rights holders' should become painters, writers, sculptors and musicians. What goes down well today with general audiences are terms like 'culture', 'creativity', 'information', 'entertainment', 'cultural heritage', 'reward for creativity', 'cultural enrichment'. And when we talk to youngsters, terms like 'fun', 'hip' and 'cool' will find an echo."

There is no pretence here that artists of various kinds are being used as little more than a camouflage by the 'copyright community'. And as Richard Stallman says, "It is interesting that WIPO is starting to find that the hypocrisy of describing a system of restricting the public as a matter of 'rights' is starting to backfire on them."[29]

Mr Yu isn't wrong though: people would be much less enthusiastic about supporting the current copyright regime if they were clearly told exactly what it was that they were supporting. Music-making and movie-making should be about 'people, imagination, fun and creative energy'. And, it is such things as 'culture', 'creativity', 'information', 'entertainment', 'cultural heritage', 'reward for creativity', 'cultural enrichment' that matter to the public.

However, if once were to do such things as look at the statements of objects and reasons which speak of why a law is passed or amended, one sees clear and entirely undisguised references to the economic and business aspects of copyright. For example, the statement explaining the need to amend copyright law in 1984, among other things, categorically says, "The emergence of new techniques of recordings, fixation and reproduction of audio programmes, combined with the advent of video technology have greatly helped the pirates. It is estimated that the losses to the film producers and other owners of copyright amount to several crores of rupees. The loss to Government in terms of tax evasion also amounts to crores of rupees." Along similar lines, one of the aims of the 1994 amendment was stated to be: 'To make provisions for licences whereby the reproduction of works by reprographic equipment or by means of devices such as tape recorders and video cassette recorders, where such reproduction would not under the existing law be infringement of copyright, shall be subject to payment or remuneration to copyright owners by means of a levy on such equipment.'

The increased commodification of creative works through the medium of copyright has resulted in access to them being decreased. Considering that much of this work comprises literature and art which are a tangible expression of culture, decreased access to them has, for all practical purposes, created very real barriers to the enjoyment of and interaction with what should have ideally been accessible and visible manifestations of culture.

FOOTNOTES

<en.wikipedia.org/wiki/Book_curse>,< litterascripta.com/bibliomania/curses.shtml>

14. Much of the material for this section has been taken from Lionel Bently's paper 'Copyright, Translations and Relations between Britain and India, 1880-1914' (ATRIP, Montreal, July 2005) and an article available at <icommons.org/articles/a-very-brief-history-of-copyright-development-in-India> by Prashant (licensed under a Creative Commons Attribution 3. 0 License) which in turn has drawn material from Upendra Baxi's magisterial work on copyright titled 'Copyright Law and Justice in India' (originally written in 1983 and subsequently revised in 1986.)

and Baxi, Upendra; Copyright Law and Justice in India; Journal of the Indian Law Institute 28. 4: 497-540.

15. <hinduonnet. com/thehindu/thscrip/print. pl?file=2007113054851100. htm&date=2007/11/30/&prd=th&>
16. Indian Proposals 1866-67, Indian Bills 1883, 1885, a Royal Commission 1875-1878
17. The early British traders and administrators in India who often adopted Indian customs and were sometimes Indophiles. William Dalrymple has written a book on them with this title.
18. Scrutton, Report to the Board of Trade on the Copyright Bills, Appendix to Select Committee on the Copyright Bill and Copyright (Amendment) Bill (HL) 1898 271,Parl Papers v.IX: "At present so far as English law is concerned, translation is probably not an infringement of copyright. There are Indian decisions to that effect, and the question is there of some practical importance, owing to the variety of Indian languages; in the UK the question might arise as between English, Welsh and Gaelic."
19. (1890) 14 Indian LR Bombay 586
20. (1895) 19 Indian LR Bombay 557
21. Bently, Lionel; Copyright, Translations and Relations Between Britain and India, 1880-1914; ATRIP, Montreal, July 2005
22. Article 8, Berlin Revision, 1908: The authors of unpublished works, being subjects of one of the countries of the Union, and the authors of works first published in one of those countries, shall enjoy, in the other countries of the Union, during the whole term of the right in the original work, the exclusive right of making or authorizing a translation of their works.
23. Report of the Joint Select Committee, The Gazette of India Extraordinary, pt. 2, s. 2, p. 907 (1956) cited in Baxi, U. See: 'Copyright Law and Justice in India' (originally written in 1983 and subsequently revised in 1986) and "Copyright Law and Justice in India." Journal of the Indian Law Institute 28. 4: 497-540.
24. Sections 7 to 12, Indian Copyright Act, 1914
25. And then, the British further sub-divided the personal/private sphere along religious lines which facilitated their 'divide and rule' policy and contributed to the formation of religious divisions which exist in India to this day.
26. AIR 2000 Bom 416
27. AIR 1998 Mad 294
28. Baxi, U., Copyright Law and Justice in India; Journal of the Indian Law Institute 28. 4: 497-540. p.503
29. <fsf. org/licensing/essays/wipo-PublicAwarenessOfCopyright-2002. html>

PART II

Snapshots of the Law

4

THE INDIAN COPYRIGHT ACT, 1957

It isn't possible to talk about what's wrong with copyright completely independently of the provisions laid down by copyright law. So, that's what this write-up aims to do: have a quick look at the basic provisions of copyright law. Here's a warning though: it's often soporific.

Should you choose to simply avoid reading this bit, here's a summary of the what the Indian Copyright Act of 1957 says: Copyright exists in a number of works including literary, dramatic, musical, and artistic works as well as computer programmes, sound recordings and films. In most cases, it subsists during the life of the author of the work and lasts for sixty years after his death. It comprises a number of rights which ensure that no one but the owner of copyright can do a number of things related to the work such as adapt, copy, translate, sell or broadcast it.

In addition to this, performers have a right in their performances which lasts for fifty years and broadcasters in their broadcasts for twenty-five years.

Copyright does not have to be registered as it subsists in a work as soon as it is created, and at most times, the person who creates a work is its owner. He can, however, assign the copyright to anyone else or bequeath it.

The person who creates a work also has certain moral rights in relation to it which exist independently of copyright and which can be protected. These moral rights continue to vest in an author even if the ownership of copyright passes from the author to someone else.

If anyone does anything which only the copyright owner is allowed to do, he must obtain a licence. Licences are usually granted for money, and licence fees may be collected on behalf of a number of copyright owners by a collective administration society such as PPL or IPRS, or by the person who licenses the copyright.

In some cases, a compulsory licence may be granted basically to ensure that a work is made available to the public.

If a licence is not obtained, the person who does what only the copyright holder has the right to do will in the ordinary course have infringed the copyright of the owner of the copyright although the law provides for some exceptions to copyright mainly for the purposes of review, research, reporting, and teaching. Infringers can be sued in civil court or prosecuted in a criminal court.

And that's the short version of the story. A longer (but by no means complete) version follows.

WORKS IN WHICH COPYRIGHT SUBSISTS

Copyright comprises a bundle of rights. It is not a right derived from Common Law. Instead, it is a statutory creation and does not have any existence beyond the limits set by the statutory law. In India, what these rights which comprise copyright are is currently defined by the Copyright Act, 1957.

According to Section 14 of the Copyright Act, 'copyright' means the exclusive right, by virtue of and subject to the provisions of the Copyright Act, to do or to authorize the doing of certain acts in relation to various works which are protected by copyright. These works include sheet music, novels, plays, sculptures, artistic buildings, handicrafts, films and paintings.

To be precise, the works in which copyright subsists[30] under the Copyright Act are:

(a) original, literary, dramatic, musical and artistic works,

(b) computer programmes,

(c) films, and

(d) sound recordings.

Copyright does not usually subsist in any of these works unless certain conditions are fulfilled. If the work is a published work, it must have been first published in India. If it is first published outside India, it can only be protected under the Indian Copyright Act if the author is a citizen of India at the date of publication. If the author is not alive when the work is published in India, he must have been a citizen of India at the time of his death. And a work of architecture is eligible to be protected under the Indian Copyright Act only if it has an artistic character and is located in India.

Computer programmes are interesting because of the deep felt desire of many in the IT community to patent them. Under Indian law, a computer programme cannot be patented per se but by exploiting the fact that the words 'per se' don't mean too much, efforts have been made to get computer programmes patented as a norm. This is despite the fact that computer programmes are protected under copyright law. The Copyright Act defines a 'computer programme'[31] as meaning 'a set of instructions expressed in words, codes, schemes or in any other form, including a machine readable medium, capable of causing a computer to perform a particular task or achieve a particular result'. Also, computer programmes are treated as literary works which means that, among other things, they cannot be adapted or translated without the permission of the owner of the copyright owner. Considering this, and the facts that copyright protection exists without registration, and that copyright protection lasts much longer than patent protection — a term of life plus sixty years v. a sum total of twenty years — in a field where even a six-month 'edge' is usually adequate to ensure profitability, it isn't entirely clear how computer programmes especially benefit by being patented under Indian law.

It could have something to do with amendments to the Indian Copyright Act introduced in the 1990s. The 1994 amendment of the Indian Copyright Act inserted a provision[32] which allowed lawful possessors to use computer programmes to make back-up copies (purely as a temporary protection against loss, destruction or damage), other copies, or adaptations of the programmes for the purposes for which they were supplied. More importantly, under an amendment introduced in 1999,[33] it became permissible for the lawful possessors of a computer programme to do any act necessary to obtain information essential for operating inter-operability of an independently created computer programme with other programmes if such information was not otherwise readily available. The amendment also made it permissible for lawful possessors to observe, study or test of functioning of computer programmes to determine the ideas and principles which underline their elements while performing acts necessary for the functions for which they were supplied. In addition to this, it became legal to make copies or adaptations of computer programmes from personally legally obtained copies for non-commercial personal use. None of these exceptions exist under patent law.

Even so, it is possible to effectively control how a computer programme is used through End User License Agreements (or other agreements which do not apply to end users) appended to software. These licences are binding legal contracts. If they are contravened, a civil action or criminal prosecution will, in all probability lie. The terms of these licences can restrict how users use the software and they may entitle those who own the licensed software to the revenue from the use of the software, the process of software development and through the trade of it.[34]

Moving away from computer programmes, there are certain works in which copyright does not subsist. For example, copyright does not subsist in any film if a substantial part of the film is an infringement of the copyright in any other work. Similarly, it does not subsist in any sound recording made in respect of a literary, dramatic or musical work, if in making the recording, the copyright in any of those works has been infringed.

The statute clearly says that the copyright in a film or a sound recording does not affect the separate copyright in any work in respect of which it is made. However, there are areas where the law is not half as clear, and has simply not kept up with changing technology. Take the case of feed aggregators, for example. Almost every blog and many other websites today publish RSS or Atom feeds which enable their readers to be aware of updates without actually having to go to the site itself. Naturally, there are feed aggregators which can be used to track a large number of feeds from individual sites. It isn't entirely clear whether they would infringe copyright. Indian statutory law does not specifically speak of RSS feeds much less of feed aggregators. While there isn't too much doubt that the restrictions which apply to content across the board would also apply to RSS and other feeds, presumably individuals accessing multiple feeds through aggregators could not possibly be accused of infringement. Licenses from content owners would almost certainly be needed for commercial use of RSS feeds though, and even if the use were non-commercial, it is possible that a licence would be needed.

This isn't the only instance of the law not keeping up with technology. Many of the most basic statutes like the Evidence Act, 1872 have had to be amended to keep up with changes in technology and, invariably, the technology has tended to leave the law far behind it. Just one example is of unsolicited commercial communication. The Telecom Unsolicited Commercial Communications Regulations, 2007[35] made it illegal for companies to arbitrarily phone persons offering everything from insurance policies to holiday homes. However, there were companies in India which, by 2007 itself, were seeking legal advice on whether they could send unsolicited commercial communication to mobile phones not by phoning subscribers but via Bluetooth. As it turned out, there wasn't anything which could easily stop them from doing so since Bluetooth does not involve transmission through a telecommunications service,[36] and the Use of Low Power Equipment in the Frequency Band 2.4 GHz to 2.4835 GHz (Exemption from Licensing Requirement) Rules say that no licence need ordinarily be obtained to send communications via Bluetooth.[37]

THE MEANING OF COPYRIGHT

A right may, in a generic sense, be defined as any advantage or benefit which the law confers on a person. Rights, like wrongs and duties may be either moral or legal or both. Bentham denied the existence of moral and natural rights saying that they were kinds of fictions. However, Salmond said that the fact that moral or natural rights are not laid down in black and white does not mean that they do not exist at all. According to Salmond, all legal rights have the following characteristics:

1	The person of inherence	Each legal right is vested in a distinguishable person; the subject of the right is the owner/the person entitled to the right
2	The person of incidence	The person upon whom the correlative duty lies; the subject of the duty is the person bound
3	The content of the right	That which places an obligation on the person of incidence to perform an act (or omission) in favour of the person of inherence
4	The object of the right	The subject matter or the thing to which the act or omission relates
5	The title of the right	The fact and/or events by which the right has become vested in its owner

Copyright is not a simple, single right. It contains within itself a number of rights. The Copyright Act not only mentions which classes of works it is that copyright subsists in but also goes on to specify precisely what rights accrue to different classes of works in which copyright subsists.

In the case of a literary, dramatic or musical work, copyright is the right to (or allow another to) reproduce the work in any material form, publish it, perform it in public, communicate it by radio-diffusion or by a loud-speaker, adapt it, or translate it and produce, reproduce, perform or publish such a translation. The copyright holder may also do any of these acts in relation to a translation or an adaptation of the work.[38]

A 'musical work'[39] means any combination of melody and harmony or either of them, printed, reduced to writing or otherwise graphically produced or reproduced, a 'dramatic work'[40] includes any piece for recitation, choreographic work or entertainment in a dumb show, the scenic arrangement or acting form of which is fixed in writing or otherwise but does not include a film, and a 'literary work'[41] includes tables and compilations.

The copyright which subsists in an artistic work allows its owner to (or authorize another to) reproduce the work in any material form, publish it, include it in any film, adapt it, and to do any of these acts in relation to an adaptation of the work.[42] An 'artistic work'[43] means: a painting, a sculpture, a drawing (including a diagram, map, chart or plan), an engraving or a photograph, whether or not any such work possesses artistic quality; an architectural work with artistic merit; and any other work of artistic craftsmanship.

While in the case of a film,[44] the copyright owner may make a copy of the film, cause the film to be seen and heard in public, make a record embodying any part of the sound track associated with the film and communicate the film by radio-diffusion. He may also grant a licence to allow anyone else to do any of these things. Under the law, a 'cinematograph film'[45] includes the sound track, if any, and 'cinematograph' is construed as including any work produced by any mechanical instrument or by radio-diffusion.

Further, in the case of a record,[46] the copyright owner has the right to do or to authorize another to utilize the record to make any other record embodying the same recording, to cause it to be heard in public and to communicate the recording by radio-diffusion.

Finally, in the case of any of these works in which copyright subsists, any reference to the doing of any act in relation to a work or to a translation or an adaptation of it includes a reference to the doing of that act in relation to a substantial part thereof. A copy which has been sold once shall be deemed to be a copy already in circulation.

It is also worth noting that there is an element of reciprocity in the grant of copyright protection to foreign works in India. If the Central Government thinks that a foreign country does not give or has not undertaken to give adequate protection to the works of Indian authors, it may direct that the provisions of the Indian Copyright Act which confer copyright on works first published in India not apply to works whose authors are subjects or citizens of that foreign country and are not domiciled in India.[47] Similarly, with reference to foreign countries which do not protect the rights of broadcasting organizations or performers, the Central Government may deny protection under the Indian Copyright Act to performers or broadcasting organizations which are based or incorporated in those foreign countries, or which are their subjects or citizens and are neither incorporated nor domiciled in India.[48]

ADAPTATIONS AND REPURPOSING CONTENT

The Indian Copyright Act defines 'adaptation' in relation to various kinds of works in the following terms:[49]

In relation to a...	
Dramatic work	the conversion of the work into a non-dramatic work
Literary or artistic work	the conversion of the work into a dramatic work by way of performance in public or otherwise
Literary or dramatic work	any abridgement of the work or any version of the work in which the story or action is conveyed wholly or mainly by means of pictures in a form suitable for reproduction in a book or in a newspaper, magazine or similar periodical
Musical work	any arrangement or transcription of the work
Any work	any use of such work involving its rearrangement or alteration

Indian law on the subject of repurposing content is unclear but considering how similar to adaptation it is, presumably, the same law would apply. In repurposing work, in addition to ensuring that neither copyrights nor trademarks are infringed, it is wise to obtain a licence from the copyright owner. The same thing applies to adaptations: only copyright owners have the right to adapt works in which they own copyright, and any unauthorized adaptation of a work would amount to copyright infringement.

In relation to the repurposing of content, the European Court of Justice has said that 'the fact that the contents of a database were made accessible to the public by its maker or with his consent does not affect the right of the maker to prevent acts of extraction and/or re-utilization of the whole or a substantial part of the contents of a database' with reference to Directive 96/9/EC.[50]

THE FIRST OWNER OF COPYRIGHT

Copyright subsists throughout India in original literary, dramatic, musical and artistic works, films, and sound records. According to Section 17 of the Copyright Act 1957, the first owner of copyright in a work is the author of the work. The Act defines who the 'author'[51] is in relation to various classes of works in the following terms:

In relation to...	
A literary or dramatic work	The author of the work
A musical work	The composer
An artistic work other than a photograph	The artist
A photograph	The person taking the photograph
A film or sound recording	The producer
Any computer-generated literary dramatic musical or artistic work	The person who causes the work to be created

There are a number of exceptions[52] to the general rule that the author of a work is the first owner of the copyright in the work though.

The proprietor of a newspaper, magazine or similar periodical is the first owner of the copyright for the purpose of publication of any literary, dramatic, musical or artistic work made by an author in the course of his employment under a contract of service or apprenticeship but in all other respects, the author is the first owner of the copyright. This, however, is subject to contract. Further, subject to contract and this provision, the person who commissions a photograph, portrait, engraving or film is the first owner of the copyright if the work has been made for valuable consideration. If neither one of these sets of circumstances exists, the employer is the first owner of the copyright if the work has been made in the course of the author's employment under a contract of service or apprenticeship.

The person who delivers an address or speech in public or the person on whose behalf it is delivered is the first owner of the copyright even if that person is employed by any other person who arranges for such address or speech to be delivered or if it is delivered on the employer's premises.

Subject to contract, the Government is the first owner of the copyright in a government work. Similarly, subject to contract, a PSU is the first owner of the copyright in a work first made or published by it or under its control. And international organizations are usually the first owners of the copyright in their own works.

As far as 'ownership' itself is concerned, 'ownership' is the relationship which exists between an owner and the copyright which he owns. It comprises a complex of rights in rem i.e. rights which can be enforced against the world at large. Salmond listed the incidents of ownership in the following terms:

The Incident	*Its Characteristics*	
1. The owner's right to possession	The owner need not actually have possession.	However, he retains a reversionary interest if he has voluntarily temporarily divested himself of possession. For example, if he has signed an exclusive licence allowing another the use of his property, during the subsistence of

		the licence, he cannot use the property. Once the licence expires, the right will revert to him.
2. The owner's right (liberty) to its use and enjoyment	The owner is not under a duty to either use or enjoy his property. He can do whatever he wants to do with it including lock it up in a vault and leave it there for all eternity.	However, others have a 'no-right' to prevent him from using/enjoying it.
3. The owner's right (power) to consume, destroy or alienate the thing		Persons other than the owner usually do not have any such power: *nemo dat quod non habet.*
4. The owner's interest is of indeterminate duration		However, the interest of a non-owner is of limited duration e.g. a licensee's interest ends with the expiry of the term of the licence.
5. Ownership has a residuary character	It is limited to the rights which remain after lesser rights have been given away.	However, the extinction of lesser rights such as licensees' rights revive in the owner all his original rights.

THE MORAL RIGHTS OF AN AUTHOR

Indian law does not speak of the moral rights of authors. However, there is a provision in the Indian Copyright Act which speaks of 'authors' special rights'.[53] These rights include the rights to paternity and integrity. They exist independently of an author's copyright. The interesting thing about these special rights is that they continue to exist even after the assignment (either wholly or partially) of the copyright. Under the law, the author of a work has the right:

(a) to claim authorship of the work; and

(b) to restrain or claim damages in respect of any distortion, mutilation, modification or other act in relation to the said work which is done before the expiration of the term of copyright if the distortion, mutilation, modification or other act would be prejudicial to his honour or reputation.

This does not apply to the making of copies or to the adaptation of a computer programme by the lawful possessor of a copy of such computer programme from such copy in order to utilize the computer programme for the purposes for which it was supplied or to make back-up copies purely as a temporary protection against loss, destruction or damage in order only to utilize the computer programme for the purpose for which it was supplied.

Failure to display a work or to display it to the satisfaction of an author is not deemed to be an infringement of his special rights. Further, the legal representatives of an author may exercise his special rights (other than the right to claim authorship of the work).

The most important thing about these Special Rights which are defined by Section 57 of the Copyright Act is that they are inalienable rights and an author cannot 'assign' them to anyone else even if he should wish to do so.

THE TERM OF COPYRIGHT

Copyright does not subsist in perpetuity. Copyright Acts in various countries govern the terms of copyright in those countries. The length of time for which copyright protection is granted can vary quite a bit. In India, copyright subsists during the life of the author. In addition to this, there also exists a posthumous copyright term of 60 years.[54] The term of sixty years, however, begins at different times depending on the type of work and on whether or not the author is known.

The term of copyright in published literary, dramatic, musical and artistic works which are not photographs

Section		*Term of Copyright*
22	The work is published within the lifetime of the author	sixty years from the beginning of the calendar year next following year in which the author dies

	In the case of a work of joint authorship, the reference to the author is construed as a reference to the author who dies last.	
23	The work is published anonymously or pseudonymously	sixty years from the beginning of the calendar year next following the years in which the work is fist published
	If the identity of the author is disclosed before the expiry of the period of the copyright term of an anonymous work	sixty years from the beginning of the calendar year next following the year in which the author dies

References to the author in the case of an anonymous work of joint authorship, are construed:

a. as references to that author if the identity of one of the author is disclosed

b. as a reference to the author who dies last from amongst such authors where the identity of more author than one is disclosed.

References to the author in the case of a pseudonymous work of joint authorship are construed:

a. where the names of one or more (but not all) of the authors are pseudonymous and his or their identity is not disclosed, as references to the author whose name is not a pseudonym, or, if the names of two or more the authors are not pseudonymous, as references to such of those authors who dies last

b. where the names of one or more (but not all) of the authors are pseudonyms and the identity of one or more of them is disclosed, as references to the author who dies last from amongst the authors whose names are not pseudonymous and the authors whose names are pseudonyms and disclosed and

c. where the names of all the authors are pseudonyms and the identity of one of them is disclosed, as references to the authors whose identity is disclosed or if the identity of two or more of such authors is disclosed, as references to such of those authors who dies last.

The identity of an author is deemed to have been disclosed, if either the identity of the author is disclosed (publicly by both the author and the publisher) or is otherwise established to the satisfaction of the Copyright Board by the author.

The term of copyright in posthumous works[55]

In the case of			*Term of Copyright*
A literary, dramatic or musical work an engraving	In which copyright subsists at the date of the death of the author or, in the case of any such work of	but which, or any adaptation of which, has not been published	sixty years from the beginning of the calendar year next following the year in which

	joint authorship, at or immediately before the date of the death of the author who dies last	before that date	the work is first published or, where an adaptation of the work is published in any earlier year, from the beginning of the calendar year next following that year

A literary, dramatic or musical work or an adaptation of any such work is deemed to have been published, if it has been performed in public or if any sound recordings made in respect of the work have been sold to the public or have been offered for sale to the public.

The term of copyright in photographs, films, sound recordings, government works, the works of public undertakings and in the works of international organizations

Section	*In the case of*		*Term of Copyright*
25	A photograph		sixty years from the beginning of the calendar year next following the year in which the photograph is published
26	A film		sixty years from the beginning of the calendar year next following the year in which the film is published
27	A sound recording		sixty years from the beginning of the calendar year next following the year in which the sound recording is published
28	A Government work	where the government is the first owner of the copyright in the work	sixty years from the beginning of the calendar year next following the year in which the work is first published
28 A	Works of public	where the public undertaking is the	sixty years from the beginning of the calendar

	undertakings	first owner of the copyright in the work	year next following the year in which the work is first published
29	Works of international organizations		sixty years from the beginning of the calendar year next following the year in which the work is first published

Even if one believed in the copyright regime, it is difficult to explain how such long copyright terms economically benefit authors especially since the bulk of the sales of most works are made within a few months of the first publication of the work. The optimal length of copyright according to Rufus Pollock of Cambridge University is fifteen years.[56] Longer terms of copyright protection achieve little but to restrict access to protected works for ridiculously long periods of time.

PERFORMERS' RIGHTS

Under the Copyright Act, performers have a right known as the 'performer's right' in relation to their performances. A 'performer' includes an actor, singer, musician, dancer, acrobat, juggler, conjurer, snake charmer, a person delivering a lecture or any other person who makes a performance[57] while a 'performance' means any visual or acoustic presentation made live by one or more performers.[58] A performer's right subsists for fifty years from the beginning of the calendar year next following the year in which the performance is made. It can be infringed by making a sound or visual recording of the performance without the performer's consent, or by reproducing such a recording. A recording of a performance also infringes the performer's right if it is made for purposes different from those for which the performer gave his consent or if it is made for purposes which so not fall within the purview of fair use even it is made from a recording which was made in accordance with fair use.

In addition to this, a performer's right can be infringed by broadcasting the performance unless the broadcast is made from a sound or visual recording not made for private use, teaching or research or is a re-broadcast by the same broadcasting organization of an earlier broadcast which did not infringe the performer's right. Subject to fair dealing exceptions, the communication of the performance to the public otherwise than by broadcast is deemed to have infringed the performer's right unless the communication is made from a sound recording or a visual recording or a broadcast.

Once a performer has consented to the incorporation of his performance in a film, the provisions of the Copyright Act which deal with performers' rights have no further application to his performance.[59]

The Copyright Act makes room for fair use in relation to performers' rights. The Act says that performers' rights are not deemed to be infringed by the making of any sound recording or visual recording for the private use of the person making such recording, or solely for purposes of bona fide teaching or research; or by the use, consistent with fair dealing, of excerpts of a performance or of a broadcast in the reporting of current events or for bona fide review, teaching or research; or such other acts, with any necessary adaptations and modifications, which do not constitute infringement of copyright.[60]

Certain provisions of the Copyright Act (which deal with the assignment of copyright, licences by copyright owners, the import of infringing copies, civil remedies for the infringement of copyright, the rights of owners against persons possessing or dealing with infringing copies, the power of police to seize infringing copies, the possession of and the disposal of plates to make infringing copies, and the disposal of infringing copies) apply in relation to performers' rights in any performance in a way corresponding to that in which they apply to copyright in a work. If copyright or a performer's right subsists in respect of any work or performance that has been broadcast, no licence to reproduce the broadcast can take effect without the consent of the owner of the copyright or the performer, as the case may be, or both of them.[61]

THE BROADCAST REPRODUCTION RIGHT

Every broadcasting organization has a special right which is known as a 'broadcast reproduction right' in respect of its broadcasts. This right subsists for twenty-five years from the beginning of the calendar year next following the year in which the broadcast is made. It can be infringed by re-broadcasting the broadcast, by causing it to be heard or seen by the public on payment of any charges or by making any sound or visual recording of it. A protected broadcast can also be infringed by making any reproduction of a sound or visual recording which was either made without a licence or which was made for a purpose not envisaged by the licence. Finally, selling or hiring any such recording to the public or offering it for sale or hire is treated as an infringement of the broadcast reproduction right. Infringement does not occur during the subsistence of the right if the act is done with a licence.[62]

A broadcast reproduction right is not deemed to be infringed by the making of any sound recording or visual recording for the private use of the person making it, or if the recording is made solely for purposes of bona fide teaching or research. Further, it is not deemed to be infringed by the use, consistent with fair dealing, of excerpts of a performance or of a broadcast in the reporting of current events or for bona fide review, teaching or research; or such other acts, with any necessary adaptations and modifications, which do not constitute infringement of copyright.[63]

Certain provisions of the Copyright Act (which deal with the assignment of copyright, licences by copyright owners, the import of infringing copies, civil remedies for infringement of copyright, the rights of owners against persons possessing or dealing with infringing copies, the power of police to seize infringing copies, the possession of and disposal of plates to make infringing copies, and the disposal of infringing copies themselves) apply in relation to the broadcast reproduction right in any broadcast in a corresponding way to that in which they apply to the copyright in a work. If copyright or a performer's right subsists in respect of any work or performance that has been broadcast, a licence to reproduce the broadcast cannot take effect without the consent of the owner of the rights or the performer, as the case may be, or both of them.[64]

ASSIGNMENTS AND VOLUNTARY LICENCES

Copyright can be assigned or licensed under the provisions of the Copyright Act. An assignment is a transfer of the ownership of the copyright from one person to another while in the case of a licence, the ownership of the copyright itself remains unchanged although the licensee is allowed to do something which would have been illegal for him to do but for the licence. The legal requirements of both assigning and licensing copyright are similar.[65]

When it comes to assignments, there should be an instrument of assignment for:

(i) the assignment of the whole copyright;

(ii) a partial assignment of the copyright;

(iii) a general assignment;

(iv) an assignment subject to limitation;

(v) an assignment for the whole term of the copyright; or

(vi) an assignment for a part of the term of the copyright.

If the agreement does not specifically state the period of assignment or licence, the law says that the period is five years and if the territorial extent of assignment or licence is not specifically stated in the agreement, it extends to the whole of the territory of India.

The owner of the copyright in any existing work or the prospective owner of the copyright in any future work may grant any interest in the right by licence in writing signed by him or by his duly authorized agent. In the case of a licence relating to copyright in any future work, the licence takes effect only when the work comes into existence. If a person to whom a licence relating to copyright in any future work is granted dies before the work comes into existence, his legal representatives are entitled to the benefit of the licence in the absence of any provision to the contrary in the contract.

The agreement automatically lapses if the assignee or licensee does not make use of the rights assigned or licensed, as the case may be, within of the assignment or licence.

If the licence is an 'exclusive licence', it confers either on the licensee alone or on the licensee and persons authorized by him to the exclusion of all other persons (including the owner of the copyright) any right comprised in the copyright. Thus, if a licensee is an exclusive licensee, it means that no one, not even the owner of the copyright, has the right to exploit the work which is protected by copyright till the expiry of the licence.

On the other hand, if a licensee is a sole licensee, both the licensee and the owner of the copyright are entitled to exploit the rights conferred by copyright in relation to the work which has been licensed. Ordinarily, a sole licensee may allow others to enjoy some of the rights which have been granted to him under the terms of the licence but the owner of the copyright cannot re-license the copyright to persons in addition to the sole licensee during the term of the licence.

Requirements

An assignment or licence must:

- be in writing
- be signed by the assignor or by his duly authorized agent
- identify the specific works and specify the rights assigned
- specify the duration and territorial extent of the assignment
- specify the amount of royalty payable, if any, to the author or his legal heirs

An assignment may be revised, extended or ended by the parties on terms they agree to.

Under Indian Copyright Law, an oral assignment of copyright is invalid.[66] There is no particular form prescribed for assignment and it may be effected even by a letter.[67] If there is a dispute, oral evidence may be admitted in court identify the subject matter of the assignment.[68]

If a publisher were to simply assert that some person owned the copyright in the work by doing something like putting a copyright notice in a book, such an assertion would by no means mean that that person owned the copyright in the work.[69] Also, for a copyright to be licensed or assigned to anyone, it would have to be licensed or assigned by all the persons who owned it. If the copyright was owned by more than one person and all of them did not assign or license the work, the assignment or licence, as the case may be, would not affect those owners who did not assign or license the work. This would mean, among other things, that although a licensee, for example, could not be sued by the licensor if he used the work according to the terms of the licence agreement, he would still be liable to be sued by the other owners for copyright infringement.

COMPULSORY LICENCES

Compulsory Licences can be obtained in certain cases such as when works are withheld from the public. These licences allow licensees to do such things as reproduce the work licensed, communicate it to the public and translate it. The grant of compulsory licences is closely linked to public policy and protecting public interest, and is among the few provisions in the Indian Copyright Act, 1957 which actively promote access to works such as those which are unpublished or which have been withheld from the public.

A compulsory license is terminated once the copyright owner himself produces the work in such a way as to do away with the circumstances which necessitated the grant of a compulsory licence. e.g. by pricing it reasonably.

The Supreme Court spoke of compulsory licences in the case of M/s Entertainment Network (India) Ltd. v. M/s Super Cassette Industries Ltd., 2008[70] in which it said:

"The scheme of the Act affirms the freedom to contract as being the primary machinery by which the copyright owner publishes his work through a voluntary license regime in terms of Section 30. Compulsory licenses are an exception to the general freedom of the copyright owner to contract.

Section 31 deals with compulsory license in works withheld from the public. Section 31A empowers the Copyright Board to issue a compulsory license in respect of an unpublished Indian work or a translation thereof in any language, whose author is dead or unknown or cannot be traced or the owner of copyright in such work cannot be found. Section 31A(4) empowers the Board to hold an enquiry and direct the Registrar of Copyrights to grant to the applicant a licence to publish the work or translation, subject to the payment of such royalty and subject to such other terms and conditions as the Copyright Board may determine.

Section 32 empowers the Copyright Board to issue a compulsory license to produce and publish a translation of literary or a dramatic work in any language after a period of 7 years from the first publication of the work.

Section 32A empowers the Copyright Board to grant a compulsory license where after the expiry of the relevant period from the date of the first publication of an edition of a literary, scientific or artistic work, copies of such edition are not made available in India. Section 32B provides for the termination of a compulsory license where it is issued under Section 32(1A) or Section 32A, on the fulfillment of the conditions mentioned in that Section.

Rule 9 of the Copyright Rules prescribed the manner in which the Copyright Board shall determine royalties payable to the owner with respect to a compulsory license for a translation under Section 32. Rule 11D provides for the manner in which the Copyright Board shall determine royalties payable to the owner of the copyright in respect of compulsory licenses issued under Section 31A, Section 32 and Section 32A.

Rule 11C (4) provides that where there are more applicants than one seeking a compulsory license for translation of a work or for reproduction of the work or for publication of an unpublished work, then the Copyright Board make grant the compulsory license to such one of the applicants, as in the opinion of the Board, would best serve the interest of the general public.

Chapter VI relates to grant of licence, which can be divided into two parts; licences by owners of copyright and compulsory licenses.

Compulsory licences can be granted by the Copyright Board subject to the limitations contained therein. It cannot be said to be an exception to the general rule in the strict sense of the term as the provisions relating to grant of license by owners of Copyright and compulsory licenses operate in different fields. It may be true that while passing an order for grant of compulsory licenses, the relevant factors as laid down therein must be kept in mind which would include the right of the owner of the copyright as a part of the right of property, but where a statute is to be construed as a balancing statute, the situation may be different."

Compulsory Licences in Works withheld from the Public

A compulsory licence which allows the licensee to republish certain published Indian works, perform them in public, or communicate them to the public by broadcast can obtained while copyright subsists in them. Specifically, the works with reference to which such licences can be obtained are: artistic works whose authors are Indian citizens, and films or records made or manufactured in India. To obtain such a licence, the prospective licensee must make a complaint to the Copyright Board regarding the work concerned. In cases where two or more persons make a complaint, a licence is granted to the complainant who (in the opinion of the Copyright Board) would best serve the interests of the general public. If the Copyright Board is satisfied that the work has been withheld from the public because the person who owns the copyright in it has unreasonably refused to republish it, allow its republication, or allow it to be performed in public, it may direct the Registrar of Copyrights to grant a licence to the complainant. Similarly, a licence can be obtained if the owner of the copyright in the work has refused to allow it to be communicated to the public by broadcast on terms which the complainant considers reasonable. Before reaching a decision, the Copyright Board must give the copyright owner a reasonable opportunity of being heard and hold an inquiry. Compulsory licences granted in this manner are subject to payment of licence fees to the copyright owner and other terms and conditions determined by the Copyright Board.[71]

Compulsory Licences in Unpublished Indian Works[72]

If the author of an Indian work referred to in Section 2(a)(iii) of the Indian Copyright Act, 1957 is dead, unknown or untraceable, or if work's copyright owner cannot be found, any person may apply to the Copyright Board for a licence to publish the work or a translation of it in any language. Section 2(a)(iii) merely says that the adaptation of a literary or dramatic work means any abridgement of it or any pictorial version of it in a form suitable for reproduction in a book, or in a newspaper, magazine or similar periodical.

Further, if the original author is dead, the Central Government may, if it considers that the publication of the work is desirable in the national interest, require the heirs, executors or legal representatives of the author to publish it within a specified period. If a work is not published within this period, the Copyright Board may, on an application made by any person for permission to publish the work and after hearing the parties concerned, permit such publication on payment of royalty it determines taking the circumstances of the case into consideration.

Before making an application, the applicant must publish his proposal in one issue of a daily newspaper in the English language having circulation in the major part of the country, and if the application is to publish a translation, he must also publish his proposal in one issue of any daily newspaper in that language. These advertisements must accompany the application. The Copyright Board may, after holding an inquiry as required, direct the Registrar of Copyrights to grant a licence to the applicant to publish the work or a translation of it in the language mentioned in the application. Such licences are subject to the payment of royalty and other terms and conditions determined by the Copyright Board. If a licence is granted, the Registrar of Copyrights may direct the applicant to deposit the royalty in the public account of India or in any other account specified by the Copyright Board so that the copyright owner or his heirs, executors or the legal representatives would be able to claim it at any time.

Compulsory Translation Licences

Any person may apply to the Copyright Board for a licence to produce and publish a translation of a literary or dramatic work in any language after a period of seven years from the first publication of the work.

In addition to this, any person may apply to the Copyright Board for a licence to produce and publish a translation of a non-Indian literary or dramatic work distributable only in India for the purposes of teaching, scholarship or research, in printed or analogous forms of reproduction, in any language in general use in India three years after the work has been published. And if the translation is in a language not in general use in any developed country, the application may be made after a period of one year. However, this does not apply to the export by Government or any authority under the it of copies of such a translation in a language other than English, French or Spanish to any country if such copies are sent to NRIs or to any NRI association outside India; or if such copies are meant to be used for purposes of teaching, scholarship or research and not for any commercial purpose; and the Government of the country to which they are exported has given permission for the export. The name of the author and the title of the particular edition of the work translated must be printed on all the copies of the translation.

Every application for a compulsory licence to produce and publish translations must state the proposed retail price of a copy of the translation of the work. After the application is made, the Copyright Board may grant a non-exclusive licence to the applicant to produce and publish a translation of the work (in the language mentioned in the application) subject to the condition that the applicant pay the owner of the copyright in the work royalties in respect of copies of the translation of the work sold to the public as determined by the Copyright Board.

A licence for translation can only be obtained if the owner of the copyright in the work has not already published a translation before the time when an application for a licence can be made, or if the translation made by the copyright owner is out of print. The applicant must prove to the satisfaction of the Copyright Board that he had requested and had been denied authorisation by the owner of the copyright to produce and publish such translation, or that he was, after due diligence on his part, unable to find the owner of the copyright. If the applicant was unable to find the owner of the copyright, must demonstrate that he had sent a copy of his request for authorisation by registered air mail post to the publisher whose name was on the work. The author must not have withdrawn from circulation copies of the work. Further, the Copyright Board must be satisfied that the applicant is competent to produce and publish a correct translation of the work and that he possesses the means to pay to the owner of the copyright the royalties payable to him.

Any broadcasting authority may apply to the Copyright Board for a licence to produce and publish the translation of a non-Indian literary or dramatic work or any text incorporated in audio-visual fixations prepared and published solely for the purpose of systematic instructional activities, for broadcasting such translation for the purposes of teaching or for the dissemination of the results of specialized, technical or scientific research to the experts in any particular field. The provisions which apply to translating non-Indian literary or dramatic works also apply to licences granted under this provision. Further, the translation must be made from a work lawfully acquired, the broadcast must be made through the medium of sound and visual recordings, the recording must have been lawfully and exclusively made for the purpose of broadcasting in India by the applicant or by any other broadcasting agency; and the translation and the broadcasting of it must be non-commercial.

Compulsory Licences for Systematic Instruction[73]

If, within a specified time, the owner of the right of

reproduction or a person he authorizes does not make copies of an edition of a literary, scientific or artistic work available in India, or put them on sale in India for a period of six months (to the general public, or in connection with systematic instructional activities) at a price reasonably related to that normally charged in India for comparable works, a compulsory licence can be obtained to reproduce and publish the works in printed or analogous forms of reproduction at the price at which such edition is sold or a lower price for the purposes of systematic instructional activities. Any person who wishes to obtain such a licence may apply to the Copyright Board for it. His application must state the proposed retail price of a copy of the work to be reproduced. After holding an inquiry, the Copyright Board may grant a non-exclusive licence to the applicant to produce and publish a reproduction of the work distributable only in India subject to the condition that he pay to the copyright owner royalties calculated at a rate determined by the Copyright Board.

The time specified by the law depends on the subject of the work.

Type of work	*The length of time after which an application for a licence can be made…*
Any work of, or relating to, fiction, poetry, drama, music or art	Seven years from the date of the first publication of the work
Any work of, or relating to, natural science, physical science, mathematics or technology	Three years from the date of the first publication of the work
Any other work	Five years from the date of the first publication of the work

Such licences do not extend to the export of copies of the reproduction of the work outside India and every copy of the reproduction must contain a notice that the copy is available for distribution only in India. The applicant must prove to the satisfaction of the Copyright Board that he had requested and had been denied authorisation by the owner of the copyright in the work to reproduce and publish such work or that he was, after due diligence on his part, unable to find such owner.

If the applicant was unable to find the owner of the copyright, he must demonstrate that he had sent a copy of his request for such authorisation by registered airmail post to the publisher whose name appeared on the work not less than three months before the application for the licence.

The Copyright Board must be satisfied that the applicant is competent to reproduce and publish an accurate reproduction of the work and possesses the means to pay to the owner of the copyright the royalties payable to him. The applicant is required to undertake to reproduce and publish the work at a price fixed by the Copyright Board, being a price reasonably related to the price normally charged in India for works of the same standard on the same or similar subjects.

The owner of the copyright in the work or any person authorized by him must not have already published a reproduction for which a licence is sought. The name of the author and the title of the particular edition of the work proposed to be reproduced must be printed on all the copies of the reproduction and the author must not have withdrawn from circulation copies of the work.

A licence to reproduce and publish the translation of a work cannot be granted under these provisions unless such a translation has been published by the owner of the right of translation or any person authorized by him and the translation is not in a language in general use in India.

However, these provisions apply to the reproduction and publication, or translation into a language in general use in India, of any text incorporated in audio-visual fixations prepared and published solely for the purpose of systematic instructional activities.

The Termination of Compulsory Licences[74]

As a general rule, compulsory licences are terminated once the circumstances which necessitated their being granted change.

If a licence to produce and publish a translation of a non-Indian literary or dramatic work distributable only in India for the purposes of teaching, scholarship or research, in printed or analogous forms of reproduction, in any language in general use in India is granted, the licence will be terminated if the owner of the copyright in the work or any person authorized by him publishes a translation of it himself.

If a licence is granted to produce copies of editions of literary, scientific or artistic works which are inaccessible in India, and the owner of the right of reproduction or any person authorized by him subsequently sells or distributes copies of the work or a translation of it, the compulsory licence will be terminated. Such a termination cannot take effect until after the expiry of three months from the date of service of a notice on the person holding the compulsory licence by the owner of the right of reproduction intimating the sale or distribution of his own copies of the editions.

In both these cases, copies of the licensed work produced and published by the holder of the compulsory licence before its termination takes effect may continue to be sold or distributed until the copies already produced and published are exhausted. Also, the holder of the right or a person authorized by him must publish a translation in same language as the compulsory licensee has done and their translation must be substantially the same in content and at a price reasonably related to the price normally charged in India for work of the same standard on the same or similar subjects for the compulsory licence to be terminated.

COPYRIGHT SOCIETIES

A copyright society is basically a Collective Administration Society which is supposed to safeguard the rights of copyright owners by administering their rights. It can grant licences for the use of copyrighted works and can collect licence fees on behalf of rights holders. Once it collects licence fees, it is supposed to pay the fees to the copyright owners ideally after deducting no more than administration charges, if at all.

The 1994 Copyright (Amendment) Act provided for separate Copyright Societies to be set up for different categories of works. There are currently four Copyright Societies:

Society for Copyright Regulation of Indian Producers of Films and Television	*for*	Films
Indian Performing Right Society Limited	*for*	Musical works
Phonographic Performance Limited	*for*	Sound recordings
Indian Reprographic Rights Organization	*for*	Books and artistic photocopy rights

These societies have their own Anti Piracy Cells and are probably most visible when they do such things as conduct raids on New Year's parties in hotels to try to curb copyright infringement and to ensure that licence fees are paid.

The registration of copyright societies is mandatory under the provisions of the Copyright Act, 1957. A copyright society may accept (from an owner of rights) exclusive authorisation to administer any right in any work by the issue of licences or the collection of licence fees or both. An owner of rights has the right to withdraw such authorisation but even if an owner did withdraw authorisation, it would not affect any of the rights which had already accrued to the copyright society under any contract.

In the case of M/s Entertainment Network (India) Ltd. v. M/s Super Cassette Industries Ltd., 2008,[75] S B Sinha, J. of the Supreme Court spoke of Copyright Societies saying:

"The provisions with respect to Copyright Societies are contained in Chapter VII of the Act which in its present form was introduced by the Copyright (Amendment) Act, 1994. Section 33 of the Act provides for the registration of a Copyright Society. Section 34 of the Act empowers a Copyright Society to accept from the owner exclusive authorization to administer any rights in any work by issue of licenses or collection of license fee or both. A Copyright Society may issue voluntary licenses under Section 30, collect fees in pursuance of such licenses, distribute such fees amongst owners of rights, and perform any other functions consistent with the collective control of the owners whose rights it administers.

The Copyright Society is required to frame a scheme to determine the quantum of remuneration payable to individual copyright owners having regard to the number of copies of the work in circulation. [Section 34A(2)]

Chapter V of the Copyright Rules, 1958 makes detailed provisions with respect to the conduct of business by Copyright Societies. Rule 14J requires that a Copyright Society shall frame a scheme of tariff to be called a 'Tariff Scheme' setting out the nature and quantum of fees or royalties which it proposes to collect in respect of such copyright or other rights administered by it. Rule 14K requires a Copyright Society to frame a 'Distribution Scheme' setting out the procedure for collection and distribution of royalty specified in the Tariff Scheme among the owners of copyright. Any distribution under the Distribution Scheme is required to be in the proportion to the income of the Copyright Society from actual use of the work or works of each owner of rights."

The Copyright Act itself does not define a copyright society in clear terms: all it says is that a 'copyright society' means a society registered under Section 33(3) of the Copyright Act, 1957.

The Copyright (Amendment) Act, 1994 prohibited any person or association of persons from commencing or carrying on the business of issuing or granting licences in respect of any work in which copyright subsisted or in respect of any other rights conferred by the Copyright Act without being registered. To be registered, the association had to apply to the Registrar of Copyrights who was required to submit the application to the Central Government.

Under this amendment, the Central Government could register such associations of persons as copyright societies having regard to the interests of the authors and other owners of rights under the Copyright Act, the interest and convenience of the public and in particular of the groups of persons who were most likely to seek licences in respect of the relevant rights, as well as the ability and professional competence of the associations. However, the law said that the Central Government could not ordinarily register more than one copyright society to do business in respect of the same class of works.

Also, the registration of copyright societies did not prevent the owner of the copyright in any work from granting licences in respect of his own work in his individual capacity in a manner consistent with his obligations as a member of the registered copyright society.

The amendment also empowered the Central Government to cancel the registration of a copyright society after an inquiry had been conducted if it was satisfied that the copyright society was being managed in a manner detrimental to the interests of the owners of rights concerned. Also, it could, by order, suspend the registration of a copyright society pending an inquiry if it thought that it was necessary to do so in the interest of the rights holders. The suspension, however, could not last for more than one year and the Government would have to appoint an administrator to discharge the functions of the copyright society during the period of suspension.

RESALE RIGHTS

The authors of certain works have the right to claim a share of the proceeds of a resale of their works if the works are protected by copyright.[76] There are certain conditions which have to be fulfilled for the author to be able to enjoy the benefit of this right though. The work must be the original copy of a painting, sculpture or drawing, or of the original manuscript of a literary, dramatic or musical work, and it must be sold for a minimum of 10,000 INR. The author of the work or his legal heirs must have been the first owner(s) of the copyright in the work.

It would not matter if the copyright in the work was subsequently assigned. The Copyright Board would make a final decision on what the author's share would be. The Act also empowers the Copyright Board to fix different shares for different classes of works although the share cannot exceed ten per cent of the resale price under any circumstances.

Disputes regarding resale rights are to be referred to the Copyright Board whose decision is final.

THE REGISTRATION OF COPYRIGHT

Copyright does not subsist in ideas; it subsists only in the expression of an idea in the form of a literary work, music, art, etc.. People often ask for instructions on 'How to copyright' various works but there is no indication in any of the provisions of the Act whether they are read individually or as a whole to suggest that registration is a condition precedent to acquiring copyright.[77] Copyright begins to subsist in a work the moment it is created. In most cases, the author-creator of the work owns the copyright. This copyright which has already come into creation can be registered. Registration is not essential under contemporary copyright law. If a work is not registered, it does not mean that the rights which are engrafted and assured under the Copyright Act will be denied.[78] Registration merely results in the names or titles of works, the names and addresses of authors, publishers and owners of copyright, and such other particulars as are prescribed by the law being entered in the Register of Copyrights. Entries in this Register are presumed to be true by courts although the presumption is rebuttable. Such entries do not create copyrights; they merely register copyrights (which have already automatically come into existence on the creation of a work).

How to Register a Copyright

A Schedule to the Copyright Act mentions what the fees for different types of works are. For example, the fees to register the copyright in a literary work is 50 INR. The fees (which can be sent by postal order or by a DD in favour of the Registrar of Copyrights) along with the application form, statement of particulars, statement of further particulars, (available online at http://copyright.gov.in/copyrightregistrationform.pdf) and the work in triplicate is required to be sent to the Registrar of Copyrights at the Copyright Office, B-2/W-3 Curzon Road Barracks, Kasturba Gandhi Marg, New Delhi 110001, India.

What the Copyright Act Says

Chapter X of the Copyright Act deals with the registration of copyright.

The author, publisher, copyright owner, or any other person interested in the copyright of a work may make an application to the Registrar of Copyrights to have the copyright registered. On the receipt of an application in respect of any work, the Registrar of Copyrights may, after holding an inquiry as he may deem fit, enter the particulars of the work in the Register of Copyrights.

In respect of an artistic work which is used or is capable of being used in relation to any goods, the application must include a statement to that effect and it must be accompanied by a certificate from the Registrar of Trade Marks saying that no trade mark identical with or deceptively similar to the artistic work has been registered under the Trade and Merchandise Marks Act, 1958 in the name of any person other than the applicant, or that no person other than the applicant has made an application for the registration of such a trade mark.[79]

The main benefit of getting a copyright registered is that the Register of Copyrights is prima facie evidence of the particulars entered in it and documents purporting to be copies of any entries in it, or extracts from it certified by the Registrar of Copyrights and sealed with the seal of the Copyright Office are admissible in evidence in all courts without further proof or production of the original.[80]

The Copyright Act makes various provisions with regard to the Register of Copyrights which is to be kept at the Copyright Office, and is required to contain the names or title of works and the names and addresses of authors, publishers and owners of copyright and such other particulars as are prescribed.[81] Indexes of the Register of Copyrights are also kept at the Copyright Office.[82]

The Register of Copyrights and indexes of it are open to inspection at all reasonable times, and any person is entitled to take copies of, or make extracts from, the register or indexes on payment of a fee.[83]

The Registrar of Copyrights may amend or later the Register of Copyrights by (a) correcting any error in any name, address or particulars; or (b) correcting any other error which may have arisen in the Register by an accidental slip or omission.[84]

The Copyright Board, on the application of the Registrar of Copyrights or of any person aggrieved, is empowered to order the rectification of the Register of Copyrights by (a) the making of any entry wrongly omitted to be made in the register, or (b) the expunging of any entry wrongly made in, or remaining on, the register, or (c) the correction of any error or defect in the register.[85] However, the rectification of an entry in the Register without giving the person against whom the entry concerned is rectified is invalid as such a rectification would be against the principles of natural justice.[86]

INFRINGEMENT

The violation of a copyright constitutes copyright infringement. Copyrights are a creation of statute and any violation is a legal wrong with legal consequences. The most commonly used tem for copyright infringement is 'piracy' which brings back echoes of pirates of yore and is presumably meant to discourage people from indulging in infringement by putting a moral element into the picture.

Most record companies etc. would have one believe that the infringement of a copyright violation is tantamount to piracy (with all the connotations of piracy on the high seas) and that it is morally wrong to infringe a copyright without seeming to realize that, among other things, they themselves often invite copyright violations by pricing their products so absurdly that the average person can't afford them. In India, some companies seem to have recognized this and have made a number of films available at lower prices. For example, Moser Baer now sells DVDs of such films as *The Passion of the Christ* for 69 INR. Moser Baer has also made VCDs of some Hindi films available for as little as 28 INR, and at that price, copyright violations obviously become a non-issue. That isn't how it works for the average DVD though which rarely costs less than 600 INR. In a country where the salaries often low, it isn't difficult to understand the temptation to buy 'pirated' music or films even if such copies are illegal.

'Infringing copies'[87] have been defined in relation to various kinds of works under the Copyright Act. In relation to a literary, dramatic, musical or artistic work, an infringing copy is a reproduction of the work which is not in the form of a cinematographic film, while in relation to a film, an infringing copy is a copy of the film made on any medium by any means. However, for the purpose of determining if infringement has been committed under Section 51 of the Copyright Act, the reproduction of a literary, dramatic, musical or artistic work in the form of a film is deemed to be an infringing copy. As far as sound recordings are concerned, infringing copies mean other recordings embodying the same sound recording made by any means. And an infringing copy of a programme or performance in which a broadcast reproduction right or a performer's right subsists is defined as 'the sound recording or a cinematographic film of such programme or performance, if such reproduction copy of sound recording is made or imported in contravention of the provisions of the Copyright Act'.

Infringing copies of works and plates which are either used or intended to be used to produce infringing copies are deemed to be the property of the copyright owner. The Court may order all such copies or plates to be delivered to the copyright owner. A police officer not below the rank of sub-inspector can seize infringing copies of a work without a warrant.

Section 51 of the Copyright Act specifically defines what constitutes copyright infringement. It says that the copyright in a work is deemed to be infringed when any person:

(1) does anything which the copyright owner has the exclusive right to do

(2) permits any place to be used for the communication of the work to the public for profit if the communication constitutes an infringement of the copyright in the work. However, he is not deemed to have infringed copyright if he was not aware and had no reasonable ground for believing that the communication was an infringement of copyright

(3) makes for sale or hire, or sells or lets for hire, or by way of trade displays or offers for sale or hire any infringing copies of a work

(4) distributes either for the purposes of trade or to such

an extent as to affect prejudicially the owner of the copyright any infringing copies of a work

(5) by way of trade exhibits any infringing copies of a work in public

(6) imports into India any infringing copies of a work. This does not apply if any person imports just one copy of any work for his own private and domestic use.

None of these acts constitute an infringement of copyright if they are done in pursuance of a licence (granted by the owner of the Copyright or the Registrar of Copyrights under the Copyright Act) or if they are done in accordance with the conditions of a licence so granted or of any conditions imposed by a competent authority under the Copyright Act.

It is a criminal offence to knowingly infringe or abet the infringement of a copyright.[88]

COMMUNICATION TO THE PUBLIC

As boring as the term 'communication to the public' sounds, it's important because such communication is often one of the key elements in infringement. Ordinarily, to communicate anything, there have to be a minimum of two parties involved: at least one which transmits information and at least one which receives that information. For example, when two people talk, for any communication to occur, there has to be one who speaks while the other listens. This bit of basic logic is completely missing in copyright law though.

Under the Copyright Act, 'communication to the public' means making any work available for being seen or heard or otherwise enjoyed by the public directly or by any means of display or diffusion other than by issuing copies of such work *regardless of whether any member of the public actually sees, hears or otherwise enjoys the work* so made available. Communication through satellite or cable or any other means of simultaneous communication to more than one household or place of residence including residential rooms of any hotel or hostel shall be deemed to be communication to the public.[89] Further, 'broadcast' means communication to the public by any means of wireless diffusion, whether in any one or more of the forms of signs, sounds or visual images, or by wire, and includes a re-broadcast.[90]

The case of Super Cassette Industries v. Sameer Kukhreja and Nirulas Cornerhouse (P) Ltd.[91] in the Delhi High Court dealt with infringing the copyright of works which are broadcast via cable (without their copyright being infringed) by subsequently communicating them to the public.

In this case, the plaintiff, Super Cassette, was the copyright holder of a number of works many of which it licenses. The defendant, Nirulas, ran restaurants. Nirulas transmitted the Super Cassette's works (which it had received via cable) to its guests without a licence from Super Cassette which caused Super Cassette to claim that its copyright in the works had been infringed and obtain an interim injunction against Nirulas.

Super Cassette relied on the explanation to Section 2(ff) — the section which defines 'communication to the public' — of Copyright Act which says that making a work available by simultaneous means of communication in hotels rooms amounts to 'communication to the public' as well as on the provisions[92] of the Copyright Act which define copyright and speak of the infringement of copyright.

With reference to *Performing Right Society* v. *Hammonds Bradford Brewery Co. Ltd.,*[93] Super Cassette contended that the provision of a cable channel to guests was analogous to making acoustic presentations to hotel guests through the wireless and that it amounted to 'communication to the public'. It also cited Garware Plastics and Polyester Ltd. v. Telelink[94] where it had been held that the broadcasting of content through cable channels to households and other places amounts to a public performance.

Nirulas first unsuccessfully tried to have the plaint rejected under Order 8 Rule 11 of the Code of Civil Procedure and later tried to avoid distinguishing between the cable operator (legally) transmitting signals to it, and its own subsequently transmitting those same signals to its guests.

The High Court of Delhi held that Nirulas had infringed the Super Cassette's copyright since Parliament intended 'to exclude the operation of such categories of [commercial] establishments from the benefit of what are obviously deemed not infringements. Such provisions should receive a restricted interpretation, having regard to the nature of the expressions used. Thus, the Court will not extend the law beyond its meaning to take care of any perceived broader legislative purpose.'

In addition to this, as held in Hubbard v. Vosper,[95] 'the court must consider the question of proportions in the case of a copyright infringement action. Therefore, for instance, the placing of a common television in a motel reception, accessible to all but without keeping a television set, in each hotel room, or placing such a set in a grocery shop for the recreation of the owner, or a wayside restaurant, may not fall within the mischief of the definition of infringement. Proportion in this context, would necessarily imply the nature of the activity of the establishment and the integral connection the infringement complained of has with it'.

EXCEPTIONS TO COPYRIGHT

Indian Law does not specifically speak of fair use. However, there are a number of exceptions to copyright which are listed in the Indian Copyright Act. The bulk of these exceptions which are in many ways analogous to fair use (although they are quite a bit more narrow) allow the use of copyrighted material without a licence for the purposes of:

- research
- review
- criticism
- education

The Act spells out exactly which acts do not constitute an infringement of copyright. Some of these acts are:

(1) a fair dealing with a literary, dramatic, musical or artistic work which is not a computer programme for the purposes of private use including research,

criticism or review, of either that work or any other work

(2) the making of copies or adaptations of a computer programme by its lawful possessor, from the copy in order to utilize the computer programme for the purposes for which it was supplied or to make back-up copies purely as a temporary protection against loss, destruction or damage in order only to utilize the computer programme for the purpose for which it was supplied

(3) the doing of any act necessary to obtain information essential for operating inter-operability of an independently created computer programme with other programmes by its a lawful possessor if such information is not otherwise readily available

(4) the observation, study or test of functioning of a computer programme in order to determine the ideas and principles which underlie any elements of the programme while performing acts necessary for the functions for which the programme was supplied

(5) the making of copies or adaptations of a computer programme from a personally legally obtained copy for non-commercial personal use

(6) a fair dealing with a literary, dramatic, musical or artistic work to report current events in a newspaper, magazine or similar periodical, or by broadcast, or in a film, or by means of photographs. (The publication of a compilation of addresses or speeches delivered in public is not a fair dealing of such works within the meaning of this provision.)

(7) the reproduction of a literary, dramatic, musical or artistic work for the purpose of a judicial proceeding or for the purpose of a report of a judicial proceeding

(8) the reproduction or publication of a literary, dramatic, musical or artistic work in any work prepared by the Secretariat of a Legislature or, if the Legislature

consists of two Houses, by the Secretariat of either House of the Legislature, exclusively for the use of the members of that Legislature

(9) the reproduction of any literary, dramatic or musical work in a certified copy made or supplied in accordance with any law for the time being in force

(10) the reading or recitation of any reasonable extract from a published literary or dramatic work in public

(11) the publication in a collection, mainly composed of non-copyrighted matter, bona fide intended for the use of educational institutions, and so described in the title and in any advertisement issued by or on behalf of the publisher, of short passages from published literary or dramatic works, not themselves published for the use of educational institutions, in which copyright subsists (Not more than two passages by the same author may be published by the same publisher in a collection during any five-year period whether the author has created the work by himself, jointly or in collaboration with any other person.)

(12) the reproduction of a literary, dramatic, musical or artistic work by a teacher or a pupil in the course of instruction, or as part of the questions to be answered in an examination, or in answers to examination questions

(13) the performance, in the course of the activities of an educational institution, of a literary, dramatic or musical work by the staff and students of the institution, or of a film or a sound recordings if the audience is limited to students, their parents and guardians, staff and persons directly connected with the activities of the institution, or the communication to such an audience of a film or sound recording

(14) the making of sound recordings in respect of any literary, dramatic or musical work, if (i) sound recordings of that work have been made by or with

the licence or consent of the owner of the right in the work or (ii) the person making the sound recordings has given a notice of his intention to make the sound recordings, has provided copies of all covers or labels with which the sound recordings are to be sold, and has paid to the owner of rights in the work royalties in respect of all such sound recordings to be made by him at the rate fixed by the Copyright Board. However, (i) no alterations can be made which have not been made previously by or with the consent of the owner of rights, or which are not reasonably necessary for the adaptation of the work for the purpose of making the sound recordings, (ii) the sound recordings cannot be issued in any form of packaging or with any label which is likely to mislead or confuse the public as to their identity; (iii) the sound recordings can only be made after the expiry of two calendar years after the end of the year in which the first sound recording of the work was made; and (iv) the person making the sound recordings must allow the owner of rights or his duly authorized agent or representative to inspect all records and books of account relating to them. If on a complaint brought before the Copyright Board to the effect that the owner of rights has not been paid in full for any sound recordings, and the Copyright Board is, prima facie, satisfied that the complaint is genuine, it may pass an order ex parte directing the person making the sound recording to cease from making further copies and, after holding such inquiry as it considers necessary, make such further orders as it deems fit, including an order for the payment of royalty

(15) the causing of a recording to be heard in public by utilizing it in an enclosed room or hall meant for the common use of residents in any residential premises (other than a hotel or similar commercial establishment) as part of the amenities provided exclusively or mainly for residents; or as part of the

activities of a club, society or similar organization which is not established or conducted for profit

(16) the performance of a literary, dramatic or musical work by an amateur club or society, if the performance is given to a non-paying audience, or for the benefit of a religious institution

(17) the reproduction in a newspaper, magazine or other periodical of an article on current economic, political, social or religious topics, unless the author of the article has expressly reserved the right of such reproduction to himself

(18) the publication in a newspaper, magazine or other periodical of a report of a lecture delivered in public

(19) the making of up to three copies of a book (including a pamphlet, sheet of music, map, chart or plan) by or under the direction of the person in charge of a public library for the use of the library if the book is not available for sale in India

(20) the reproduction, for the purpose of research or private study or with a view to publication, of an unpublished literary, dramatic or musical work kept in a library, museum or other institution to which the public has access. If the identity of the author of any such work or, in the case of a work of joint authorship, of any of the authors is known to the library, museum or other institution the reproduction can only be made at a time more than sixty years from the date of the death of the author or the last surviving author whose identity is known.

(21) the reproduction or publication of (i) any matter which has been published in any Official Gazette except an Act of a Legislature; (ii) any Act of a Legislature subject to the condition that the Act is reproduced or published together with any commentary on it or any other original matter; (iii) the report of any committee, commission, council, board or other like body

appointed by the Government if the report has been laid on the Table of the Legislature, unless its reproduction or publication has been prohibited by the Government

(22) any judgment or order of a court, tribunal or other judicial authority, unless its reproduction or publication is prohibited by the court, the tribunal or other judicial authority, as the case may be

(23) the production or publication of a translation in any Indian language of an Act of a Legislature and of any rules or orders made under it if no translation of such Act or rules or orders in that language has previously been produced or published by the Government; or if the translation of the Act or rules or orders in that language has been produced or published by the Government but is not available for sale to the public. The translation must contain a statement at a prominent place to the effect that it has not been authorized or accepted as authentic by the Government

(24) the making or publishing of a painting, drawing, engraving or photograph of a work of architecture or the display of a work of architecture

(25) the making or publishing of a painting, drawing, engraving or photograph of a sculpture, or any other work of artistic craftsmanship if the work is permanently situated in a public place or any premises to which the public has access

(26) the inclusion in a film of any artistic work permanently situated in a public place or any premises to which the public has access, or any other artistic work, if the inclusion of the work is only by way of background or is otherwise incidental to the principal matters represented in the film

(27) the use by the author of an artistic work, if he is not the owner of the copyright in the work, of any mould, cast, sketch, plan, model or study made by him for

the purpose of the work provided that he does not thereby repeat or imitate the main design of the work

(28) the reconstruction of a building or structure in accordance with the architectural drawings or plans by reference to which the building or structure was originally constructed provided that the original construction was made with the consent or licence of the owner of the copyright in such drawings and plans

(29) in relation to a literary, dramatic or musical work recorded or reproduced in any film, the exhibition of such film after the expiration of the term of copyright therein in certain cases

(30) the making of an ephemeral recording by a broadcasting organization using its own facilities for its own broadcast by a broadcasting organization of a work which it has the right to broadcast; and the retention of such recording for archival purposes on the ground of its exceptional documentary character

(31) the performance of a literary, dramatic or musical work or the communication to the public of such a work or of a sound recording in the course of any bona fide religious ceremony (including a marriage procession and other social festivities associated with a marriage), or an official ceremony held by the Central Government, a State Government or any local authority.

These provisions apply to the doing of any act in relation to the translation of a literary, dramatic or musical work or the adaptation of a literary, dramatic, musical or artistic work as they apply in relation to the work itself.

PENALTIES AND REMEDIES

If the provisions of the Copyright Act are contravened, three types of action can be taken: civil, criminal and administrative. The person whose name appears on the work as being its author or publisher is assumed to actually be its author or publisher, as the case may be, and can initiate proceedings.

Infringing copies of any copyrighted work and all the plates which have been used or are intended to be used to produce such infringing copies are deemed to be the property of the owner of the copyright.

Administrative Action

In addition to civil and criminal proceedings, an administrative remedy in the form of an Anton Piller Order can be obtained. These orders direct opponents to allow applicants to search their premises for evidence (of infringement) and seize such evidence.

The suspected infringer is not given notice of the search. However, Anton Piller Orders are granted only if there is:

(a) a very strong prima facie case against the opponent

(b) a risk that the opponent will destroy or conceal evidence which he has been shown to possess

(c) serious potential or actual damage to the applicant.

The order is named after the case of Anton Piller KG v. Manufacturing Processes Limited, 1976 although it was first granted by Templeman J in EMI Limited v. Pandit, 1975. It does not grant the applicant the right to search the opponent's premises. As Lord Denning put it, "[T]he order sought in this case is not a search warrant. It does not authorize the plaintiff's solicitors or anyone else to enter the defendants' premises against their will. It does not authorize the breaking down of any doors, nor the slipping in by a back door, nor getting in by an open door or window ... The plaintiffs must get the defendants' permission. But it does do this: It brings pressure on the defendants to give permission. It does more: It actually orders them to give permission — with, I suppose, the result that if they do not give permission, they are guilty of contempt of court."

Criminal Prosecution

Knowingly infringing or abetting the infringement of copyright is a criminal offence,[96] and infringers can be punished with:

(1) imprisonment

(2) fines

(3) the seizure of infringing copies of the work

Specifically, the Copyright Act says that any person who knowingly infringes or abets the infringement of the copyright in a work is punishable with imprisonment for a term which shall not be less than six months but which may extend to three years and with a fine which shall not be less than fifty thousand rupees but which may extend to two lakh rupees. This penalty is enhanced on second and subsequent convictions to a term which is required not be less than one year but which may extend to three years and with fine of not be less than one lakh rupees but which may extend to two lakh rupees.[97]

Any person who knowingly uses a pirated copy of a computer programme is liable to be imprisoned for a term of not less than seven days but which may extend to three years and be required to pay a fine of not less than fifty thousand rupees but which may extend to two lakh rupees.[98]

Any person who knowingly makes, or has in his possession, any plate for the purpose of making infringing copies of any copyrighted work is liable to be punished with imprisonment which may extend to two years and is also liable to fine.

A police officer not below the rank of a sub inspector may seize infringing copies of a work without a warrant. The person from whom they have been seized may apply to a Magistrate to have them restored.

No court inferior to that of a Metropolitan Magistrate or a Judicial Magistrate of the First Class can try any criminal offence under the Copyright Act.[99]

Civil Action

Civil proceedings can be initiated against a person who infringes copyright. The owner of the copyright can pray to the Court for:

(1) an injunction

(2) damages

(3) an account of profits

4. damages for conversion

Proceedings may be initiated by the copyright owner or an exclusive licensee. However, Section 56 of the Act says that where the several rights comprising the copyright in any work are owned by different persons, the owner of any such right may individually enforce such right by means of any suit, action or other proceeding without making the owner of any other right a party to such suit, action or proceeding. He is entitled to remedies provided by this Act to the extent of the right he owns.

The costs of the parties in any proceedings in respect of the infringement of copyright are at the discretion of the court. If the infringer were able to prove that at the date of the infringement he was not aware of and had no reasonable ground to believe that copyright subsisted in the work, the person who went to court because of his right having been infringed would not be entitled to any remedy except an injunction in respect of the infringement and a decree for the whole or part of the profits made by the infringer from the sale of the infringing copies as the court deemed reasonable in the circumstances.[100]

The District Court concerned has the jurisdiction in suits against copyright infringement. This includes a district court within the local limits of whose jurisdiction, at the time of the institution of the suit or other proceeding, the person(s) instituting the suit or other proceeding actually and voluntarily reside or carry on business or personally work for gain.[101] This is one of the provisions of the Indian Copyright Act which truly gives it teeth. Generally, civil proceedings can be initiated where the cause of action took place or where the person complained against voluntarily resides, carries on business or personally works for gain. By allowing a suit to be filed wherever the person who claimed his copyright had been infringed lived, the law makes life much more difficult for those who are accused of infringing copyright. For example, if a person who lived in Bombay was accused by a person living in Delhi of infringing his copyright at Kolkata, the suit for copyright infringement could be filed in Delhi. Apart from increasing costs exponentially for the alleged infringer, it could also create massive logistical problems for him.

The flip side, of course, is that the starving artist would be able to protect his copyright by filing a suit in his local court and would therefore not have to pay as much. Filing a suit anywhere though does cost money as does pursuing any matter, and its unlikely that impoverished persons would benefit greatly by not having to pay transport costs. Assuming that this is another one of those provisions which are supposed to protect starving artists, presumably those artists would travel by train. Compare a train fare of about 500 INR from Bombay to Delhi with the tens of thousands charged by good lawyers, do the math and wonder how this allowing suits to be filed where copyright owners live helps artists.

On the other hand, consider a major company which routinely files its infringement suits in, say, Delhi, where it is headquartered — and most infringement suits are filed by companies which accumulate copyrights. The alleged infringer who would probably not have comparable resources and could in fact well be a personification of the starving artist would then not only have to pay legal fees but also transport costs.

If it is looked at from this point of view, it is difficult to justify this provision regarding the jurisdiction of courts in the Copyright Act.

FOOTNOTES

30. Section 13, Indian Copyright Act, 1957
31. Section 2(ffc), Indian Copyright Act, 1957
32. Section 52(1)(aa), Indian Copyright Act, 1957
33. Section 52(1)(ab), Indian Copyright Act, 1957
34. <mit.gov.in/default.aspx?id=717>
35. <trai.gov.in/trai/upload/Regulations/65/Regulation5june07.pdf>
36. Under Rule 2(q), Telecom Unsolicited Commercial Communications Regulations, 2007, an 'unsolicited commercial communication' is defined as any message, through telecommunications service, which is transmitted for the purpose of informing about, or soliciting or promoting any commercial transaction in relation to goods, investments or services which a subscriber opts not to receive, but does not include any message (other than promotional message) relating to a service or financial

transaction under a specific contract between the parties to such contract; or any messages relating to charities, national campaigns or natural calamities transmitted on the directions of the Government or agencies authorized by it for the said purpose; or any message transmitted, on the directions of the Government or any authority or agency authorized by it, in the interest of the sovereignty and integrity of India, the security of the State, friendly relations with foreign States, public order, decency or morality.

37. Under R 3 of the Use of Low Power Equipment in the Frequency Band 2.4 GHz to 2.4835 GHz (Exemption from Licensing Requirement) Rules, <dot.gov.in/wpc/Gazette%20(%202.4%20GHz)_Outdoor.doc> notwithstanding anything contained in any law for the time being in force, no licence is required by any person to establish, maintain, work, possess or deal in any wireless equipment, on non-interference, non-protection and shared (non-exclusive) basis, in the frequency band 2.4 GHz to 2.4835 GHz with the maximum out power of the transmitter being less than 1 W (30 dBm) in Spread of 10 MHz or higher, maximum effective radiated power being less than 4 W (36 dBm), and the height of antenna being within five metres above the roof top of an existing authorized building.
38. Section 14(a), Indian Copyright Act, 1957
39. Gramophone Co. of India v. Super Cassette Industries Ltd. 1995 (58) DLT 99; Section 2(p), Indian Copyright Act, 1957
40. Section 2(h), Indian Copyright Act, 1957
41. Section 2(o), Indian Copyright Act, 1957
42. Section 14(b), Indian Copyright Act, 1957
43. Section 2(c), Indian Copyright Act, 1957
44. Section 14(c), Indian Copyright Act, 1957
45. Section 2(f), Indian Copyright Act, 1957
46. Section 14(d), Indian Copyright Act, 1957
47. Section 42, Indian Copyright Act, 1957
48. Section 42A, Indian Copyright Act, 1957
49. Section 2(a), Indian Copyright Act, 1957
50. The British Horseracing Board Ltd and Other's v.William Hill Organization Ltd (November 9, 2004) <eur-lex.europa. eu/LexUriServ/site/en/oj/2005/c_006/c_00620050108en00040004.pdf>;Also see: Fixtures Marketing Ltd v. Oy Veikkaus Ab (November 9, 2004)<eur-lex.europa.eu/LexUriServ/site/en/oj/2005/c_006/c_ 00620050108 en 00020002.pdf>
51. Section 2(d), Indian Copyright Act, 1957
52. Section 17, Indian Copyright Act, 1957
53. Section. 57, Copyright Act, 1957
54. Section 22 to 29, Indian Copyright Act, 1957
55. Section 24, Indian Copyright Act, 1957
56. <hinduonnet.com/thehindu/thscrip/print.pl?file =2007113054851100.htm&date=2007/11/30/&prd=th&>, <tinyurl.com/37g5eo>
57. Section 2 (q), Copyright Act, 1957

58. Section 2 (qq), Copyright Act, 1957
59. Section 38, Copyright Act, 1957
60. Section 39, Copyright Act, 1957
61. Section 39 A, Copyright Act, 1957
62. Section 37, Copyright Act, 1957
63. Section 39, Copyright Act, 1957
64. Section 39 A, Copyright Act, 1957
65. Sections 18, 19 and 30, Indian Copyright Act, 1957
66. Venugopal Setty v. Suryakanta, 1992
67. London Printing and Publishing Alliance v. Cox, 1891
68. E.W.Savoy v. World of Golf, 1914
69. AIR 1967 Ass 70
70. <judis.nic.in/supremecourt/qrydisp. aspx?filename=31596>
71. Section 31, Indian Copyright Act, 1957
72. Section 31A, Indian Copyright Act, 1957
73. Section 32A, Indian Copyright Act, 1957
74. Section 32B, Indian Copyright Act, 1957
75. <judis.nic.in/supremecourt/qrydisp. aspx?filename=31596>
76. Section 53A, Indian Copyright Act, 1957
77. AIR 1976 Mad 22
78. (1987) 2 ALT 699
79. Section 45, Indian Copyright Act, 1957
80. Section 48, Indian Copyright Act, 1957
81. Section 44, Indian Copyright Act, 1957
82. Section 46, Indian Copyright Act, 1957
83. Section 47, Indian Copyright Act, 1957
84. Section 49, Indian Copyright Act, 1957
85. Section 50, Indian Copyright Act, 1957
86. AIR 1977 Del 41
87. Section 2(m), Indian Copyright Act, 1957
88. Section 63, Indian Copyright Act, 1957
89. Section 2 (ff), Indian Copyright Act, 1957
90. Section 2 (dd), Indian Copyright Act, 1957
91. CS (OS) 1096/2007, <nsaikia.files. wordpress. com/2008/03/super-cassette-v. -nirulas-corner-house-ia_no_10742_2007_and_ia_no_6882. pdf>; Copyright Infringement In Playing Television Channel by Manisha Singh Nair <mondaq. com/article. asp?articleid=58634>
92. Sections 14 and 51, Indian Copyright Act, 1957
93. (1934) Ch. 121
94. AIR 1989 Bom 331
95. 1972 (1) All ER 1072
96. Section 63, Indian Copyright Act, 1957
97. Section 63A, Indian Copyright Act, 1957
98. Section 63B, Indian Copyright Act, 1957
99. Section 70, Indian Copyright Act, 1957
100. Section 55, Indian Copyright Act, 1957
101. Section 62, Indian Copyright Act, 1957

5

CONTRACTS

"This contract is so one-sided, I am astonished to find it written on both sides of the paper."

— *Lord Evershed, M R*[1]

DAVID AND GOLIATH

An independent artist negotiating with the corporate owner of a copyright could quite easily be the equivalent of a serf attempting to negotiate with his overlord: one party has all the power, the other party has none.

Under the law, a legally valid agreement is a contract. To be valid, an agreement must be entered into by competent parties, for a lawful object, with free consent and for a valid consideration. Other agreements may either be void or voidable depending on how they are arrived at.

The law does not recognize agreements which are void. Void agreements include those which restrain marriage and trade. Also, all contracts entered into by minors are void-ab-initio. Voidable agreements, on the other hand, are agreements which do receive a degree of acceptance by the law. They are treated as contracts provided they are not avoided by a party to them who has the right to do so. For example, if one person forces another to agree to sell his house at gunpoint, the person who was held at gunpoint has the right to avoid the contract.

Thus, there exists a framework within one must function but that framework is skeletal at best and doesn't say much beyond such things as an impossible agreement is a void agreement. One of the most important features of contract law is the freedom to negotiate commercial terms.

That, however, doesn't help very much if one party is far more powerful than the other is and exercises its power to the detriment of the weakerparty. The Doctrine of Unconscionability is supposed to come into play in such cases where bargaining power is not evenly distributed. It is one of the exceptions to the freedom of parties to contract. As a general rule, as long as a contract involves some form of consideration i.e. quid pro quo, courts do not get involved. However, if a contract is excessively one-sided, courts are willing to step in and come to the aid of the injured party.

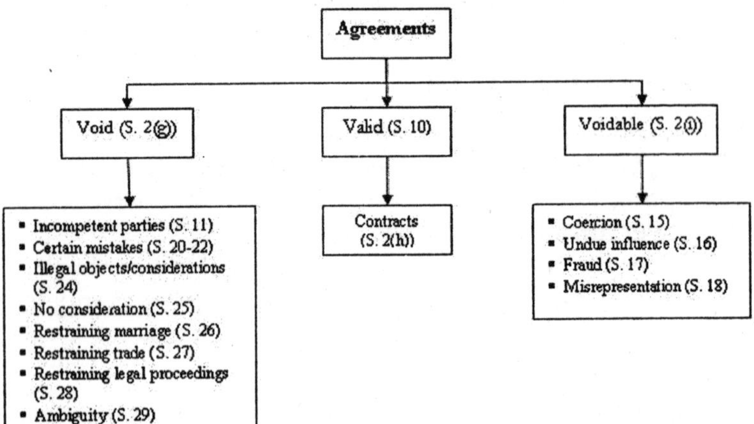

The Indian Contract Act, 1872

Section 16 of the Indian Contract Act deals with 'undue influence'. It says that a contract is said to be induced by undue influence if one of the parties is in a position to dominate the will of the other and uses that position to obtain an unfair advantage over the other. For example, a person who is in a position of authority over another, or who stands in a fiduciary relation to the other, or who makes a contract with a person of sub-normal mental capacity is deemed to be in a position to dominate the will of that other person. If, in such situations, the transaction appears, on the face of it or on the evidence adduced, to be unconscionable the person who is in a position to dominate the will of the other is required to prove that the contract was not induced by undue influence.

The standard fiduciary relationships which are recognized are those which exist between such persons are parent and child, student and teacher, patient and doctor, lawyer and client, trustee and beneficiary, and priest and parishioner. That friendship is a form of fiduciary relationship isn't something which is ordinarily considered but as Ethan J Leib[2] says, "[T]he case for thinking of friends as fiduciaries is exceedingly persuasive and underappreciated, both in the law and in our lives."[105]

Under Section 19A of the Indian Contract Act, the party whose consent was obtained by undue influence may choose to avoid the contract. The Court may set the contract aside either absolutely or, if the party entitled to avoid it has received any benefit under it, upon such terms and conditions which the Court thinks are just.

Even though a fiduciary relationship clearly does not exist between the average artist and record company, the mere difference in bargaining power can in itself lead to an unconscionable contract being drafted. Also, the application of the doctrine under Indian statutory law is on a much firmer footing under Section 23 of the Indian Contract Act which says that the consideration or object of an agreement is not lawful if it is immoral, or opposed to public policy. And if the consideration or object is not lawful, the contract is void and unenforceable.

Deciding whether or not a contract is unconscionable though is often difficult to do — in some instances, it is obvious such as in Employment Contracts which contain absurdly broad non-compete clauses or in boilerplate contracts which favour sellers, insurers and other such persons to an unimaginable degree. In others, however, it is more difficult to tell the difference between a well-negotiated deal (for one party) and the imposition of an unconscionable contract term on another party to the contract. Also, the decision as to whether or not a contract is actually unconscionable relies heavily on morality. As such, the factors which come into play to reach a decision are decidedly subjective.

Augusto C Lima says, "The defense of freedom of contract, which finds contemporary resonance in the economic analysis of contract law, usually entails the narrow application of unconscionability. The concept of unconscionability for such a purpose is narrowed by the assignment of a procedural, rather than substantive, nature to it. In such a procedural view, unconscionability is but a device to fill in the gap between a defect in contract formation (such as fraud or duress) and unconscionability as substantive unfairness (focused on the morality of the transaction)," in 'When Harry Met Kreutziger: A Look into Unconscionability Through the Lenses of Culture'.[106]

Indian courts have generally been willing to interfere in boilerplate contracts on the ground that they are unconscionable.[107] However, proving unconscionability in other situations can be an uphill task in the absence of clear evidence either within the agreement itself or otherwise.

ASSIGNMENTS AND CONTRACTS

The doctrine of privity mandates that a third party cannot enforce a contract. Assignment is in a way an exception to this doctrine. It has been defined by Black's Law Dictionary to mean a 'transfer or making over to another of the whole of any property, real or personal, in possession or in action, or if in estate or in right therein'.

A party to a contract can assign the benefits which are to accrue to him under the contract to a third person. The third person is not a third party beneficiary and he can, once the assignment is complete, enforce the contract of his own accord. The assignor may, subject to the terms of the contract, still be liable on it. However, post-assignment, the contract retains its bilateral character with the contract virtually becoming one between the other party to the contract and the assignee.

Section 37 of the Indian Contract Act, 1872 (which speaks of the obligations of parties to contracts) enables parties to assign their contractual obligations by saying:

'The parties to a contract must either perform, or offer to perform, their respective promises, unless such performance is dispensed with or excused under the provisions of this Act, or of any other law.

Promises bind the representatives of the promisors in case of the death of such promisors before performance, unless a contrary intention appears from the contract.'

However, although some statutes such as the Copyright Act speak of assignments, there is no explicit provision in the Contract Act which allows for the assignment of a contract in spite of the fact that Common Law countries usually allow for much freedom in the assignment of contracts.

Under Indian law, the matter of whether or not a contract can be assigned is determined by considering the intention of the parties as spelt out by the contract if at all it has been spelt out. Assignments may be of the rights under a contract or of the obligations under the contract. Generally, rights under a contract can be assigned unless the rights in question cannot be assigned under law.

In addition to this, the obligations under contracts of a personal nature invariably cannot be assigned and must be performed by the parties who have contracted to perform them. The classic example is that of a commission to paint a portrait — the artist in such a contract cannot have someone else perform his obligation viz. have someone else paint the required portrait.

This obviously does not apply where a would-be assignor obtains the consent of the other party to the contract. In the case of Khardah Co. Ltd. v. Raymon and Co. (India) Pvt. Ltd., 1962[108] the Supreme Court laid down the law quite clearly by saying:

"An assignment of a contract might result by transfer either of the rights or of the obligations thereunder. But there is a well-recognized distinction between these two classes of assignments. As a rule, obligations under a contract cannot be assigned except with the consent of the promisee, and when such consent is given, it is really a novation resulting in substitution of liabilities. On the other hand rights under a contract are assignable unless the contract is personal in its nature the rights are incapable of assignment either under the law or under an agreement between the parties. ... An arbitration clause does not take away the right of a party to a contract to assign it if it is otherwise assignable. ... There is, in law, a clear distinction between assignment of rights under a contract by a party who has performed his obligations thereunder, and assignment of a claim for compensation which one party has against the other for breach of contract. The latter is a mere claim for damages which cannot be assigned in law; the former is a benefit under an agreement, which is capable of assignment."

While the substantive provisions of Indian law are almost invariably in favour of honouring the intention of the parties to a contract, figuring out exactly what their intention vis-à-vis a contract is has often proved to be difficult. As a matter of practical expedience, it is therefore advisable to include a clause in every contract stating exactly what the intention of the parties is with respect to assignment.

FOOTNOTES

102. <bcli.org/pages/projects/unfairterms/Unfair_Contract_Terms_Interim _Rep. pdf>

103. Fiduciary relationships are relationships in which trust is an important component and in which the price of distrust could be very high. The fiduciary is often in a position of authority or power, and it is difficult to keep a close eye on him — what do you do when your doctor or lawyer begins to spout Latin other than hope that they know what they're talking about?

Fiduciary relationships are also relationships in which the price of distrust is often extremely high — think of the consequences of having a doctor talk about one's medical issues to all and sundry. The possible consequences of a breach of trust make it essential for fiduciaries to be required to act with some minimal degree of care.

If one looks at the relationships which one shares with one's friends, the similarities are striking. There is trust involved. If there wasn't, one would never be able to exchange confidences with one's friends. Friends are expected not to be entirely selfish and self-absorbed. They have an obligation to keep their word whether that obligation is simply to the extent of not standing one up for dinner or in relation to something more important. They have a duty to be loyal particularly since a breach of the obligations of friendship can have extremely serious consequences for the person aggrieved.

One of the first things one learns of civil procedure is that civil courts have jurisdiction to try all suits of a civil nature and that suits involving what are merely social obligations do not qualify as being of a civil nature. There is no reason, however, for friends not to be subject to the same liabilities as a fiduciary. When one friend makes a promise to another and that other acts in reliance of that promise, he should be required to keep his word. He should not take advantage of the friendship or exercise undue influence for his own benefit. And if he does do so, there should be some way the person aggrieved can remedy the situation particularly if he is harmed by it.

Many people would probably cringe at the thought of having the State interfere in the private sphere. Apart from arguing from a purely moral position that trust should be honoured or from a legal point of view saying that if trust could be dishonoured with impunity, it'd destroy the socio-legal structure within which we function, the bottom line for me is that it is now accepted that abuse cannot be tolerated in either the public or the private sphere.

All of us trust our friends (in varying degrees, it must be admitted). We are usually far more vulnerable to them than we are to most other people. The very nature of our relationship with them requires that we let down our guard. And it is difficult to see how a breach of trust in friendship, the betrayal of the relationship itself isn't a form of abuse.

104.Associate Professor of Law, at the University of California's Hastings College of the Law

105.Friends as Fiduciaries: <ssrn. com/abstract=1115668>

106. <papers. ssrn. com/sol3/papers. cfm?abstract_id=1124922>

107.Chairman and MD, NTPC Ltd. v. Reshmi Constructions, Builders and Contractors, 2004 <judis. nic. in/supremecourt/qrydisp. aspx? filename =25736>; LIC of India v. Consumer Education Research Centre, 1995 <judis. nic. in/supremecourt/qrydisp. aspx?filename=10745>; Delhi Transport Corporation v. DTC Mazdoor Congress, 1990 <judis. nic. in/ supremecourt/qrydisp. aspx?filename=7431>; Bihar SEB v. Green Rubber Industries, 1989 <judis. nic. in/supremecourt/qrydisp. aspx? filename=7734>; Central Inland Water Transport Corporation Ltd. v. Brojo Nath Ganguly, 1986 <judis. nic. in/supremecourt/qrydisp. aspx? filename=9073>; Pierce Leslie and Co. Ltd. v. Violet Ouchterlony Wapshare, 1968 <judis. nic. in/supremecourt/qrydisp. aspx? filename=1865>

108.<judis. nic. in/supremecourt/qrydisp. aspx?filename=3822>

PART III

The Law at Work

6

REGULATION BY FEAR

The aspect of copyright law which is most important to most people is not the protection of works but the infringement of works which are protected. True, there are a small number of companies and superstars who rake in millions thanks to copyright but for every handful of persons who make money, there are hundreds of thousands who worry about whether or not they have infringed the copyright of someone who has the means and the inclination to sue them for infringement. They may be independent artists who have no desire to use other works in their own work for fear of being accused of infringement or simply members of the general public who think several times over before they download music illegally off the Internet.

The Recording Industry Association of America infamously spent years suing random online music file sharers in an effort to discourage infringement. Towards the end of 2008, it was reported that the Association planned to stop its suing spree — in a five-year period between 2003 and 2008, it sued some 35,000 people for copyright infringement. In what could have been construed as being good news for Internet users, the RIAA said that it would stop suing random Internet users who downloaded music without a licence (or who stole it, if one were to use the lingo of popular anti-'piracy' campaigns).

The RIAA announced that it planned to adopt some form of 'three strike programme' to curb copyright infringement. It said that it planned to work with — or possibly through — Internet service providers to get the job done. As of December 2008, it wasn't clear which service providers had agreed to work with it.

The Association said that ISPs would send warnings to persons who illegally downloaded music asking them to stop doing so. If the warnings were heeded, well and good. If not, action which could ultimately be the cancellation of their Internet connections could be taken against the users concerned.

While the good thing about this was that it signalled that the distinctly distasteful suing campaign would be over, the bad part was that one couldn't help but get the feeling that the recording industry was getting service providers to do its dirty work for it. Also, the new strategy did come with a disclaimer: the RIAA reserved the right to sue Internet users, and it had no intention of not pursuing pending law suits.

Speaking specifically about infringement, there is no infringement which occurs if the person 'using' a work has obtained permission from the owner of the copyright to do so. The most obvious way to obtain such consent is through a licence from the copyright owner. It is, however, worth noting that there may be more than one person who owns the copyright in a work, and in such a case, it would be necessary to obtain consent from all of the owners. For example, consider the case of a sound recording. To use it, depending on what the ownership of rights situation is, it may be necessary to obtain a licence from the lyricist, the composer, the producer et al.

Figuring out who owns the copyright though is, at times, no easy matter especially in the case of old works in relation to which there exist only skeletal contracts which do not clearly indicate who exactly the owner of the copyright is.

In such cases, a title search needs to be conducted using relevant route documents. Sometimes also referred to as an intellectual property audit, this involves examining records, deeds, contracts, wills and other documents by which property can be transferred. The Indian Copyright Act clarifies that if a person is bequeathed a manuscript[109] of an unpublished literary, dramatic or musical work, or an artistic work, the bequest includes the copyright in the work as far as the testator owned the copyright immediately before his death unless a contrary intention is indicated in the will or any of its codicils.[110]

The purpose of conducting an intellectual property audit is to find out who owns the relevant copyright and to check if there is any likelihood of having anyone claim that they own the copyright of the work. If such a possibility exists, a decision on whether or not to go ahead with using the work protected by copyright would depend on the risks involved and whether or not one was willing to assume those risks.

If no assignment agreements are available to trace the ownership of the intellectual property, an affidavit and an indemnity bond would ideally have to be obtained. If the producer was a company, a board resolution should have been obtained. It would be necessary to ensure that stamp duty had been paid and an indemnity clause would have to be included in each agreement.[111]

'An intellectual property audit (an intellectual property legal Due Diligence) is vital' before acquiring property either through a licence or a franchising agreement, or by a purchase. It must be conducted because it is the only viable method with which to gauge the rights of whoever claims to own the property and to enable a person to make appropriate decisions before using or acquiring the work in question.[112] If the audit were to show that the ownership of copyright was disputed, for example, the person considering acquiring or using the intellectual property in the work could decide not to go ahead with doing so if he were unwilling to assume the risks involved in doing so. If, however, the audit were simply not conducted, he would be blissfully unaware of the risks involved.

One saving grace is that when it comes to publishing third party content online, a network service provider is not always automatically liable for third party content if he can prove that he did not approve it.[113] Nonetheless, a person who publishes third party content may be liable for:

(1) Copyright infringement
(2) Contributory copyright infringement
(3) Vicarious copyright infringement
(4) Trademark infringement

Contributory infringement and vicarious infringement are both types of indirect copyright infringement. To commit contributory infringement, a person is required to have not only known or had reason to know of the infringement but also to have actively participated in it. In contrast to this, to commit vicarious infringement, a person is not required to actually have knowledge of the infringing activity or to take part in it: all that is required is for him to have a direct financial interest in the infringement and to have the ability to control it.

Not too surprisingly, it isn't difficult to wind up infringing someone's copyright, and the consequences of doing so can be severe. As a result, there are many people who will avoid touching works protected by copyright unless they have obtained an explicit licence from whoever owns the copyright in the work. They will not record a dance rehearsal with, say, 'The Simpsons' being watched in the background by a few dancers taking a break just in case they wind up violating the copyright which subsists in the cartoon. They will not make a film using music which they are uncertain is in the public domain. They will not take part in a non-commercial performance of a contemporary play just in case they infringe the playwright's copyright. In short, they won't do anything which just might be able to get them accused of having infringed copyright despite the fact that living without ever infringing someone's copyright in today's world is almost impossible.

In 2007, it was reported[6] that John Tehranian, a professor of law at the University of Utah, tracked all the times he could have infringed copyright in any given day by doing things as simple as forwarding eMail, and found that if all copyright owners sued for copyright infringement, he'd have to pay $12 million a day in fines — excluding fines for peer-to-peer downloads. Multiply that by 365 days a year and you have an annual fine of $ 4.5 billion. And that's just with reference to one person in one year.

It's a terrifying figure. Copyright holders know that, and, in all probability, they rely on it to ensure that ordinary people think not just twice but several times over before infringing copyright. They do such things as file suits for infringement against random individuals to make the fear of having infringed copyright not just a latent and abstract fear but a real and present danger. Whether or not those accused of infringing copyright are held guilty of doing so, there are legal fees with which to contend. And should they be held guilty, the penalties are rarely light.

FOOTNOTES

109.'Manuscript' means the original document embodying the work, whether written by hand or not.

110.Section 20, Indian Copyright Act, 1957

111.Ryder, Rodney, Intellectual Property and the Internet, LexisNexis, 2002, pp.562

112. Ryder, Rodney, Intellectual Property and the Internet, LexisNexis, 2002, pp.560

113.Section 79, Information Technology Act, 2000

114.<hinduonnet. com/thehindu/thscrip/print. pl?file=20071130548511OO. htm&date=2007/11/30/&prd=th&>

7

COPYRIGHTABILITY

Not every work under the sun automatically gets copyright protection. It has to be a work which can be protected by copyright according to copyright law. It cannot be an idea. It must be expressed in some form. It must be original and it must be 'contemporary'. In other words, no one can suddenly pull up a copy of the Canterbury Tales and claim that they are protected by copyright — copyright lasts only during the lifetime of the author and for sixty years after his death.

THE REMNANTS OF THE ANCIENT WORLD

Copyright certainly doesn't subsist in paintings of the 17th century,* in manuscripts which are two hundred years or in buildings which were erected hundreds of years ago. Once copyright in a work protection expires, the work falls into the public domain, and anyone can exploit the intellectual property which earlier subsisted in it. And if the work was created long before copyright itself was created, it would under no circumstances be protected (having always belonged to the 'intellectual commons' and, in all probability, to the public domain).

This, however, seems to have been completely lost on some of those who would either like to commercially exploit what is our common cultural legacy, or, at any rate, prevent others from doing so.

In December, 2007, it was widely reported that Egypt apparently planned to copyright the pyramids and its other antiquities despite the fact that they had been in the public domain for thousands of years.[115] No one knew quite how they planned to do so or, for that matter, how they planned to take action against would-be infringers. After a while, the reports died down and no one seemed to be quite certain of what happened to the government's plans.

The issue was partly whether a photograph or other reproduction of an old work in the public domain constitutes a new work with independent intellectual property rights. Bridgeman Art Library, Ltd. v. Corel Corp.[116] clarified the situation in the United States. However, that precedent does not help much when it comes to other countries; in the case of the Sistine Chapel, the Japanese TV network NHK reportedly paid between three and four million for its restoration in return for exclusive film and publication rights. The Vatican thus managed to turn an ancient artistic work into a commercial property.[117]

The Indian High Commission at Dhaka seemed to have missed both the controversy and the amusement Egypt's plan gave rise to in legal circles though. According to an editorial in the Times of India,[118] in December 2008, the High Commission (or perhaps just its spokesman) threatened to invoke copyright laws against a Bangladeshi businessman named Ahsanullah Moni who was building a replica of the Taj Mahal in Bangladesh.

Indian copyright law does protect works of architecture to an extent: their artistic character or design is protectable and so are models for buildings provided the buildings are located in India. In other words, buildings which look like boxes cannot be protected by copyright law, and whether or not the buildings are shaped liked boxes, copyright protection does not extend to processes or methods of construction or to buildings which are not located in India.

Most importantly, copyright protection for artistic works — and buildings are treated as artistic works by the Indian Copyright Act — lasts for sixty years after the death of the author if the work is published during the lifetime of the author. By no stretch of the imagination can copyright exist in the Taj Mahal. If not anything else, it was built long before copyright protection existed. Never mind the practical implications of claiming that structures such as the Taj have such protection. Every keychain and model maker would then have to obtain a licence before selling their wares whether to tourists or others. It would be well nigh impossible to enforce such a requirement.

And even if, just for the sake of argument, one were to assume that copyright subsisted in the Taj, and that a regime comparable to the modern copyright regime (with ludicrously long terms of protection) existed during the Mughal Period, it wouldn't be too hard to make a convincing argument that the Taj itself was some form of derivative work. The design of the Taj is inspired by that of Humayun's Tomb (built in 1565) which inspired the designs of tombs all the way down to the time of Safdarjung's 1754 tomb which is often described as 'the last flicker in the lamp of Mughal architecture at Delhi'. And if one made that argument, it would follow that having infringed the copyright in an earlier work itself, the Taj would not be entitled to copyright protection.

There's also the matter that if copyright protection did exist in the Mughal Period, far from ensuring, encouraging, and facilitating creativity, it would probably have ensured that the Mughal architectural style remained entirely undeveloped and that the Taj would not have been created.

THE EXPRESSION OF AN IDEA

Copyright does not exist in an idea regardless of how brilliant it may be. To be protected by copyright the idea must be expressed. It is the expression of the idea, and the expression alone which can be protected. So, if someone were to think of writing a book about — let's be mundane — a couple falling in love, he could do so. He would not be able to copyright his idea itself but the resulting book, that is to say, the expression of his idea, would be entitled to copyright protection. If someone else were to write a book on the same subject, he too would be entitled to copyright protection for his own book.

In India, the law was clearly defined in what is probably the most famous Indian copyright case: R G Anand v. Delux Films, 1978. In this case, a playwright alleged that his copyright in a play had been infringed by a film. Breaking down the film into its constituent elements and saying that those ideas could be used by anyone, the Supreme Court held that no such thing had happened. It was in this case that the basic principles of copyright law and infringement were clearly defined in the following terms:

(1) There can be no copyright in an idea, subject matter, themes, plots or historical or legendary facts and violation of the copyright in such cases is confined to the form, manner and arrangement and expression of the idea by the author of the copyrighted work.

(2) Where the same idea is being developed in a different manner, it is manifest that the source being common, similarities are bound to occur. In such a case, the courts should determine whether or not the similarities are on fundamental or substantial aspects of the mode of expression adopted in the copyrighted work. If the defendant's work is nothing but a literal imitation of the copyrighted work with some variations here and there, it would amount to violation of the copyright. In other words, in order to be actionable the copy must be a substantial and material one which at once leads to the conclusion that the defendant is guilty of an act of piracy.

(3) One of the surest and the safest tests to determine whether or not there has been a violation of copyright is by seeing whether the reader, spectator or the viewer after having read or seen both the works is clearly of the opinion and gets an unmistakable impression that the subsequent work appears to be a copy of the original.

(4) Where the theme is the same but is presented and treated differently so that the subsequent work becomes a completely new work, no question of violation of copyright arises.

(5) Where, however, apart from the similarities appearing in the two works, there are also material and broad dissimilarities which negate the intention to copy the original and the coincidences appearing in the two works are clearly incidental, no infringement of the copyright comes into existence.

(6) As a violation of copyright amounts to an act of piracy, it must be proved by clear and cogent evidence after applying the various tests laid down by case law.

(7) Where, however, the question is of the violation of the copyright of stage play by a film producer or a Director, the task of the plaintiff to prove piracy becomes more difficult. It is manifest that unlike a stage play a film has a much broader prospective, a wider field and a bigger background where the defendants can by introducing a variety of incidents give a colour and complexion different from the manner in which the copyrighted work has expressed the idea. Even so, if the viewer after seeing the film gets a totality of impression that the film is by and large a copy of the original play, violation of the copyright may be said to be proved.

The Supreme Court relied on the works of a number of jurists to formulate these principles. It inter alia referred to Copinger who in the 11th Edition of his book had pointed out that what is protected is not the original thought but expression of thought in a concrete form saying: "What is protected is not original thought or information, but the original expression of thought or information in some concrete form. Consequently, it is only an infringement if the defendant has made an unlawful use of the form in which the thought or information is expressed. The defendant must to be liable, have made a substantial use of this form; he is not liable if he has taken from the work the essential, ideas however original, and expressed the idea in his own form, or used the idea for his own purposes."

The Court also quoted Mr Ball who said: "When two authors portray in literary or dramatic form the same occurrence, involving people reacting to the same emotions under the influence of an environment constructed of the same materials, similarities in incidental details necessary to the environment; or setting are inevitable; but unless they are accompanied by similarities in the dramatic development of the plot or in the lines or action. Of the principal characters, they do not constitute evidence of copying. They are comparable to similarities in two works of art made by different artists from the same original subject, and in the usual case are too trivial and unimportant to amount to a substantial appropriation of copyrighted material."

The result is that as far as the law is concerned, copyright cannot possibly subsist in an idea by itself. For copyright to exist, there must necessarily be a work and not simply an idea. [5] If ideas can be taken from a work without copying the work, the owner of the copyright in the work from which the ideas are taken cannot interfere with the use of those ideas.[120]

MERIT AND ORIGINALITY

Although copyright nominally protects literary works among others, the works do not actually have to be 'literary', or for that matter, be any form of literature. All that the term means is that the works need to be expressed in writing.

It cannot be said, by any stretch of the imagination, that a work must be good to be worthy of copyright protection. It simply means that the work must not be the equivalent of a list which says: 'Sugar 1kg, Rice 2 kg'. Artistic merit plays absolutely no role in whether or not a work is entitled to copyright protection so even an appallingly bad novel or a truly grotesque picture would be entitled to copyright protection. It's another matter that it may not 'need' protection simply because no one would want to copy it. (As the Privy Council held in the 1923 case of Macmillan v. Cooper:[121] 'what is worth copying is prima facie worth protecting'.)

Nonetheless, the standard of originality required for a work to be capable of being protected by copyright is also abysmally low. In the case of Associated Publishers v. K. Bashyam,[122] the Madras High Court held that 'to constitute original artistic work neither original thought nor original research is essential and the standard of originality is a low one. It is original skill or labour in execution and not originality of thought which is required'.

This premise has been repeated in various forms in a number of cases. For example, in Macmillan & Co. v. K & J Cooper, it was held that the test was whether sufficient labour, skill and capital had been extended in creating the work while in Agarwala Publishing House v. Board of Higher Secondary and Intermediate Education, UP,[123] it was held that all that was needed was for a work to be expressed in print or writing irrespective of literary quality. Specifically, in Macmillan v. Cooper, it was held: ". . . it is the product of the labour, skill and capital of one man which must not be appropriated by another, not the elements, the raw material, if one may use the expression, upon which the labour and skill and capital of the first have been expended. To secure copyright for this product it is necessary that the labour, skill and capital expended should be sufficient to impart to the product some quality or character which the raw material did not possess, and which differentiates the product from the raw material."

As was quoted in the case of P R Viswanatha Iyer v. A Muthukumaraswami Pillai and Others,[124] 'the word 'original' does not in this connection mean that the work must be the expression of original or inventive thought. Copyright Acts are not concerned with the originality of ideas, but with the expression of thought, and, in the case of 'literary work,' with the expression of thought in print or writing. The originality which is required relates to the expression of the thought. But the Act does not require that the expression must be in an original or novel form, but that the work must not be copied from another work'-that it should originate from the author. What is the precise amount of the knowledge, labour, judgment or literary skill or taste which the author of any book or other compilation must bestow upon its composition in order to acquire copyright in it within the meaning of the Copyright Act, 1911, cannot be defined in precise terms. In every case, it must depend largely on the special facts of that case, and must in each case be very much a question of degree.'

Copyright also subsists in translations provided the author of a translation has expended sufficient skill and labour on it.[125] However, if copyright subsists in a work, and that work is translated, the translation will have infringed the copyright of the original work unless the owner of the copyright in the original work has given permission for the original to be translated.

The basic principle, however, remains unchanged: to be entitled to copyright protection, a work must have some level of originality or display some form of creativity or be the result of some amount of skill and labour being expended on it. So, even something like a compilation of a list of customers would be protected by copyright.[126] But an ordinary diary containing a calendar and a certain amount of miscellaneous information regarding postal rates, weights and measures, lighting up times and so on, all accessible in official publications and a feature of all diaries of the kind, would not be entitled to copyright protection. In Cramp & Sons Ltd. v. Frank Smythson Ltd.,[127] the Lord Chancellor explained why he thought this was the case saying: "There would, indeed, as it seems to me, be considerable difficulty in successfully contending that ordinary tables which can be got from, or checked by, the postal guide or the Nautical Almanac are a subject of copyright as being original literary work. One of the essential qualities of such tables is that they should be accurate so that there is no question of variation in what is stated. The Sun does in fact rise, and the Moon set, at times which have been calculated, and the utmost that a table can do on such a subject is to state the result accurately. There is so far no room for taste or judgment. There remains, I agree, the element of choose as to what infórmation should be given, and the respondents contend that the test of originality is satisfied by the choice of the tables inserted; but the bundle of information furnished in the respondents' diary is common place information which is ordinarily useful and is, at any rate to a large extent, commonly found prefixed to diaries, and, looking through the respondents' collection of tables, I have difficulty in seeing how such tables, in the combination in which they appear in the respondents' 1933 diary, can reasonably claim to be 'original work'. There was no evidence that any of these tables was composed specially for the respondents' diary. There was no feature of them which could be pointed out as novel or specially meritorious or ingenious from the point of view of the judgment or skill of the compiler. It was not suggested that there was any element of originality or skill in the order in which the tables were arranged. My own conclusion is that the selection did not constitute an original literary work."

Generally, works which are based on a standard template are not entitled to copyright protection. However, in January 2008, an Idaho court ruled that cease-and-desist letters are protected by copyright. [14] This surprised many people because they do follow a pretty standard template: 'Cut it out or I'll sue.' and there's precious little creativity involved in writing them. The effect of this ruling would seem to be that (a) if someone received such a letter and posted it on their web-site or blog, they would have violated the sender's copyright and (b) no one would be able to merely tweak a letter written by someone else a little bit and use the result.

Not requiring any artistic or literary merit for a work to be copyrightable can sometimes be a little confusing though because there do exist cases where works cannot be protected by copyright law even if they do have 'literary merit'. At one point of time, it was held[129] that there could not, for example, exist copyright in advertising slogans although subsequent judgments appear to have changed that decision.

So, although the 'no merit necessary' rule sounds clear enough at first glance, it is fraught with loopholes. Perhaps that isn't too surprising though considering that there is very little in the legal world which isn't subject to a number of exceptions.

FOOTNOTES

115.<news. yahoo. com/s/afp/20071225/lf_afp/egyptantiquitieslaw>

116.36 F.Supp.2d 191 (S.D.N.Y.1999); <law.cornell.edu/copyright/cases/36_FSupp2d_191.htm>

117.Eric Scigliano, Inglorious Restorations, Harper's Magazine:<harpers.org/archive/2005/08/0080699>

118.<timesofindia.indiatimes.com/World/Bangladeshi_Taj_irks_India/articleshow/3820838.cms>
119.Jefferys v. Boosey 1854 4 HLC 815
120.AIR 1972 Cal 533
121.1923, 40 T. L.R. 186; AIR 1924 PC 75
122.AIR 1961 Mad 114
123.AIR 1967All 91
124.AIR 1948 Mad 139
125.AIR 1959 Mad 410
126.Burlington Home Shipping (P) Ltd. v. Rajnish Chibber 1996 (61) DLT 6
127.(1944) 1944 A.C. 329 differentiated in AIR 1948 Mad 139; Deepak Printers v. ForwardStationery Mart 1981 PTC 186
128.<yro.slashdot.org/article. pl?sid=08/01/26/0351225>,<prweb.com/releases/DozierInternetLaw/InternetLawyer/prweb650951. htm>, <techdirt.com/articles/20080125/18070575.shtml>
129.Pepsi Co. Inc. and Anr. V. Hindustan Coca Cola and Ors. 2001 (21) PTC 699; Also See: Pepsi Co., Inc. and Ors. V. Hindustan Coca Cola. 2003 (27) PTC305(Del); Enercon System Pvt. Ltd. V. The Registrar of Copyrights MANU/CP/0001/2008.

8

LITERARY SQUABBLES

Throughout history, writers have drawn off each other's works. Shakespeare was 'inspired' by Chaucer, William Yeats had Pierre de Ronsard to fall back on. While neither Chaucer or de Ronsard were at any time protected by copyright law, the basic working ethos is clear: originality in literature is rare. Most authors draw on works which have already been written. Ideas endure, only their expressions change. Few literary works are not derivations in some sense of the work, and it is these derivations which are the most easily accessible because they contain identifiable motifs, ideas to which one can relate.

The problem with copyright law though is that it can restrict writers from using works in existence if those works are protected by copyright. As early as 1890, it was held that plays which were based on novels which were themselves based on original plays infringed the copyright which subsisted in the original plays.[130]

Not all disputes in the literary arena have to do with direct copyright infringement though. There are also issues such as the nature of fair use and the problem of plagiarism with which to contend.

FAIR USE

One of the most recent fair use disputes involved Warner Bros. Entertainment and J K Rowling in a dispute they had with RDR Books and Steve Vander Ark. This was the case in which the author and Warner Bros. sued to prevent a small publisher from publishing 'The Harry Potter Lexicon'[131] as a book.

'The Harry Potter Lexicon began as a website on which contributors collected information about people, places and things that inhabited the Harry Potter Universe as described in J K Rowling's books, the movies based on those books and associated products. It grew into what is widely regarded into the most complete and authoritative guide to the world of Harry Potter and attracts upwards of 25 million visitors a year. In 2004, it won a fansite award from Ms Rowling herself. In light of the website's popularity, its editor, Steve Vander Ark, decided to publish it in book form and RDR books agreed to do so. Upon learning of this, Warner Bros. Entertainment and J K Rowling filed a suit against RDR alleging trade mark and copyright infringement and seeking to stop publication of the book.'[132] Warner Brothers and J K Rowling were successful in having the publication of the book stopped.

A new manuscript was later drafted which addressed the concerns raised at the trial, and professing themselves to be happier with the new manuscript than they were with the original one, RDR decided not to appeal.

Anthony Falzone and his team from Stanford University's Fair Use Project represented RDR in the matter because they believed that the fair use doctrine protected the lexicon and other publications like it. Leaving aside the decision of the judge, the case generated a lot of debate on the nature of fair use and the extent of copyright protection; it hinged on fair use, and on where fair use becomes copyright infringement.

A few issues which immediately came to mind were:

(1) Can content which accompanies some other work and which has been published online and endorsed by the copyright holder of that other work subsequently be accused of violating copyright simply because the author of the second work plans to publish it in a more traditional manner?

(2) What is the relationship between an online work available to readers without charge and a book sold to readers if both of them contain the same material?

(3) Can a copyright holder actually stop the publication of a companion work considering that the copyright in the original work does not extend to preventing the publication of companion works? Can a copyright holder legitimately claim that their work has merely been repackaged? And can that claim be made after the work has already been endorsed by the copyright holder?

The New York Times[133] said that 'though the case pits a billionaire author against a tiny publishing house, the Potter fan base seems to have little sympathy for RDR' although in an earlier article,[134] it described Ms Rowling as a copyright hog. It was somewhat surprising that Harry Potter fans were not overwhelmingly in support of RDR considering that most Harry Potter fan sites exist in part due to the right of fair use. Also, it was unclear how such a derivative work in which an author put a substantial amount of effort into could infringe a copyright simply because it was not available at no cost to readers.

Fair Use is an interesting concept. It does not exist in India although the Indian Copyright Act contains several exceptions to copyright. It is, however, spoken of in Title 17 of the USC as follows:

'107. Limitations on exclusive rights: Notwithstanding the provisions of sections 106 and 106A, the fair use of a copyrighted work, including such use by reproduction in copies or phonorecords or by any other means specified by that section, for purposes such as criticism, comment, news reporting, teaching (including multiple copies for classroom use), scholarship, or research, is not an infringement of copyright. In determining whether the use made of a work in any particular case is a fair use the factors to be considered shall include —(1) the purpose and character of the use, including whether such use is of a commercial nature or is for nonprofit educational purposes;(2) the nature of the copyrighted work;(3) the amount and substantiality of the portion used in relation to the copyrighted work as a whole; and(4) the effect of the use upon the potential market for or value of the copyrighted work. The fact that a work is unpublished shall not itself bar a finding of fair use if such finding is made upon consideration of all the above factors.

Under the law, 'in determining whether the use made of a work in any particular case is a fair use the factors to be considered include —

(1) the purpose and character of the use, including whether such use is of a commercial nature or is for nonprofit educational purposes;

(2) the nature of the copyrighted work;

(3) the amount and substantiality of the portion used in relation to the copyrighted work as a whole; and

(4) the effect of the use upon the potential market for or value of the copyrighted work.'

Whether or not what Ms Rowling asked for was entirely fair with reference to the RDR case, she undoubtedly really asked for copyright protection to be stretched to what could well have been unprecedented lengths. That being said, the case could easily have gone either way both on facts and on law. In a poll on the WSJ Law Blog,[135] 301 readers believed Rowling would prevail, while 246 thought RDR Books would prevail.

The proceedings turned into an emotional drama. One could only suspect that the case needed to be made emotive (with Rowling going on the stand calling her books her children) for her to be certain to win. Many people spoke of her moral rights having been violated at the time although far from being a moral right, copyright is a legal right which just happens to have some moral rights associated with it viz. those of integrity and paternity and, in this instance, neither of those moral rights appeared to have been violated.

Also, if it comes down to derivation, Ms Rowling's books are pretty much a patchwork of older stories involving magic. As A S Byatt put it: "Auden and Tolkien wrote about the skills of inventing 'secondary worlds'. Ms. Rowling's world is a secondary world, made up of intelligently patchworked derivative motifs from all sorts of children's literature — from the jolly hockey-sticks school story to Roald Dahl, from "Star Wars" to Diana Wynne Jones and Susan Cooper. Toni Morrison pointed out that clichés endure because they represent truths. Derivative narrative clichés work with children because they are comfortingly recognizable and immediately available to the child's own power of fantasizing."[136]

One concern with having J K Rowling win was whether any literary work which accompanied another book protected by copyright would, as a result of her success, automatically be considered to be a derivative work and necessarily infringe the copyright of the book it accompanied.

The good thing about the ruling in the matter was that although Rowling did win, the Court recognized that as a general matter, authors do not have the right to stop the publication of companion books and reference guides to literary works, and said that reference guides are not derivative works.

PLAGIARISM

The other problem in the literary world is that of plagiarism. Copyright infringement is nothing more than the violation of copyright. Plagiarism, on the other hand, is an ethical issue which involves copying another person's ideas or work without giving them credit, and, usually, passing them off as one's own. In most cases, there is no plagiarism involved in copyright infringement — it's unlikely that anyone would photocopy 'David Copperfield', for example, and pretend that the work had been written not by Charles Dickens but by himself, or that someone would attach their own name to a copy of Beethoven's Fifth Symphony. Plagiarism of a copyrighted work does, however, also constitute copyright infringement. So, if someone were to attach their own name to, say, a work by a contemporary author such as Amitav Ghosh or Vikram Seth, he would not only have plagiarized that author's work but also infringed its copyright.

Although there is a clear difference between the two, very often, the terms 'plagiarism' and 'infringement' are used interchangeably and are confused. On January 13, 2009, for example, the Times of India ran a piece which said that a well-known Tamil writer, Indira Parthasarathy, had accused a Bengali playwright, Mohit Chattopadhyay of plagiarizing his 1974 play 'Aurangzeb'. The plagiarized play was scheduled to be performed at the National School of Drama on January 15, 2009 as part of the School's 11th Annual Theatre Festival by a Kolkata-based group called 'Rangapat'. Parthasarathy apparently asked the Madras High Court for an interim injunction against the staging of the play but Justice M Jeyapaul of the High Court declined to grant the injunction.

The newspaper report had four short paragraphs, and used the word 'plagiarism' three times in it including once in a quote from the Tamil playwright. The word 'infringement' was not used once. If Chattopadhyay did in fact use Parthasarathy's idea, he would have plagiarized his work, and since the work appears to be protected by copyright, he would have also infringed the copyright in the work. It is against the infringement of copyright for which legal proceedings can be initiated, not against plagiarism per se (as unethical as plagiarism is). There is not one mention in the piece about copyright infringement though and the word plagiarism seems to have been treated as being synonymous with infringement.

Another author who was involved in a plagiarism scandal was the romance writer Cassie Edwards who, in early 2008, was accused[137] of recycling material from older academic works. There was, at that point of time, much discussion about fair use and copyright, and one of the biggest names in the romance fiction genre, Nora Roberts,[138] issued a strongly worded statement saying: "By my definition, copying another's work and passing it as your own equals plagiarism. As a writer, a reader and a victim of plagiarism, I feel very strongly on this issue. I'm not a lawyer, but I can't see it as fair use or fair anything when one writer takes another's work."

Signet which published Cassie Edwards' books had this to say:[139] "The copyright fair-use doctrine permits reasonable borrowing and paraphrasing of another author's words, especially for the purpose of creating something new and original. Also, anyone may use fact, ideas and theories developed by another author as well as any material in the public domain. Ms Edwards's researched historical novels are precisely the kind of original, creative works that this copyright policy promotes."

Weighing in on the subject, copyleft activist, Karl Fogel said: "That fair use statute, vague as it is, is at least clear on one point: that it is about copying, not attribution. That is, "fair use" is about whether one can redistribute (or publish derivative works based on) some original work, independently of whether one also claims credit for the work.

Nora Roberts is spot on when she says 'copying another's work and passing it as your own equals plagiarism'. But then she conflates crediting with copying: 'I can't see it as fair use, or fair anything when one writer takes another's work'. She would have expressed her meaning much more precisely had she said '...when one writer takes another's credit'. Credit is a finite resource: the degree to which one person takes another's credit is exactly the degree to which that other person loses the credit. But the texts themselves are not a finite resource: if someone makes a copy of Nora Roberts' book (leaving Nora Roberts' name on the cover, of course), that doesn't diminish Nora Roberts' own supply of the book, even though it may still be copyright violation under today's laws.

Copyright violation and plagiarism are two different things. (Another way to put it: when people download songs illegally off the Internet, they do not replace the artists' name with their own!)

So if Cassie Edwards recycled material from older romance novels, then she is indeed guilty of plagiarism — but she would be guilty of it regardless of whether her sources were still under copyright or not. The two are unrelated, and this controversy is not really about fair use doctrine. It would be great if Signet and its critics would make this distinction too, and not associate copyright violation (questionable whether it should even be an offense) with the much more serious crime of plagiarism (few would disagree that theft of credit is bad)."

The list of authors accused of plagiarism isn't short, and sometimes, the passages they are accused of having plagiarized are so wretchedly mundane that one can only wonder why they bothered. Take Kavya Vishwanathan who was accused of plagiarizing passages from Megan McCafferty's books 'Sloppy Firsts' and 'Second Helpings' in her debut 'How Opal Mehta Got Kissed, Got Wild, and Got a Life'. Opal Mehta, after the plagiarism scandal, Got Shelved.

At other times, authors say that they have so internalized other people's works that they were not even aware of having committed plagiarism. This is entirely possible to do but it could just as easily be a convenient excuse, and there's no one but the person who has plagiarized material who would be in a position to know what had actually happened. In January 2009, for example, the story broke that Neale Donald Walsch, the author of the best-selling work 'Conversations with God' had plagiarized a story. Walsch said that someone performing at the dress rehearsal of a Winter Pageant in his son's school had held the letter 'M' upside down in the message 'Christmas Love' thereby turning it into 'Christ Was Love'. Although Walsch conceded the error, the actual author of the story, Candy Chand, who had published it in 1999, wasn't amused. Speaking to the New York Times, she questioned whether the man who writes best-selling books about his conversations with God had heard God's commandments. 'Thou shalt not steal. Thou shalt not lie, and thou shalt not covet another's property.'[140]

Plagiarism may sometimes be completely unintentional (insofar as the original work is copied subconsciously) and, possibly, excusable. However, it is doubtful that habitual plagiarism is forgivable.

FOOTNOTES

130.Schlesinger v.Turner, (1890) 63 LT 764

131.<hp-lexicon.org/>

132.<cyberlaw.stanford.edu/case/rowling-v-rdr-books> published under a CC Attribution Licence from which some of the data for this section of the book has been taken.

133.<nytimes.com/2008/04/14/books/14potter. html ?_ r= 1 & ei = 5090 & en=960332b363f2f96c & ex=1365912000 & partner = rssuserland & emc = rss & pagewanted=all & oref=slogin>

134.<nytimes.com/2008/02/09/business/09nocera. html?_r=1&ref= business & pagewanted = all>

135.<blogs. wsj. com/law/2008/04/18/final-for-now-reflections-on-the-harry-potter-trial/?mod=WSJBlog" rel="nofollow>

136.A S Byatt, 'Harry Potter and the Childish Adult', New York Times, 7 July 2003 (subscription needed) through 'The Legal Soapbox'

137.<smartbitchestrashybooks.com>

138.<news.yahoo.com/s/ap/20080110/ap_en_ot/books_romance _ writer;_ ylt =AltTCIINgmpQ8xiRK_WAxV1xFb8C>

139.<smartbitchestrashybooks. com/index. php/weblog/finally_heard_ back_from_signet>

140.<mobile. nytimes. com/article?a=292384&f=78&p=3>

9

ACADEMIA AND EDUCATION

It's often said that if you copy from one person, it's plagiarism and, possibly, infringement. If you copy from a number of persons though, it's research.

There is no copyright in information or in facts. There is, however, a copyright in the way those facts are presented. This is partly based on public policy. In the 1980 case of Ravecraft v. Herbert,[141] for example, it was pointed out that in a historical work, the purpose of the work was not just to contribute to the reader's enjoyment but also to increase the sum total of human knowledge.

Nonetheless, as far as educational material is concerned everything from textbooks[142] and guides[143] to examination question papers[144] are protected by copyright.

Lecturers have a copyright in their lectures. However, there is a caveat to this: the lectures must be in written form. If a lecture is made extempore, the lecturer cannot claim copyright protection but if someone were to transcribe the lecture and publish it, a civil action for breach of confidence would in all probability lie. Also, in an 1887 case,[145] it was held that the intellectual property of lectures delivered in a classroom belong to the lecturer and students are not supposed to make a (monetary) profit off it.

In addition to this, a lecturer is the first owner of copyright in his lecture even if the lecture is delivered by someone else on his behalf. He is a performer as far as the Copyright Act of

1957 is concerned. This means that he is entitled to the benefit of performers' rights as defined by Section 38 of the Act.

When it comes to students, that the copyright in a student's assignments and other works belongs to him isn't disputed; he has the right to control how or if his work is published. Having the right to do so, however, as with all legal rights, does not ensure beyond doubt that he can do so.

In America, an IIT student — that's the Illinois Institute of Technology — Roman Kofman, didn't seem to have been able to convince one of his professors who has posted some of his work online of this[146] and, writing on his blog, he said that he wasn't sure of what to do next as he wondered: "Should I serve my professor with a formal "cease and desist"? Should I go to legal counsel with a Digital Millennium Copyright Act (DMCA) takedown notice? The DMCA notice would make IIT (as the Internet service provider for the site) liable if the content was not removed. Surely, this would produce results. I doubt I would actually sue the school, but who knows?" Mr Kofman went on to say, "Winning a case of willful copyright infringement would net me a nice payout to help me with my student loans."

This is a problem which Indian students typically face. If they did have such a problem, although their rights would be similar, it's doubtful whether, practically speaking, their remedies would be comparable.

In the Indian scenario, it's extremely difficult to see a student actually choose to send a legal notice to a professor who controlled his grades for something which he probably did not consider an extremely serious issue. If he tried to file a suit, he may not actually achieve very much beyond antagonizing the teacher and the institute in which he was studying. Even if he was successful, he would, in all likelihood have to devote a great deal of time, money and effort into enforcing his rights. He would probably not get much (if at all anything) in the way of damages. And the fall out could involve his failing courses because of the professor or the institute being unable to refrain from holding his actions against him. Not to mention that his future employability could be adversely affected if he was thought of as being litigious.

Owning a copyright doesn't automatically ensure that one can easily keep others from infringing it. Nonetheless, students do own the copyright which subsists in work they have created.[147]

There are also various exceptions to copyright embedded in the law.[148] The reproduction of a literary, dramatic, musical or artistic work by a teacher or a pupil in the course of instruction, or as part of the questions to be answered in an examination, or in answers to such questions does not violate the copyright in those works.

The staff and students of an educational institution can also perform a literary, dramatic or musical work protected by copyright, or play a film or a sound recording in the course of the activities of the institution, if the audience is limited to students, their parents and guardians, the staff and persons directly connected with activities of the institution without having infringed the copyright in the works they have performed or played.

In addition to this, in certain cases, compulsory licences can be obtained for the purpose of reproducing works protected by copyright for systematic instruction.

And when it comes to research and access to protected works, the Copyright Act allows the making of not more than three copies of a book (including a pamphlet, sheet of music, map, chart or plan) which is not available for sale in India by or under the direction of the person in charge of a public library for the use of the library.

Further, the reproduction, for the purpose of research or private study or with a view to publication, of an unpublished literary, dramatic or musical work kept in a library, museum or other institution to which the public has access does not violate the copyright in that work. However, if the library, museum or other institution knows who the authors are, this applies only if the reproduction is made more than fifty years after the date of the death of the last surviving author.

The general impression these provisions give is that although all the works which are created in the course of education or research whether they be theses or question papers are themselves protected by copyright, educators, students and researchers have more leeway than others when it comes to using the works of third persons which are protected by copyright in the course of their own activities which are related to teaching, studying and conducting research.

FOOTNOTES

141.1980 RPC 193
142.Misra Bandhu Karyalaya v. Shiv Ratan Lal KoshalAIR 1970 MP 261
143.E M Forster v. A N Parasuram AIR 1964 Mad 331
144.Jagdish Prasad v. Parameshwar Prasad Singh AIR 1966 Pat 33; Univ. of London Press v.Univ. Tutorial Press (1916) 2 Ch 601
145.Caird v. Sime 1887 GLP 526
146.technews.iit.edu/index.php?id=973
147.Fateh Singhal Mehta v. Singhal 1990 1PLR 69(Raj)
148.Section 52(1), Indian Copyright Act, 1957

10

PERPETUAL YOUTH AND PERPETUAL COPYRIGHT

Copyright being a creation of statute ensures that the legislature can determine for how long copyright will subsist in any particular work or class of works. In most countries, copyright protection subsists during the life of the author and extends for between fifty and seventy years after his death. The length of time for which copyright subsists though is entirely dependent on for how long the legislature decides it should subsist.

Peter Pan, for example, enjoys not only Perpetual Youth but also Perpetual Copyright. The work is an exception to the rule that copyright cannot subsist in any work in perpetuity. J M Barrie's famous character is not only renowned for never growing up but also for never having to lose copyright protection in the UK thanks to a special exception campaigned for in the Copyright, Designs and Patents Act, 1988 by former British Prime Minister, James Callaghan whose wife, Audrey, was a chairwoman of the Great Ormond Street Hospital which owns the copyright in Peter Pan. This exception says that the trustees of the Great Ormond Street Hospital are entitled to a royalty or some other agreed form of remuneration in respect of any public performance, commercial publication, broadcasting or inclusion in a cable programme service of the whole or any substantial part of the play 'Peter Pan' by Sir James Matthew Barrie or an adaptation of it.[149]

The play is already in the public domain in some countries such as Canada which has a copyright term which extends for fifty years after an author's death. (In this case, the author, J M Barrie, died in 1937 although he assigned the copyright to the hospital in 1929.) There are, nonetheless, copyright issues which exist in relation to the publication of works produced in countries where Peter Pan is still protected by copyright as have been seen in the case of Emily Somma v. Great Ormond Street Hospital for Sick Children — the case involved a dispute about a book in which the author, Emily Somma, spoke of Peter Pan as an adult.[150]

This exception which allows Peter Pan to enjoy perpetual copyright protection, thankfully, does not apply to the rest of the world and, and apart from in the UK, Peter Pan will soon lose copyright protection in the rest of the world. And as time runs out for the boy who refused to grow up, perhaps one will see more books like Somma's enter the market.

As the legal wrangles which Somma ran into show, although copyright is widely perceived as encouraging creativity there are, without a doubt, also instances where copyright protection does precisely the opposite. True, there is nothing on the face of the Earth which can prevent any author or artist from creating a work which involves a character that enjoys copyright protection but the fact of the matter is that very often, legal problems ensure that that work cannot be distributed to the public. And the average creator does not produce works which he or she would like to see being shoved into the bottom drawer of a desk and being kept there for all eternity — or till copyright protection is exhausted, at any rate.

This is, in many ways, a free speech issue. The owners of copyright do have much control over their works and the use of those works under the current copyright regime. However, the rights which really matter: those of paternity and integrity which require works to be attributed and not abused exist independently of copyright and continue to vest in authors even if the authors transfer ownership of the copyright to others. It may not be easy for the average artist to simply say that he has no problem with allowing others to use or build on his work without knowing how they will do so. However, if it came down to it, and his work was actually used in an entirely repugnant manner, he could always rely on the moral right of integrity to protect his work.

Under the law, with reference to the right of integrity, an author has the right to restrain or claim damages in respect of any distortion, mutilation, modification or other act in relation to his work which is done before the expiration of the term of copyright if it is prejudicial to his honour or reputation. And it is curbing such distortion, mutilation, modification of their work that is most important to most artists, not making their work inaccessible as copyright does.

FOOTNOTES

149.<opsi.gov.uk/acts/acts1988/Ukpga_19880048_en_28. htm>

150.Please See:<cyberlaw.stanford. edu/attachments/Amended%20 Complaint%201-07-03.pdf>

11

THE SUPREMACY OF THE WRITTEN WORD

If you were to ask the average person, "When was the last time you signed a contract without reading it?" they'd probably say never.

They've also probably never read the terms and conditions which are in a little scrolly box before they've signed up for an eMail account. And it's unlikely that they know what Orkut's terms of service are. Or for that matter, what Facebook's or Twitter's are.

Facebook's Terms of Service[151] inter alia say: "By posting User Content to any part of the Site, *you automatically grant,* and you represent and warrant that you have the right to grant, *to the Company* an irrevocable, perpetual, non-exclusive, transferable, fully paid, worldwide *license (with the right to sublicense) to use, copy, publicly perform, publicly display, reformat, translate, excerpt (in whole or in part) and distribute such User Content for any purpose,* commercial, advertising, or otherwise, on or in connection with the Site or the promotion thereof, to prepare derivative works of, or incorporate into other works, such User Content, and to grant and authorize sublicenses of the foregoing."

One can only assume that not too many people know that by posting their content on to Facebook, they automatically licence it to the company in such a broad manner. It isn't clear what fully paid means in this context though since no money changes hands — one would ordinarily have assumed that the consideration for the licence was the provision of a service but the words 'fully-paid' are confusing.

This is in contrast to Automattic's Terms of Service[152] which say: "By submitting Content to Automattic for inclusion on your Website, you grant Automattic a world-wide, royalty-free, and non-exclusive license to reproduce, modify, adapt and publish the Content solely for the purpose of displaying, distributing and promoting your blog. If you delete Content, Automattic will use reasonable efforts to remove it from the Website, but you acknowledge that caching or references to the Content may not be made immediately unavailable."

Whether or not one thinks of it, these are legally binding contracts. In 2008, such a contract was used against someone in Megan Meier's suicide case. Megan killed herself at the age of thirteen after being rejected online by a person she thought was a sixteen-year-old boy. That person, however, turned out to be Lori Drew, the mother of one of her friends.

Strangely enough, there were no laws which could readily be applied to prosecute the woman so she was ultimately charged with violating MySpace's terms of use which, among other things, do not allow 'promoting information users know to be false or misleading, or soliciting personal information from anyone under the age of eighteen or using information gathered from the Web site to 'harass, abuse or harm other people'.

Presumably, Ms Drew had no idea of what the terms of service were although, in all probability, knowing them would not have stopped her from acting in the way she did.

The point, though, is not merely that she didn't know what she had signed up for but that the contract was treated as being binding on her and was enforced.

This is, by no stretch of the imagination, the only case in which a contract which has been signed (probably without considering its ramifications) has been given such force. In India, in the 2008 case of the overweight air hostesses, a single judge bench of the Delhi High Court described the employment contract the air hostesses has signed as their nemesis.

Nonetheless, despite being aware of what the pitfalls of signing agreements without knowing what their contents are or without wanting to be bound by them could be, it's something most people do without thinking twice. Think of all the times people have signed loan agreements which say that they will repay money at 20% interest just because their moneylender says, "But I'll charge you only 14%, just let this be there on paper."

The problem with just letting things be on paper is that if a person signs them, they will be bound by them. It doesn't matter if they have entered into a separate oral agreement with different terms. It doesn't matter if the other party claims that he won't enforce the terms on paper.

The law of evidence very clearly says that oral evidence is excluded by the existence of documentary evidence. There are a few exceptions and provisos but they apply so rarely that it's hardly worth taking them into consideration at all. For example, if the whole agreement is not written down, while interpreting it and deciding whether or not oral evidence about a supplementary oral agreement which is not written down and which does not go against anything which is written down is admissible, the court will take into consideration 'the degree of formality' of the contract i.e. basically, who drafted it. And the contract will be interpreted differently depending on whether it was drafted by two laymen over coffee or by two dozen overpaid lawyers since it will be probably be presumed by a Court that two laymen may have left out something by accident but if it isn't mentioned in a contract drafted by two dozen lawyers, it was probably left out intentionally.

As a general rule, the only thing which a court will take into consideration is the written contract. And if one of the parties to that contract has inadvertently signed away your copyright or any other right because he didn't read what he was signing, well, tough luck.

The moral of the story: sign what you mean, and mean what you sign.

FOOTNOTES

151.<facebook. com/terms.php>
152.<wordpress. com/tos/>

12

COMMENTS ON BLOGS

What does one do if someone leaves distasteful comments on one's blog? The law regarding comments is actually a bit dicey: if a blog owner's Terms of Service clearly say that they allow unmoderated comments, that they bear no responsibility, and if they remove nasty comments once they're brought to their notice, they generally won't be held liable for nasty comments made by other people. The picture changes, however, if the comments on a blog are moderated: if a blog's owner chooses to take on the responsibility of not allowing nasty comments, then they will be liable if any appear. The result is that absurdly enough, the less care you take, the less liable you could be. This is, however, drawn from case law in non-Indian jurisdictions; the Indian position is unclear.

In the case of a blog written by an Indian blogger in India, if one were to focus on contract law, there would be two different agreements.

One is between the owner of the blog and Wordpress/ Blogger/Blogware/whichever service is used i.e. the fascinating Terms of Service which hardly anyone ever reads. In the case of blogs hosted by Wordpress/Automattic, that agreement is governed by US law. As far as the choice of forum is concerned, there seem to be three aspects, briefly: (a) that disputes regarding the access to/use of the site are to be settled at a San Francisco court, (b) that disputes regarding the terms of the Terms of Service themselves are to be settled by specified arbitrators and (c) that injunctions can be obtained and intellectual property claims settled at any competent court.

The Automattic Terms of Service does not speak of which law applies to the intellectual property claims and one can only suspect that the issue is arguable since according to the agreement, all intellectual property remains with authors and is not assigned to Automattic. So, the content of a blog may not automatically be treated as a part of the site to which the Terms of Service applies.

However, the Terms of Service is a boilerplate contract so presumably it could be challenged in an Indian Court which probably wouldn't be too useful since in the absence of something like unconscionability, Indian Courts are not particularly enthusiastic about interfering with contractual choices of law or fora.[153]

The second agreement would be between the owner of the blog and their visitors. In such a case, the owner of the blog could be the one to impose a standard contract saying that the use of their blog is governed by so-and-so law. Or that all disputes in relation to it are to be settled at such-and-such place.

If the owner of a blog did not have such an agreement, if a case was to be filed, it could be done wherever the cause of action was to arise. The country where it was filed would generally apply its own law. The court could choose to override the Terms of Service of the owner of the blog. The only thing the Terms of Service would do would be to give the owner of the blog much firmer ground to stand on while arguing his case.

The bottomline is that there's nothing to stop anyone from filing anything anywhere. The best the owner of a blog can hope for if that happens is that the case gets thrown out in a hurry.

If one were to consider a case where a third party was to sue for a nasty comment about him, continuing with the same example, Automattic, if it could be sued, would probably have to be sued in the US because that's what its Terms of Service mandates. The owner of the blog could theoretically be sued in India. Or the blog service provider and the owner of the blog could be sued wherever the comments were viewed and the damage was done (although an Australian Court refused to allow a plaintiff to sue in such circumstances in Australia in 2008 because the Terms of Service agreement said that all disputes must exclusively be settled in the US). In India, case law is still emerging and statutory law is woefully inadequate at the moment.

One saving grace is Section 79 of the Information Technology Act, 2000 which deals with the liability of 'webmasters' and says: "Network service providers not to be liable in certain cases: For the removal of doubts, it is hereby declared that no person providing any service as a network service provider shall be liable under this Act, rules or regulations made thereunder for any third party information or data made available by him if he proves that the offence or contravention was committed without his knowledge or that he had exercised all due diligence to prevent the commission of such offence or contravention."

A 'network service provider' means an intermediary, and under Section 2(w) of the Act, an 'intermediary' with respect to any particular electronic message means any person who on behalf of another person receives, stores or transmits that message or provides any service with respect to that message.' Third party information' means any information dealt with by a network service provider in his capacity as an intermediary.

If a person were to initiate legal proceedings though, he would in all probability sue for defamation. Defamation is a broad term which includes slander and libel.[154] In India, it is both a criminal offence and a civil wrong, and there is nothing to stop someone from suing the owner of a blog. And if that person showed that the action/inaction of the owner contributed to the defamation, presumably, that person would probably be awarded damages in a civil suit although it is hugely unlikely that the owner of a blog would ordinarily be held to be guilty.

As far as defamation as a criminal offence is concerned,[155] the position is somewhat different; the 1860 Penal Code was obviously not drafted taking the creation of the Internet into account.

A comment could also infringe the copyright which subsisted in someone else's work. It's unlikely that anyone in their right mind would even consider taking legal action. But should someone get it into their head to do so, the position would be quite different and the owner of the blog could quite easily be held liable especially since infringement need not always be direct infringement but could also be indirect. True, the Indian Copyright Act makes no mention of indirect infringement. Nonetheless, the judiciary — specifically Supreme Court — did recognize it in the case of Garware Plastics and Polyester Ltd. v. Telelink, 1989[156] where it held that assisting in infringement would amount to the infringement of copyright.[157] And the Constitution says that the law declared by the Supreme Court is binding on all other Indian courts.

The fact of the commenter owning the copyright in his comment may not ensure that no legal action can be taken though. Defamation could conceivably be linked to the violation of the rights to publicity and privacy (although they can create liability issues entirely independently of defamation and of each other). The right to privacy is recognized as one of the fundamental rights under Article 21 of the Constitution while the right to publicity allows a person to control in what way he will be represented in public (usually for profit). Although Indian statutory law does not speak of the right to publicity, the right has been recognized by the Indian judiciary,[158] and its infringement is a commercial tort and a form of unfair competition.[159]

So, if a photographer took a picture of a person, he would probably own the copyright in it but to use that photograph. However, he would probably have to get the permission of the person photographed to exploit the photograph. For example, if he took a picture of a non-photogenic obese person, he would be begging for trouble if he allowed an anti-obesity campaign to use the photo to demonstrate the ills of pigging out on greasy food since, presumably, the obese person would not be amused to have his image used in that manner, and could go to court either to restrain such use or to obtain damages for it.

As usual, to be safe, one should not do anything which one does not have permission to do, and ideally, a blog's terms of service should, as ridiculous as it may sound, contain some form of indemnity clause saying that those who leave comments will be liable for the legal consequences of the comments they leave.

FOOTNOTES

153. The substantive provisions of Contract Law give immense freedom to parties to decide on the terms of any agreement they might reach. There are a few provisions which are inflexible – for example, an agreement to do something illegal is not, under any circumstances, a legally enforceable contract.

That being said, as long as parties do not go against the tenets of contract law, they have immense freedom to choose such things as the time of performance, the place of performance, the manner of performance, how disputes are to be settled etc.

One of the areas which parties can choose what works best for them is that which deals with the law that governs the contract. Indian courts, however, appear to have blown hot and cold on the issue, in a way. In most cases where contracts governed by a non-Indian law have come up before it, the courts have said that although they do have jurisdiction to try the case, they will not do so.

In the case of Messrs. Lakhinarayan Ramniwas v. Lloyd Triestino Societa Per Azinni (AIR 1960 Cal 155), the contract involved stated that if a dispute arose, the suit would be filed in Italy and tried according to Italian Law. The Calcutta High Court held that such a clause cannot oust the jurisdiction of the Indian courts to try the suit although considering the circumstances of the case, it stayed the suit instituted in India.

The Calcutta High Court reiterated this principle in the case of Swedish East Asia Co. Ltd. v. B P Herman and Mohatta (AIR 1962 Cal 601) in which a contract which chose Swedish law and courts was involved.

In Lakshminarayan Ramniwas v. Compagnia Genovese D'Esportazione (AIR 1960 Cal 545), a suit was brought in India regarding a Bill of Lading which limited jurisdiction to Italy. The suit was stayed but the Court said 'if no proceedings are taken in Italy, the defendants will be at liberty to mention the matter for that purpose'. Quoting Dicey quoting The Fermarh (1957) 1 WLR 815, the judgment said: "It is well established that where there is a provision in a contract providing that disputes are to be referred to a foreign tribunal, then prima facie, this court will stay proceedings instituted in this country in breach of such agreement, and will only allow them to proceed when satisfied that it is just and proper to do so."

The clause of the contract involved in the case of Union of India v. Navigation Maritime Bulgare (AIR 1973 Cal 526) said, "Any dispute arising under this Bill of Lading to be decided in Bulgaria according to Bulgarian Law." This forum selection clause was not interpreted to mean that the jurisdiction of the Courts of India was ousted. However, considering the balance of convenience and the law applicable, the court concluded that the dispute should be decided in a Bulgarian Court.

And in the case of Black Sea Steamship U L Lastochkina Odessa, USSR v. Union of India (AIR 1976 AP 103), a dispute arose in the course of the operation of an international trade contract which stated that disputes would be adjudicated in the USSR. Considering the small size of the claim and the availability of the defendant, the Vishakapatnam court decided that the balance of convenience and interest of justice were in favour of its deciding the suit. The jurisdiction clause in the contract involved in this case did not appear to choose any law though. It merely said, "All claims and disputes arising under and in connection with this bill of lading shall be judged in the USSR."

Regarding the choice of law in a contract, as the Andhra Pradesh High Court pointed out, 'the firm conclusion is that it is perfectly open to the court to consider the balance of convenience, and interests of justice and like circumstances when it decides the question of jurisdiction of a court in the light of a clause in the agreement between parties choosing one of several courts or forums which were available to them'.

154.Incidentally, libel can also occur in fiction. The most famous libel in fiction case is that of Princess Irina Youssoupoff v. MGM [1934] 50 TLR 581 (CA) in which the Princess successfully claimed that she had been defamed in the 1932 movie 'Rasputin and the Empress'.

The film showed a Princess in it called Natasha having been seduced. The Princess in the film was, however, clearly 'identifiable' as Princess Irina Youssoupoff who had in fact been raped and not seduced. One of the defences MGM used was that the Princess had indeed been shown to have been raped and therefore could not be blamed which in turn meant that she had not been defamed. (While this does demonstrate the attitudes towards women which prevailed at the time, that's something best left for another discussion.)

Slesser LJ held that the test should not be whether the plaintiff had been exposed to ridicule, hatred and contempt but if — expanding the Parmiter v. Coupland definition — the defamation had caused the plaintiff to be shunned and avoided. He thought that the film was defamatory whether it suggested rape or seduction and said:

"I, for myself, cannot see that from the plaintiff's point of view it matters in the least whether this libel suggests that she has been seduced or ravished. The question whether she is or is not the more or the less moral seems to me immaterial in considering this question whether she has been defamed, and for this reason, that, as has been frequently pointed out in libel, not only is the matter defamatory if it brings the plaintiff into hatred, ridicule, or contempt by reason of some moral discredit on her part, but also if it tends to make the plaintiff be shunned and avoided and that without any moral discredit on her part. It is for that reason that persons who have been alleged to have been insane, or to be suffering from certain disease, and other cases where no direct moral responsibility could be placed upon them, have been held to be entitled to bring an action to protect their reputation and their honour. One may, I think, take judicial notice of the fact that a lady of whom it has been said that she has been ravished, albeit against her will, has suffered in social reputation and in opportunities of receiving respectable consideration from the world. .... When this woman is defamed in her sexual purity I do not think that the precise manner in which she has been despoiled of her innocence and virginity is a matter which a jury can properly be asked to consider."

The WSJ Law Blog <blogs. wsj. com/law/2008/03/20/libel-in-fiction-claim-rarely-successful-survives-summary-judgment/?mod=WSJBlog> speaking of another case on the issue which has just been filed says:

"To make out a libel-in-fiction claim — a somewhat counterintuitive theory in which a plaintiff claims that something that is fictional is not factually accurate — Batra [the plaintiff] must demonstrate that the identities of the real and fictional characters are "so complete that the defamatory material" becomes a "plausible aspect" of the plaintiff's real life."

See: <bulk. resource. org/courts. gov/c/F2/364/>

155. Under Section 499 of the Indian Penal Code, whoever, by words either spoken or intended to be read, or by signs or by visible representations, makes or publishes any imputation concerning any person intending to harm, or knowing or having reason to believe that such imputation will harm, the reputation of such person, is said to defame that person. However, it is not defamation to impute anything which is true concerning any person, if the imputation should be made or published for the public good. Whether or not it is for the public good is a question of fact. In addition to this, it is not defamation to express in a good faith any opinion whatever respecting the conduct of a public servant in the discharge of his public functions, or respecting his character, so far as his character appears in that conduct, and no further. It may amount to defamation to impute anything to a deceased person, if the imputation would harm the reputation of that person if living, and is intended to be hurtful to the feelings of his family or other near relatives. It may amount to defamation to make an imputation concerning a company or an association or collection of persons as such. An imputation in the form of an alternative or expressed ironically, may amount to defamation. No imputation is said to harm a person's reputation, unless that imputation directly or indirectly, in the estimation of others, lowers the moral or intellectual character of that person, or lowers the character of that person in respect of his caste or of his calling, or lowers the credit of

that person, or causes it to be believed that the body of that person is in a loathsome state, or in a state generally considered as disgraceful.

156.AIR 1989 Bom 331

157.Ryder, Rodney, Napster and beyond,<tata.com/0_knowledge_centre/ipr/articles/20010711_net_effects11.htm>

158.ICC Development (International) Ltd. v. Arvee Enterprises and Anr., MANU/DE/0053/2003; 2003VIIAD(Delhi) 405; 2003(26) PTC245 (Del); 2004(1) RAJ10

159.McCarthy, The Right of Publicity and Privacy 28:3, West Group; Midler v. Ford Auto Co. 849 F. 2d 460, 7 U S P Q 2d 1398 (9th Cir. 1988); Factors Etc., Inc. v. Creative Card Co., 444 F Supp 279,283 (SDNY 1977)

13

ADVERTISEMENTS

Ordinarily, all the regulations and restrictions which apply to general content also apply to advertisements as well. However, advertisements are subject to several extra restrictions to attempt to ensure that they are not entirely untruthful and that they give consumers enough information to be able to make an informed choice. Many of these restrictions are laid down either in statutory enactments and in executive rules. And where there are lacunae in the law, such as when it comes to ambush advertising, the courts have stepped in.

Ambush marketing is the practice of running a marketing campaign around an event without actually being an official sponsor of the event or paying any fees to the person who conducts the event. One of the most well known examples of this happening in recent history is in the case of Pepsi's 'Nothing Official About It' campaign during the 1996 World Cup in which Coca-Cola was the official sponsor.

It is often thought of as a form of unfair competition and can be carried out in any number of ways: through the use of slogans, through endorsements from participants such as sportspersons involved in the event concerned or by simply purchasing advertising space in the vicinity of the venue of the event.

Those who engage in ambush marketing do not (and cannot legally) explicitly represent themselves as being sponsors of the event. However, their tactics are often designed to implicitly create the impression in the minds of the general public that such an association exists.

At other times, they parody the ads of official sponsors who are competitors. Such parodies are often seen independent of any event, but when a third party is involved and the target of the parody has paid a lot of money to be associated with that third party (or an event organized by the third party) the dynamics of the relationship between the competitors changes.

In the case of parodies, copyrights in the original would probably not be infringed. (Trade marks are another matter though.) In addition to this, fair use and the right to freedom of speech and expression would usually ensure that parodies were legal which means that those targeted by ambush marketing would not automatically be able to successfully sue for copyright infringement, trademark infringement or passing off although they might be able to sue under unfair competition laws, and possibly, if one were to really stretch one's imagination for corporate disparagement.

India, like many other countries, does not have a law which specifically deals with ambush marketing or advertising. Nonetheless, in 2003, the Delhi High Court said that ambush marketing is legal under Indian law in the case of ICC v. Arvee Enterprises and Philips.

The Indian advertising industry is governed by a code for self-regulation among advertisers which has been adopted by the Advertising Standards Council of India. Under this code, the representations and claims made by advertisements must be truthful, and must not be offensive to generally accepted standards of public decency. In addition to this, the code aims to provide safeguards against the promotion of products which are regarded as hazardous or harmful to society or to individuals, particularly minors, to a degree or of a type which is unacceptable to society at large. Advertisements addressed to minors cannot contain anything, whether in illustration or otherwise, which might result in their physical, mental or moral harm or which exploits their vulnerability. Advertisements must observe fairness in competition such that the consumer's need to be informed on choice in the market place and the canons of generally accepted competitive behavior in business are both served.[160]

However, this code does not have the force of law and it does not, by any stretch of the imagination, comprise all the regulations and restrictions to which advertisements are subject. In other words, it merely supplements the law; it does not supplant it.

The law governing is a mixture of statutory and judicial law. For example, puffing in advertising has been held to be illegal by the Madras High Court in December 2008 in a dispute between Colgate and Palmolive.

In addition to this, there are a various statutory provisions and executive rules which affect advertisements. Rule 7 of the Cable Television Networks Rules, 1994, for example, contains an advertising code unto itself which pertains to advertisements carried on cable services.[161] It says that advertisements must conform to the laws of the country and should not offend morality, decency or the religious susceptibilities of subscribers.

There are also special restrictions with regard to specific kinds of advertisements. Insurance advertisements, for example, must comply with the Insurance Regulatory and Development Authority (Insurance Advertisements and Disclosure) Regulations which prohibit unfair or misleading insurance advertisements. While the Drugs and Magic Remedies Act not only prohibits misleading advertisements of drugs in general but also contains a blanket ban on the advertisement of drugs for the treatment of certain diseases. A first offence under the Act is punishable with imprisonment which may extend up to six months or fine with both.[162]

And when it comes to promoting films, the Cinematograph (Certification) Rules require persons advertising a film by means of insertion in newspapers, hoardings, posters, handbills or trailers to indicate the category of certification of the film.[163] Non-compliance of this rule is a cognizable and non-bailable offence.[164]

And if that weren't enough, all the standard laws which relate to content also apply to advertisements i.e. don't infringe copyrights or trademarks, don't make defamatory statements, don't show images which portray women in a derogatory light etc.

Further, advertisements may also be subject to local laws. Consider just New Delhi. Under the New Delhi Municipal Council Act, only one advertisement board may be displayed at the site of any establishment. Prior written permission from the Chairman, NDMC is required to put up any additional board.[165] Also, the Delhi Police Act says that no person can carry or place bulky advertisements, pictures, figures or emblems in any street or public place which may cause any obstruction to passengers or annoyance to the residents in the vicinity in contravention of any regulation made by the Commissioner of Police.[166] Any person who contravenes such a regulation made by the Police Commissioner may be punished with a fine of up to one hundred rupees, or, in default of payment of such fine, with imprisonment for a term not exceeding eight days.[167]

However, there are areas where the law in India is less than crystal clear. For example, take seeding and viral ads. Legislation to fine and/or imprison brand owners who blog, use brand ambassadors or seed viral ads online without making their origin clear came into force across Europe on January 1, 2008 and on May 26, 2008 in the UK. Under the rules, bloggers are required to disclose if they are being paid to write about any particular product. Campaigns like the "All I want for Christmas is a PSP" by Sony and its agency, Zipatoni, will be illegal.[168] Indian law, however, seems to be oblivious to viral ads.

Similarly, it is unclear how advertorials would be treated by the law. While copyright infringement in advertorials would probably be a relatively straightforward issue, with an advertorial being treated as a literary work in most circumstances, there are other areas where the law is not quite as clear.

FOOTNOTES

160.<ascionline.org/regulation/code.htm>

161.Section 2 (b), Cable Television Networks (Regulation) Act, 1995: 'Cable service' means the transmission by cables of programmes including re-transmission by cables of any broadcast television signals.
Section 2 (b), Cable Television Networks (Regulation) Act, 1995: 'Programme' means any television broadcast and includes —
(i) exhibition of films, features, dramas, advertisements and serials through video cassette recorders or video cassette players; (ii) any audio or visual or audio-visual live performance or presentation, and the expression 'programming service' shall be construed accordingly.
162.Section 3, Drugs And Magic Remedies Act, 1954
163.Rule 38, Cinematograph (Certification) Rules, 1983
164.Section 7, Cinematograph Act, 1952
165.Section 89, The New Delhi Municipal Council Act, 1994
166.Section 85, The Delhi Police Act, 1978
167.Section 97, The Delhi Police Act, 1978
168.<adage. com/digital/article?article_id=126667>

14

ONLINE PRIVACY

Online privacy is an interesting issue mainly because it highlights the fact that the words personal and private are not synonymous. And quite frankly, it's only a tiny fraction of the material that's put online is actually private, and even if the person who uploads it thinks it's private, it may not take more than a thirteen-year-old who knows what he's doing to access it.

There are some websites like Privnote[169] which try to offer increased privacy by doing such things as offering to send notes which self-destruct. A reading of its website in June 2008 seemed to explain how the service worked: persons wrote notes and then posted them. The notes were stored somewhere — the site, at that point of time, didn't say where — and senders were given links where they (or someone they gave / mailed the link to) could read the notes. The links worked just once after which the notes were destroyed. Privnote said that the service provided 'a little extra privacy at zero cost'.

The company also said in a disclaimer which showed up when users clicked on a link Privnote sent that they 'store the notes encrypted in a way that only the sender and receiver know how to decrypt'. This meant, they said, that they could not themselves read the notes sent through Privnote. And, obviously, Privnote said that it did not shoulder 'any responsibility for the views and opinions expressed in the note'.

However, as Brian Beckham[170] pointed out, the site does not specify exactly what happens to the data sent through its system and asked some pretty important questions: 'Can the company retrieve information which has supposedly been destroyed? Is it compiling a profile on those who use the service? Would it turn the info over to the feds or anyone else armed with a subpoena?'

Most websites and companies have privacy policies nowadays and it seemed strange that a service which was all about privacy didn't have a policy at the time — or a policy that was easily visible to visitors at any rate — answering those questions.

As a result, one could only think that perhaps the service was best suited to the needs of teenagers who'd like to spice things up a bit by sending each other supposedly private notes. Somehow, it didn't seem to be a very bright idea to send confidential professional information across without actually knowing what was happening to it.

Privacy Policies are unusual documents in themselves. They're common but that's not the same as being 'usual'. They are among the few instances where companies and others take it upon themselves to restrict their own freedom by saying that they will use the information they receive only in certain specified ways. The promises contained in Privacy Policies are binding on those who make them, and liability can be incurred if they are broken.

Another important question though when it comes to online privacy is 'what it private material'?

The issue was widely discussed when the Judge Kozinski and the porn / non-porn / (?) mess[171] surfaced. It appeared that an attorney (who was been widely reported to be disgruntled) accessed the judge's family server and got the LA Times to print a story about some of its contents which were supposedly pornographic. There were also some mp3s on the server. Some claimed that the judge had violated copyright by having them there.

If the story had broken in India, there is little doubt that the material on the judge's server would be perceived as being obscene both legally and otherwise, and that there would have been a massive outcry. Although, that being said, it's somehow doubtful whether the average Indian judge would ordinarily maintain a server and, if he did, whether he would have anything worth mentioning on it.

The content, however, seemed to have been legal in the US. Nonetheless, the episode raised some interesting questions about privacy, in particular, whether, if you have a server which you use for your own personal use, you have a reasonable expectation of privacy. Some scholars like Larry Lessig[172] weighed in in favour of Judge Kozinski inter alia saying that privacy is not determined technology. One can't help but suspect that it'd probably be more accurate to say that privacy should not be determined by technology although, in reality, it is — the virtual equivalent of having someone go through what's on your desk. If your personal desk is locked, it is evidently private. If it isn't, in theory, it should ordinarily be private but there are a number of people who won't respect that privacy.

And that brings one to the question of whether it matters if privacy is determined by technology in that sense that if you consider something online to be private and someone, possibly by because of a superior knowledge of technology, accesses that material, has your privacy been violated? What would you need to do in order to ensure that your material was in fact private? Would you need to restrict search engine access to it or would you have to password protect it?

When it comes to documents, some professionals do not use much (or any) technology worth mentioning to protect documents they transmit online and instead rely on merely having a notice which clearly says that the contents of the document are private. In some jurisdictions, that is enough to ensure that the document is acknowledged to be private and (with some luck) respected as such. And although such notices do not prevent persons from accessing documents, they do limit liability and other similar issues.

In the Kozinski episode, the judge seems to have placed material on a personal server which he seemed to have assumed was private. At first glance, his actions don't seem to have been illegal but they do seem to have been naive. Personal material is not the same as private material and a personal server certainly isn't the same as a private server.

However, if you have something online — in this case, there were mp3s on the server — on a personal server and someone accesses it, can any consequences follow from that person's having accessed the material if you didn't authorize him to access it? Would it be analogous to placing CDs on your bookshelf which if a trespasser accessed would certainly not cause you to be accused of having infringed the copyright in the music? There are good reasons to put personal collections of music online. For example, one would be able to access one's own music for one's own use from anywhere say, when one were travelling, without actually having to carry three hundred CDs along with one.

Considering how undeveloped both cyber law and the law of privacy are in India, one can't be absolutely certain of the outcome if a person made no attempt to restrict access to their server. That, however, doesn't prevent one from hoping that good sense would prevail and that one would not be held to have committed infringement.

FOOTNOTES

169.< privnote.com/about/>

170.<blog.internetcases.com/2008/07/08/wouldnt-privnote-be-better-if-it-had-a-privacy-policy/>

171.<patterico.com/2008/06/23/the-material-from-judge-kozinskis-websiteserver-part-two-including-videos/#more-9000>

172.<lessig.org/blog/2008/06/on_privacy_in_the_cyberage_ii.html>

15

WHAT YOU WEAR

There isn't too much doubt about the fact that the application of make up, no matter how artistic, cannot be copyrighted. But when it comes to certain other facets of looking good — or trying to — there has been some amount of debate.

Take clothes, for example. In early 2008, there were reports[173] from Australia of a dispute about the design of a dress having been copied. The SMH said that "The case has ended with a victory — and an award of $17,500 damages — for Melbourne fashion label Review over the Sydney company behind fashion labels Charlie Brown and Lili. Justice Christopher Jessup found that the Lili dress sold in Sydney had been copied from the Review dress."

Around the same time, it was widely reported[174] that the US Senate and Congress had both been discussing extending special copyright protection to the fashion industry — it was unclear what exactly they were trying to achieve considering that the fashion industry is an industry which thrives on the lack of copyright protection in several ways. Their logic was rather obscure insofar as one of the reasons they thought that copyright protection should be so extended was to ensure that 'Terrorists Don't Win'. If there's one thing no one can accuse Bush's Washington of, it's inconsistency on that score. It'd probably be equally difficult to praise it for being sensible on the same score.

While this was going on, across the pond, the Scots were looking for a way to protect the kilt.[175] They didn't try to go down the copyright route though. The Independent reported that the campaign was 'the idea of an Edinburgh-based kilt-maker, Howie Nicholsby, who, exasperated by the influx of cheap, foreign imports calling themselves Scottish kilts, got in touch with the Scottish Member of European Parliament Alyn Smith to see if they could persuade the European Commission to give the Scottish kilt protected designation of origin (PDO) status.' The protected designation of origin status is usually used to protect food though under EEC regulation 2081/92.[176]

Back in India, at the end of 2008, the Delhi High Court came up with an interesting decision in the matter of Masrani v. Tahiliani Design which dealt with copyright, clothes and the connection between the Copyright Law and the Designs Act.

Designs receive protection as intellectual property under the law. However, the Copyright Act does not always protect them; they may be protected by the 2000 Designs Act. Under this Act, designs are defined as only the features of shape, configuration, pattern, ornament or configuration of lines/colours applied to any article in 2D or 3D or both by any manual, mechanical, chemical industrial process/means which appeal to the eye and are judged solely by the eye.[177] So, a design is often a work which could be protected by copyright.[178] However, a provision in the Copyright Act says that copyright cannot subsist under it in any design which is registered as a design. If the design is capable of being registered as a design but has not been registered as one, copyright ceases to subsist in it as soon as any article to which it is applied has been reproduced more than fifty times by an industrial process either by the copyright owner or his licensee.[179] So although the two statutes may appear to overlap at first glance, they do not offer protection to any work simultaneously.

There is no copyright in the designs of clothes so what the designer who filed this suit effectively did was get protection slipped in rather innovatively in a way which made one wonder why foreign pharmaceuticals generally sue only for patent infringement instead of also suing for copyright infringement.[180] He claimed that designs of the clothes which he had made in the course of making clothes and accessories were artistic works in which copyright subsisted. In addition to this, he claimed that the patterns made on the cloth involved were also artistic works in their own right in which copyright protection subsisted. The other party obviously did not agree but a Single Judge Bench of the Delhi High Court did, and issued an interim injunction in favour of the designer who filed the suit.

There were a few interesting issues which came up in the course of the proceedings which primarily had to do whether the work was protected at all. One was that no copyright subsisted in the works as they should have been registered as designs.[181] This didn't hold too much water since the designs of the clothes were in fact for couture and were not even reproduced twenty times — copyright law requires a work to be reproduced fifty times before it loses the protection of the Copyright Act.

The other was whether the work was an artistic work at all. In the case of Microfibre v. Girdhar, it had been held that 'What cannot be lost sight of is the very object with which such arrangements or works had been made. The object is to put them to industrial use. An industrial process has to be done to apply the work or configuration to the textile. It is not something which has to be framed and put on the wall or would have any utility by itself. The two important objects are the object with which it is made (which is industrial) and its inability to stand by itself as a piece of art.' In Masrani v. Tahiliani, however, the Court decided that this did not apply since the circumstances were different: in Microfibre, a floral textile design which had been registered in the UK and had been applied more than fifty times was sought to be protected.

It therefore appears that the Indian judiciary is not averse to the idea of protecting designer clothes. The injunction being granted does not mean that copyright has been infringed though; it merely means that there is a good chance of there being copyright infringement. Personally, I think that couture is often art (and that it is sometimes *godawful*). However, it's extremely doubtful that it's a good idea for access to couture (or any other form of art whether or not specifically protected by the Copyright Act) to be limited. The path from the runway to the high street is lined with imitations in various forms, and to cut off access to designer clothes in such a manner would probably be counter-productive to the industry as a whole.

FOOTNOTES

173.<theage. com. au/news/national/what-the-frock-a-designers-costly-essing-down/2008/03/08/1204780131643. html>, <smh. com. au news/life—style-home/the-fashion-swindle/2008/03/08/1204780127303. html>

174.<techdirt. com/articles/20080215/135455266. shtml>, <techdirt. com/articles/20070810/030915. shtml>, <nytimes. com/2007/08/09/fashion/09ROW.html?ex =1344398400 & en = 1075a5b43c787fd8 & ei = 5124 & partner = permalink & exprod=permalink>

175.<independent. co. uk/news/uk/home-news/hands-off-our-kilts-scots-bid-to-copyright-their-national-dress-789340. html>

176.<eur-lex.europa.eu/LexUriServ/LexUriServ.do?uri=CELEX: 31992 R 2081:EN:HTML>

177.Section 2(d), Designs Act, 2000

178.Under Section 4 of the Designs Act, certain designs cannot be registered. They are those designs which:
(a) are not new or original
(b) have been disclosed to the public in tangible form
(c) are not significantly different from known designs or a combination thereof
d) comprise / contain material which is scandalous or obscene.

179.Section 15, Indian Copyright Act, 1957

180.Indian pharmaceutical companies reported make much use of the documentation of foreign pharmaceuticals to make products which the copy and to get them approved.

181.Section 5 of the Designs Act deals with the registration of a design.
1. An application in the prescribed form is filed in the Patent Office in the prescribed manner with the prescribed fee.
2. A design can only be registered in one class; the controller decides the class in case there is a doubt.
3. The Controller refers the design to an examiner under Section 3 to see if the design can be registered and considers his report. The design should be new and/or original, not previously published in any country and consistent with public order and morality. Also, under Section 4, it should be distinguishable from known designs or a combination thereof.
4. The Controller may refuse registration. If he does so, the person aggrieved may prefer an appeal to the High Court.

5. If the Controller registers the design, it is registered as of the date of the application and, under Section 7, the Controller then causes the publication of the particulars of the design and it is open to public inspection.
6. The Controller grants a certificate of registration to a registered design under Section 9.
7. An entry regarding the registration of the design is then made in the register of Designs as required by Section 10.

An application which has not been completed because of any neglect or default on the part of the applicant so as to enable registration to be effected within the prescribed period is deemed to have been abandoned under Section 5.

Corrections and substitutions may be made in the application under Section 8.

Under Section 6, a design may be registered in respect of all or any of the articles which belong to a particular class, and:

(a) the proprietor of the design may later register it in respect of one or more articles belonging to the same class although the subsequent registration does not extend the period of copyright in the previous registration.

(b) If a proprietor wants to register a design which is identical or similar to a design registered by some other person in respect of some other article then, if the applicant becomes the proprietor of the earlier design while the application for the latter one is pending, the applicant is treated as though he had been the registered proprietor of the earlier design at the time of making the application.

Under Section 3, the Controller of Patents, Designs and Trademarks appointed under Section 4 is the Controlled of Designs.

16

HARDLY MUSIC TO THE EARS

Copyright subsists in music just as it does in literary works. However, to merely say that copyright subsists in music is a deceptive simplification: copyright subsists in what one would normally think of as music — say a Bryan Adams' song — not as one composite copyright but as several copyrights which protect different elements such as the score and the lyrics of the song.

A 'musical work'[182] is defined by the law as a work consisting of music and it includes any graphical notation of the work. However, it does not include any works or any action intended to be sung, spoken or performed with the music. What this means is that even if one were to simply consider the sheet music of a song alone, there would already be on one sheet of paper, two different copyrights: one for the musical notation itself and the other for the lyrics. The notation is what would be considered a musical work while the lyrics would be a literary or dramatic work.[183] The two different works would probably be written by two different people. The law[184] says that the person who wrote the lyrics would be their author while the composer of the music would be considered to be its author whether or not he had recorded the music in any form of graphical notation.[185]

Assuming that the lyricist and the composer were working independently, they would both own the copyrights in their respective works and the rights in the sheet music, containing both musical notation and lyrics, would be owned by both of them. They would not own it jointly though: they would each own separate elements in the music and their ownership would be distinct and divisible.

If, however, they, or either one of them was employed by someone else under a contract of service, and created that work under the contract, the picture would be slightly murky. Under some circumstances, the employer would then be the 'first' owner of copyright in the work although the author of the work would not entirely lose his rights in it. The exact situation would depend on the terms of the contract between the author and the employer. That is why, if one wanted to use the work, it would be imperative to conduct an intellectual property audit to figure out who owned the rights. Only if one knows who the rights holders are in any work can one obtain appropriate consent for the use of the work from the right people and ensure that one isn't guilty of infringement.[186]

And so far, we're still talking about music on a sheet of paper which hasn't been sung by anyone, or recorded by anyone.

Now, if a third person were to sing the song so as to communicate it to the public without obtaining permission from the owners of the work, he would, technically, usually be an infringer. If, however, he were to sing it after obtaining the appropriate licences, he would be considered a performer[187] under the law. As a performer, he would have his own right in relation to his performance,[188] namely, the performer's right. This right would last for fifty years from the time of the performance and would ensure that no one could legally record the performance without his consent or do such things as reproduce unauthorized recordings of the performance. If the performance was incorporated in a film though, the performer's right would cease to exist.

Finally, to record the song, permission would have to be obtained from all the rights holders. If the contracts between the performer, the lyricist and the composer said that the performer could have his performance recorded, this wouldn't be necessary but if they didn't say so, it would be required. It wouldn't make any difference how the performance was proposed to be recorded: a 'sound recording' means a recording of sounds from which such sounds may be produced regardless of the medium on which the recording is made or the method by which the sounds are produced.[189]

The producer of the sound recording would be considered to be its author,[190] with the producer being the person who took the initiative and responsibility for making the work.[191] As the author of the work, the producer would own the copyright which subsisted in the sound recording although, of course, if he made it under a contract either of or for service, his ownership of the copyright would be subject to the terms of the contract.

Once the sound recording was made, any other recording made by any means which embodied it would infringe it.[192] No one but its owner would be able to communicate it to the public without a licence and it would be illegal to sell or hire an infringing copy of the recording. Obviously, as a result, it would be necessary to obtain a licence from all the rights holders to broadcast the record, and once it was broadcast, a new right called the broadcast reproduction right which lasted for twenty-five years would come into being.

Also, depending on what the contracts signed by the various rights holders said, it would be entirely possible for the music as a composite work not to be owned by any one person: the composer, lyricist, performer, producer and, possibly, their employers could all have some stake in the rights of the 'end product'. If one were to avoid infringing any of their rights, one would have to get permission from each of them to use their works during the subsistence of the term of copyright in their works.

Since performers' rights last for fifty years (compared to the life plus sixty-year term for which music, lyrics and sound recordings are protected), one could easily wind up in a situation where although the performer's rights no longer subsisted, the rights of the others were still in existence.

Considering this, even in the traditional course, it isn't difficult to infringe the copyright in music. Bring the Internet and other new technologies into the picture and the landscape changes considerably by making it much easier, and much more tempting to infringe copyright.

Sharing music files online is a common example, and there's much that has been said about it. A breathless recapitulation of the peer-to-peer or P2P file-sharing story is: people share files, and record companies and other rights holders do not like this. Various rights holders filed suits for copyright infringement to stop files from being shared online. They went after unlikely individuals and accused them of copyright infringement and they went after entities such as Napster which facilitated file sharing on a massive scale. The music rights holders succeeded.

A number of attempts were made to defend online file sharing. Sharers started off by using the 'time shifting' defence which was seen in the case of Sony v. Universal Studios[193] in which the users of a Sony Betamax Video Recorder were allowed to shift the time slot of programmes which were broadcast. By analogy, in Universal v. MP3.com,[194] a company which built an online library of MP3s and allowed persons to access it said that it had not committed copyright infringement because it had merely 'space shifted' the music involved. The judiciary wasn't too impressed with this and said that the company had committed copyright infringement.

After this, came the Napster case[195] where a website did essentially the same thing as MP3.com but did not maintain an online library so to avoid being held guilty of infringement. All it did was manage a searchable database of music files. And sure enough, when the matter went to court, Napster was not held guilty of direct infringement. It was, however, held guilty of indirect infringement since it had facilitated and contributed to direct infringement.

In the next round, the sharers[196] got rid of not only the online library but also the searchable centrally-managed database believing doing so that would protect them. It did protect them from being held guilty of both direct and indirect infringement.[197] Nonetheless, it didn't prevent them from being held to have committed an offence which no one had earlier heard of: 'active inducement to commit piracy'.

India has, however, not seen P2P cases which have made headlines possibly because Internet penetration in the country is low.

Leaving aside file-sharing though, the accessibility of new technology has made such things as creating remixes extremely easy. Although it takes talent to make a good remix, it doesn't take much more than access to a computer to make a remix in the first place.

Remixes exist in a grey area of copyright law: to commit infringement, there has to be substantial copying of the original work. What 'substantial copying' would be though is a question of fact. And if a person who made a remix hadn't got appropriate licences from all the rights-holders, he would have to rely on not having used 'much' of a copyrighted song or other piece of music to avoid being accused of infringement. That is a strategy which may or may not work though.

In addition to this, apart from trying to rely on fair dealing, one possible way to avoid being held guilty of copyright infringement would be to say that the amount of music copied was negligible and so, a Court should not interfere since the law does not, according to the ancient maxim, care for trivialities: *de minimis non curat lex.*[198] Although this defence is not available to those who 'sample' sound recordings,[199] the Beastie Boys did successfully manage to use it in a case involving the use of three notes in a song 'Pass the Mic'.[200]

The problem is that even three notes can amount to substantial copying. For example, it is absolutely impossible to play the three notes E♭, E♭, G without evoking Beethoven's Fifth Symphony. True, Beethoven's Fifth is not protected by copyright but the principle remains the same: three notes can define a piece of music even if that piece is as long and as complex as a symphony.

And so, the bottom line is that the only way one can be absolutely certain of not being accused of having infringed the copyright in music is to do nothing with music without obtaining a licence unless all the rights which subsist in it are firmly in the public domain.

FOOTNOTES

182. Section 2(p), Indian Copyright Act

183.A 'Dramatic work' includes any piece for recitation under Section

2(h),Indian Copyright Act, 1957.
184.Section 2(d), Indian Copyright Act, 1957
185.Section 2(ffa), Indian Copyright Act, 1957
186.An 'Infringing copy' of literary, dramatic, or musical work means a reproduction of it which is not in the form of a cinematographic film under Section 2(m), Indian Copyright Act, 1957.
187.Section 2(qq), Indian Copyright Act, 1957
188.A 'Performance' in relation to performer's right means any visual or acoustic presentation made live by one or more performers under Section 2(q), Indian Copyright Act, 1957.
189.Section 2(xx), Indian Copyright Act, 1957
190.Section 2(d), Indian Copyright Act, 1957
191.Section 2(uu), Indian Copyright Act, 1957
192.Section 2(m), Indian Copyright Act, 1957
193.Sony Corp. of America v. Universal City Studios Inc. 464 US 417 (1984)
194.Universal Recordings Inc. v. MP3. com Inc. 92 F Supp 2d 349 (SDNY 2000)
195.A & M Records Inc. v. Napster Inc. 239 F 3d 1004 (9th Circuit 2001)
196.Grokster, Aimster, eDonkey
197.MGM Studios Inc. v. Grokster Ltd. 545 US 913 (2005)
198.This does not mean that Courts do not decide 'trivial' issues. Consider Justice Scalia's dissenting decision in US Supreme Court case, PGA v. Martin which he didn't think should have been brought before a court at all. While the majority held that Casey Martin, a professional golfer suffering from a degenerative circulatory condition, could use a motorized cart during tournaments under the Americans with Disabilities Act, Justice Scalia had this to say: "It has been rendered the solemn duty of the Supreme Court of the United States to regulate Commerce with foreign Nations, and among the several States, to decide What Is Golf. I am sure that the Framers of the Constitution, aware of the 1457 edict of King James II of Scotland prohibiting golf because it interfered with the practice of archery, fully expected that sooner or later the paths of golf and government, the law and the links, would once again cross, and that the judges of this august Court would some day have to wrestle with that age-old jurisprudential question, for which their years of study in the law have so well prepared them: Is someone riding around a golf course from shot to shot really a golfer? The answer, we learn, is yes. The Court ultimately concludes, and it will henceforth be the Law of the Land, that walking is not a "fundamental" aspect of golf. Either out of humility or out of self-respect (one or the other) the Court should decline to answer this incredibly difficult and incredibly silly question. ... many, indeed, consider walking to be the central feature of the game of golf—hence Mark Twain's classic criticism of the sport: 'a good walk spoiled'."
199.Bridgeport Music Inc.v. Dimension Films 410 F 3d 792, 802 (6th Circuit 2005)
200.Newton v Diamond 388 F 3d 1189 (9th Circuit 2004)

PART IV

Beyond Copyright

17

COPYRIGHT AND ACCESS TO THE LAW

People have been claiming copyright in 'the law' for a long time, and at times, they've been able to make a halfway convincing case for it. While there are good answers to these arguments, they're not always the first ones that come to hand. It's really only the arrival of the Internet that genuinely puts the long-standing goal of free and unencumbered access to the law within our grasp.

There are exceptions[201] in the India Copyright Act which enable laws to be republished without infringing their copyright. The reproduction or publication of any matter which has been published in any Gazette except an Act of a Legislature is allowed by the Copyright Act, 1957. Any Act of a Legislature can also be reproduced or published provided it is accompanied by any commentary on it or any other original matter. The report of any committee, commission, council, board or other like body appointed by the Government if the report has been laid on the Table of Legislature can be reproduced or published as long as the Government has not prohibited such reproduction or publication.

An Act of a Legislature and any rules or orders made under it can also be translated into any Indian language if the Government has not already done so or if the Government's translation is not available for sale to the public. Translations must, however, contain a statement at a prominent place saying that they have not been authorized or accepted as authentic by the Government.

Further, any judgment or order of a court, tribunal or other judicial authority may be reproduced or published unless it is prohibited by the court, the tribunal or other judicial authority. This is vital to the functioning of the legal system because a large chunk of Indian law is case law i.e. law as it is laid down in the judgments of cases. If it were to be copyrightable and if access to it were restricted, it would in effect mean that people would be required to follow laws they did not know about.

Despite the law clearly saying that judgments can be republished, there have been disputes on the matter in Court as early as 1915. At the time, the Calcutta High Court in Jagdish Chandra v. Mohim Chandra[202] held that although judgments are themselves not protected by copyright, the selection of cases and their arrangement is protected by copyright.

This did nothing to resolve the issue and in recent years, there has been a fresh spate of litigation on the subject. In 2001, with reference to judgments, it was held that there cannot be any monopoly in subject matter which the author has borrowed from the public domain in a case filed by Eastern Book Company, the company which publishes SCC, a reporter of Supreme Court judgments, against Navin J Desai.[203]The Court said that since there was no copyright in judgments, a plaintiff could not claim copyright in them merely by publishing them in his journal, and another person could copy the judgments from the journal instead of copying them from the 'raw source'.

A few years later, in Eastern Book Company v. D B Modak,[204] EBC filed a suit against Spectrum Business Support Ltd. run by D B Modak which collates judgments from a number of legal reporters and makes them available on CDs (which they call Grand Jurix and sell for about 28000 INR). In this case, the Supreme Court ruled (in December 2007) that EBC holds a copyright in its own internal referencing of judgments and headnotes although court judgments themselves are not copyrighted as Section 52(1)(q) of the Indian Copyright Act also makes clear.

Not even this was enough to ensure that the matter would be settled. In 2006, Eastern Book Company filed yet another case against Deepak Kapoor and claimed copyright in the copyedited text of judgments. Mr Kapoor did not admit this claim but to resolve the matter amicably, the suit was settled (without prejudice) in terms of a compromise with Mr Kapoor agreeing to replace or remove the offending texts within six months.[205]

Issues about access to the law are not limited to India though. In April 2008, the State of Oregon sent Justia a cease-and-desist letter[206] telling it to either enter into a licensing agreement with it (and pay Oregon for the privilege of posting its Revised Statutes) or to remove the Oregon Revised Statutes from its site.

James Grimmelmann, Associate Professor at the New York Law School wrote an essay[207] in June 2008 after this happened. In it, he speaks of the importance of access to the law, the history of access to the law, copyright in the law, and new principles for the Internet Age. The chapter comprises an edited version of his essay.

WHY ACCESS?

"But the plans were on display..."
"On display? I eventually had to go down to the cellar to find them."
"That's the display department."
"With a flashlight."
"Ah, well, the lights had probably gone."
"So had the stairs."
"But look, you found the notice, didn't you?"
"Yes," said Arthur, "yes I did. It was on display on the bottom of a locked filing cabinet stuck in a disused lavatory with a sign on the door saying 'Beware of the Leopard'."

—*Douglas Adams, The Hitchhiker's Guide to the Galaxy*

Why do we care so much about access to the law? It's clearly wrong to make the documents that constitute the law accessible only by putting them on display on the bottom of a locked file cabinet stuck in a misused lavoratory with a sign on the door saying "Beware of the Leopard." But why? What's wrong with this approach to government? At least four things:

- *Democracy:* Rule by secret law is perhaps indistinguishable from rule by no law whatsoever. It's fundamental to democracy and the rule of law that rules be announced and applied prospectively. A government that only uses secret laws can rule with impunity; it can change the laws on the on the fly; it can simply act and make up the laws in hindsight so that whatever it does turns out to be allowed. Thus, requiring laws to be published acts as a restraint on the exercise of arbitrary government power. It's the first measure of transparency and accountability, the one on which every subsequent measure depends.
- *Fairness:* Even in a functioning democracy, deficient access to law is dangerous. The rule of law only works if people actually know the laws. There are legal maxims that express this idea, such as "Everyone is presumed to know the law" and "Ignorance of the law is no defense." These maxims are only fair—they are only reasonable principles rather than cruel jokes—if the public in fact has an opportunity to learn the content of the law. It's ridiculous, both morally and pragmatically, to expect someone to comply with a set of rules that he has no reasonable chance of learning. It's literally Kafkaesque, and incidentally violates the Due Process Clause of the US Constitution.
- *Consistency:* Access to the law is also vital to the idea of law as a system of rules. You can't act consistently if you have no memory of what happened last time. While either of two rules might be fair if applied consistently, oscillating back and forth between them is pure chaos. There's a rule in administrative law that agencies aren't free to reverse their own prior decisions without providing some reason for the switch. This is the rule of stare decisis in the courts and it obviously depends on having some accurate information about what happened in previous cases.
- *Equality:* Unequal access to the law creates substantive inequality. If law is only available to those who have

the resources to go and seek it out—a well paid lawyer, a better library, access to expensive services like Westlaw and Lexis—then people who can afford better access can afford better outcomes. This means that the rich can take advantage of law in ways that the poor can't. Worse, it means that they can set traps to ensnare their less legally educated opponents. Law becomes the servant of those with better access to it; it takes their side, exacerbating inequality.

A PAGE OF HISTORY

None of these things are new problems.

Babylon

Consider the Code of Hammurabi which is inscribed on a rock. It's a bit under four millennia old and even there, you can see some very modern things. While this is a highly visible artifact—8 feet tall and carved out of solid black basalt—literacy in Babylonian society was low. Only members of the priestly caste and a few others were able to read this and even a skilled reader would have a difficult time reading the 282 laws inscribed on the surface. That doesn't, however, stop the code from declaring in its epilogue that "Hammurabi did teach the land these laws." Even at this early stage, the Babylonian legal system was taking the problem of notice seriously.

Note also a few other features of this piece of legal access technology:

Quality: There's a technological choice here. The laws are inscribed on an 8-foot stele, rather than on clay tablets. Hammurabi wanted to make sure that his laws were permanent and that their authenticity was indisputable. He succeeded. Today, we still know the contents of almost all of his laws (except for the one or two that have been chipped away over the years).

Organization: Technology isn't just what you write on; it's also how you arrange and index the things you write. The Code uses some clever organizational technologies. In an early example of a citation system, the Code's laws are consecutively numbered from 1 to 282. The Code also contains what we'd call today headnotes or legislative history. True, they're mostly accounts of Hammurabi's deeds and dedications to the gods, but they still provide us extra information about the history of the Code and its purposes.

Cost: Something this large and substantial doesn't come cheap. It took a substantial investment to physically produce this stele; it also took labour to compile the laws themselves. Hammurabi could have used those resources to engage in additional smiting, but instead he chose to spend them on distributing his laws.

Copyright (!): Lest anyone else think to tamper with his Code, Hammurabi calls down the curses of the gods on any later ruler who should "corrupt my words, change my monument, efface my name, write his name there, or on account of the curses, commission another to do so." It's not exactly a copyright, but it comes from the same impulse to exercise control over words. (Perhaps it is best compared to the moral rights associated with contemporary copyright.)

England

Fast-forward a few millennia, and legal publication is still grappling with these same issues. Here are a few snapshots from England's long and halting progress towards widespread access to the law. If there's a recurring theme, it's that good legal publishing is hard.

Within 150 years after the Norman Conquest, England's royal courts started keeping parchment plea rolls to track the results of cases. They reported the nature of the lawsuit and who won, but in formulaic terms that provided no factual details or legal explanation. They were thus completely inadequate at meeting the needs of actual lawyers and their clients—who need to know which arguments will win in court and which will lose.

Instead, by 1300 or so, lawyers were consulting anonymous and often sketchy outlines of the arguments made in court, compiled in volumes called the 'year books'. While they became standard sources for lawyers and judges to consult in looking up the law, over the years their disorganization became a serious problem. It's a painful task to have to search through centuries of handwritten volumes without an index, especially when you're looking for rough analogies rather than exact matches.

Eventually, the anonymous yearbooks were displaced by nominative (or 'named') reports, i.e. volumes of cases produced by specific editors who named their reports after themselves. This is a familiar shift in copyright history; going from script to print means both that the author becomes more important and that charging for copies becomes the dominant business model. By modern standards, the early nominative reports were woefully incomplete. In 1571, Edmund Plowden produced two carefully-edited volumes, but they covered a grand total of sixty-two cases. The second attempt was a 1582 collection of notes by Sir James Dyer (who had died in 1579), which mixed reports of actual cases with reports of dinner conversations. Sir Edward Coke, another judge, reported many cases starting in 1606, but sometimes falsified precedents, when doing so would support his position in a case. After Coke, no one tried again until the 1640s. Meanwhile, the yearbooks had petered out in the 1530s, which leaves quite a gap.

Over the years, there were more and more of these nominative reports. Some were excellent; many were terrible. An 1849 report on the system noted the inconsistencies among various competing reporters, the resulting inaccuracies and gaps, and the enormous cost to lawyers who needed to buy copies of multiple reporters' sets in order to have everything relevant. It concluded: "To sum up in a few words the evils and inconveniences of the existing system of Law Reporting, there is no guarantee afforded to the public that the judicial exposition of the law will be reported at all, or reported correctly—or in time to prevent mistakes—or in such a manner, with respect to conciseness, form, and price, as to be accessible to those whom it so vastly affects."

The Law Reports produced by the independent, unpaid committee ultimately set up in response to the report became the English standard. And yet the profession hated them for many decades: they were slow, badly indexed, badly arranged, and—astonishingly enough—printed some cases repeatedly and other, important ones not at all. Nonprofit, quasi-public reporting turned out to have most of the same defects as private control over case law had.

Types of Legal Materials

'The law', he says, comes in many forms. Lawyers commonly talk about three major kinds, which correspond to the three branches of government. If one were to take the US federal government as an example, these kinds of law would be:

1. *Legislative:* Bills passed by the Senate and the House and signed by the President (or passed over a veto) are statutes. The legislative history of how a bill becomes a law contained in such things as hearing testimony, amendments, debates, and committee reports, often includes important information about what Congress meant by it.
2. *Executive:* Agencies like the FDA, the FCC, and the TSA issue regulations that tell the public, for example, what frequencies they can broadcast on, or what size bottles of gel they can bring onto airplanes. Agencies also issue thousands of adjudications on matters ranging from whether to grant a refugee asylum to whether to grant someone Social Security disability benefits.
3. *Judicial:* A court that hears a case will issue a judgment at the end of the matter, and orders disposing of issues along the way. For any significant decision, the court will usually also issue an opinion explaining its reasoning. This list is massively incomplete, but it provides an idea of the range of things that government does that create law. Statutes, regulations, and opinions are the big three: These are the ones that a lawyer who needs to know what the law is on a given point will typically consult first. States, counties, cities, and other units of government are also in the lawmaking game and produce their own legal materials.

Another instructive example involves not case law, but legislation. Consider the Statutes of the Realm, the first official attempt to provide a comprehensive collection of the legislation passed by Parliament in all of English history. It appeared in nine volumes and took twelve years to compile. The result of this extensive effort, completed in 1822, was to produce a relatively complete set of laws all the way up through ... 1714. The Statutes of the Realm were over a century out of date on the day they first came off the printing presses! Perhaps unsurprisingly, practicing English lawyers turned instead to a privately-produced set: Chitty's Statutes of Practical Utility. This is an important point, and it bears repeating. From the perspective of the people who most regularly needed to consult these legal materials, a private editor did a better job than the men with the official governmental commission to make the laws widely available.

THE ABRIDGMENTS

One way the legal profession responded to the disorganization of the year books was to produce abridgments: volumes of abbreviated case reports, arranged by topic. The abridgments employed organizational techniques that included alphabetical arrangement by topic, hierarchical indices, and notes in the margin to aid quick browsing. While some editors produced abridgments by hand, they really only became competitive around 1500, with the availability of the printing press. It's hard to produce and maintain all that organizational material without the technological assistance of movable type.

For all their virtues, the abridgments had their own issues. Despite the great labour involved in producing an abridgment of ten or twenty thousand cases, or perhaps because of it, their editorial quality was often poor. Here's a passage from (US Supreme Court Justice) Joseph Story's review[208] of Charles Viner's 24-volume 18th-century abridgement: "It is a cumbrous compilation, by no means accurate or complete in its citations, and difficult to use, from the irregularity with which the matter is distributed, and from the inadequacy, and sometimes the inaptness of the subdivisions. Indeed everything appears to have been thrown into it, without any successful attempt at method or exactness."

REPORTERS IN THE US

Henry Wheaton

Enough ancient history. Let's cross the Atlantic and continue our story by looking at the roots of modern American copyright doctrine on legal materials.

Legal publication in the US didn't get off to a good start. In its early years, the US Supreme Court didn't produce printed opinions. Even today, we don't have copies of all Supreme Court cases. The first published reports of Supreme Court cases come from Alexander Dallas, who was actually reporting Pennsylvania cases and decided to report the US Supreme Court because it was sitting at the time in Philadelphia. His first volume, published in 1798, contained a grand total of five cases from the Supreme Court—decided between 1791 and 1793. As for his accuracy, the best that we can say is that we have nothing to compare it against, since we don't have the originals. This sad state of affairs continued through the term of Dallas and his successor, William Cranch, until Henry Wheaton, entered the picture in 1816. If this story has a hero, it's Henry Wheaton. If it has a villain, it's also Henry Wheaton. His 11-year tenure as Supreme Court reporter was marked by a number of innovations, some of which may sound interestingly familiar.

Quality: He achieved nearly unheard-of standards of timeliness and accuracy. His reports of a given year's Supreme Court term would typically be produced before the start of the next term.

Organization: His enthusiasm also extended to the organization of his reports. He produced marginal notes and scholarly essays following the cases that put the opinions in a broader context.

Cost: These high standards of scholarly editorial quality came at a quite literal cost: his volumes were expensive. A single volume of Wheaton's reports cost $7.50, which works out to over $100 today, an even more princely sum considering the distribution of income at the time. Only a small group of lawyers could afford his reports.

Copyright: Perhaps most interestingly for our story, Wheaton used copyright to fight lower-cost competitors.

In 1829, Wheaton's successor, Richard Peters, brought out inexpensive, smaller versions of cases first reported by his predecessors. He omitted the marginal notes and deleted the scholarly essays, but he took the text of Wheaton's cases word for word. Wheaton sued. The resulting case, Wheaton v. Peters, decided by the Supreme Court in 1834, is famous in American law as the first Supreme Court case on copyright. (Among other things, it's the source of the statement that United States copyright is exclusively statutory. Copyright covers only those things that Congress wishes it to cover.) Right at the end, almost as an afterthought, the Court says: "It may be proper to remark that the Court is unanimously of opinion that no reporter has or can have any copyright in the written opinions delivered by this Court, and that the judges thereof cannot confer on any reporter any such right."

So, this is the initial statement of rule that the law is not a proper subject for copyright. Wheaton tried to get a copyright by intermingling his additions with the public domain texts underneath. Peters got around Wheaton's trick by extracting the underlying material, reprinting only the stuff that came from the court. So Wheaton v. Peters, in effect, says that Wheaton's intermingling doesn't take the underlying kosher public domain materials and render them treyf. Peters was free to publish his cheaper editions.

But think about the incentives that this decision gives to potential reporters. Until Henry Wheaton's innovations, Supreme Court reporting had been a money-losing business. No one had been able to make it work. Dallas's and Cranch's reports were too slow and too inaccurate to meet lawyers' needs. Wheaton did the job right. But doing the job right proved to be nearly impossible without copyright's incentives. While Peters nominally won, the decision left him and his successors with no clear way to assert copyright in their work. For the next several decades, the general consensus was that the Supreme Court reports were no good.

Reverse Citations

Another important landmark in legal publishing technology from the late 19th century was Shepard's Citations. To appreciate its importance, it helps to understand the problem it solves.

Lawyers are always looking for legal 'authorities' (e.g. cases, statutes, regulations, and so on) that support their positions. For an authority to be useful, it needs both to say something relevant and to be 'good law', that is, not to have been rendered obsolete by later developments. New statutes replace old ones, higher courts overrule lower ones, and so on. This evolutionary process means that even a lawyer holding in her hands a legal document that would perfectly, completely resolve her question isn't out of the woods. Even if it's only a week old, something might have happened since then to transform it from a gold-plated authority into worthless scrap paper.

In one direction, the problem is comparatively easy. If a court is overruling its earlier decision in Joe v. Blow, its opinion will typically contain a sentence such as, "Therefore, we now choose to overturn the rule of Joe v. Blow, 23 Foo. 2d 400." The reader of this passage knows that it affects Joe v. Blow; the court is kind enough to name it and cite it. The hard part is going in the opposite direction. Starting from Joe v. Blow, how do you know which later cases cite it? It's not as though the Joe v. Blow court can look into the future, see that ten years hence State v. Hutz will come along, and insert a citation to it.

In 1875, Frank S. Shepard started constructing a reverse index. As each new case came along, he'd make notes of which cases it cited. As long as he caught every new case, he could be sure that he'd catch every case citing Joe v. Blow. His company sold the reverse index to lawyers, first as stickers (to paste into the lawyer's copy of a case report) and then as actual printed volumes. The lawyer looking up Joe v. Blow in one of Shepard's — 'citators' would see a list of citations, each of them referring to a later case citing Joe v. Blow. Other cases might still call it into question indirectly, but a lawyer using a good citator can be confident that she's looked at every later case that explicitly refers to the case she cares about. This kind of exhaustive search is a regular part of careful legal research; it's a way of avoiding nasty surprises.

For our purposes, three things are worth noting about Shepard's: Others had tackled the problem in more ad hoc ways before; Shepard was just the first to deal with it comprehensively. At the time he started his work, preparing a reverse index of citations required an immense investment of labor. Someone had to read every new case and extract each citation. Today, digital technologies have made the problem profoundly easier. Computers are very good at building reverse indices.

John West

Coming back to the story of how later reporters in the 19th century figured out how to do, more or less, what Wheaton hadn't. Starting in 1876, John B West produced a series of reporters tied to geographic regions. Each reporter covered several states' worth of courts (including the federal courts in those states). By 1887, he had expanded to national coverage, very much on Wheaton's model; careful editing, lots of additional material, and strong copyright claims. His production process was a good example of late 19th century information workflow. Very carefully structured, it took the handwritten decisions as they came from the judges and passed them through a group of clerks who not only typeset the opinions but also proofread them and arranged them. The process took advantage of substantial economies of scale in printing and in managing the clerical work.

To this, West added a system of key numbers, essentially a hierarchical taxonomy of legal topics, the idea being that any legal question whatsoever could be classified using some number. For example, 99 is 'Copyrights and Intellectual Property,' 99.I is 'Copyrights,' 99.I(A) is 'Nature and Subject Matter,' and 99.I(A)k14 (which can be abbreviated to 99k14) is 'Statutes and Law Reports,' the key number that covers essentially this entire essay. If you look under that number in one of West's printed indexes (or on Westlaw, its online service), you'll find Wheaton v. Peters and other cases dealing with these issues of copyright in the law.

A fairly typical page from a modern reporter in the West system contains a number of constituent elements. We have, for example, the text of the opinions themselves. Thanks to

Wheaton v. Peters, these are public domain. Banks v. Manchester,[209] later in the century, extended the rule to state courts, such as the Kansas courts. We also have a number of things that copyright law would classify as 'facts': the names of the parties in the case, the court deciding it, the court's own number for the case, and the date. All of these things are treated as uncopyrightable; they're not considered original to the reporter writing them down.

On the other hand, there are some things in here that are indubitably copyrightable in a typical page from a modern reporter. The headnotes written by West and his employees consist of summaries of the points of law discussed in the opinion, rephrasing the court's reasoning and making it shorter and more concise. They make it easier for a lawyer to skim through quickly, looking for relevant cases. (In the system of West Digests, which extract the headnotes and link them with the key numbers, you'd simply read through a list of headnotes until you'd found one reasonably close to what you were looking for, and then go consult the entire case.)

But we're missing one other very important thing that West added to this system: the page numbers. And this is the key to the American system of legal citation. The tradition hereabouts is that one cites a case by listing the name of the reporter in which the version cited appears, the volume number within that series, and the number of the page on which the case starts. Thus, State v. Commemorative Services Corporation would be reported as '823 P. 2d 831'. That's volume 823 of the second series of the Pacific Reporter (abbreviated to P. 2d) at page 831.

While technically, a lawyer could cite to any reporter in which the case appears, there are enormous network effects at work. If you produce a reporter that's more commonly used than other reporters are, as West's reporters were by the early twentieth century, then courts come to expect citations to those reporters. Lawyers stock the dominant reporter in their libraries; the value of providing citations to any other reporter drops. Ultimately, the citation system becomes the hook that makes West's reporters the ones every lawyer has to buy.

Today, there are about 20 states in the US where the West reporter is the only available source for published court decisions.

This standardization on West page numbers gives West ammunition to argue that it has a copyright not merely in its editorial additions, but also its arrangement of cases within the volumes. More precisely, the page numbers become artifacts of the order of cases in a volume, and the editorial decisions West makes in choosing how to order them become the basis of a claim to copyright.

THE STATE OF PLAY

West is hardly the only one trying something like this. Plenty of other entities are claiming that their annotations of the law or citations to the law are copyrighted. West has gone computerized, and so has its archrival, LexisNexis. Both of them have extensive online databases of primary and secondary legal materials. These databases—which one used to access via direct dial-up are now on the Web, wrapped in dire copyright warnings and extensive terms of service.

The American Medical Association produces a standardized taxonomy of medical billing codes. The taxonomy is privately drafted, but the federal government requires that Medicare and Medicaid reimbursement paperwork use its codes. The AMA claims that its taxonomy is copyrightable. A federal appeals court agreed[210] as did one considering[211] a similar code produced by the American Dental Association.

Similarly, cities require that all new buildings be constructed to standards specified in building codes. The private construction industry trade associations that draft the building codes assert copyright over them. In a closely contested 8-6 decision,[212] a federal appeals court threaded the needle: It's legal to make copies of a town's law, but not of a building code as such. Thus, what would otherwise be an infringing copy of a building code becomes legal if it's made as a copy of 'the law'.

How about tax maps? New York City makes maps of property lines to determine the assessment boundaries for property taxes. It's gone to court to assert its copyright in those maps—and won. (That case isn't publicly accessible online, oh the irony, but an earlier one[213] on the same issues is.)

Out in Wisconsin, a private company even attempted to use copyright to limit the use of tax assessment data. Not data that it created, not data that it gathered, but just data that city employees used its software to gather. The court that heard this case rejected this argument, saying, "It would be appalling if such an attempt could succeed."[214]

The lay reader may be forgiven for wondering whether lawyers have lost their minds, that such claims are not immediately laughed out of court. So, let's talk briefly about why these things are not obviously forbidden under copyright law.

Copyright Law

The first line of defense is 17 USC. § 105: "Copyright protection under this title is not available for any work of the United States Government, but the United States Government is not precluded from receiving and holding copyrights transferred to it by assignment, bequest, or otherwise."

If the United States government writes it, it's not copyrightable. This is in one sense a natural consequence of the rule from Wheaton v. Peters. But the rule is both broader and narrower than we'd like if we're thinking about access to the law. It's broader in that there are lots of other federal works that are not copyrightable. For example, NASA's space photographs aren't copyrighted and they're freely usable by anyone. But the rule is limited to the federal government. Congress hasn't prohibited states or cities from taking copyright in the works they produce.

Another common approach is to emphasize 17 USC. § 103, which deals with 'compilation' copyrights. If you gather together a bunch of uncopyrightable things, the things themselves don't suddenly become copyrightable merely because you collected them. If you take a group of public domain poems, such as Shakespeare's sonnets, you can't recopyright them. This is an important principle, but it's also limited. The rule that compilation copyrights don't cover underlying material is part of a larger provision that says that copyright is available for the compilation as a whole. If I took Shakespeare's sonnets and arranged them into an original order that I thought displayed the logical progression of the author's emotional relationship with the Dark Lady, that arrangement might well be copyrightable as an original arrangement. The same would be true if I wrote an introductory essay, or short summaries of each sonnet. Add additional material, and you get a copyright in that additional material.

The result is that these modern Wheatons engage in a process of intermingling. They take public-domain legal material, add some copyrightable bells and whistles, and make their combined version the easiest, most accessible form of the law. If it should so happen that their copyrightable contributions are now hard to separate from the underlying public-domain matter, well, that's just too bad for the rest of us.

Copyright Theory

Let's look at the usual kinds of policies that people in law talk about when they talk about whether we should or shouldn't give copyright in certain kinds of works. There are three standard patterns for arguments against particular copyrights. If we plug 'laws' into those patterns, we get:

Authorship: Copyright is reserved for original works, but laws lack originality.

Incentives: Copyright gives people an incentive to make things they wouldn't otherwise make, but the government doesn't need further incentives to pass laws.

Access: The public's need for access to the laws is too great for the laws to be locked up behind a copyright.

The problem is that each of these standard moves comes with a standard counter-move. Arguments that are internal to copyright's Bizzaro-world logic have a weird way of wimping out when they're asked to challenge other copyright policies. Let's take them up in turn.

Authorship

The standard argument here is that copyright protects the originality of the human mind. It protects things that express the author's unique personality. Here's a famous passage from Justice Holmes's Supreme Court opinion in Bleistein v. Donaldson Lithographing Co.:[215] "The copy is the personal reaction of an individual upon nature. Personality always contains something unique. It expresses its singularity even in handwriting, and a very modest grade of art has in it something irreducible which is one man's alone."

Under this theory, the government isn't a person. It has no personality. The author of the laws is the populace as a whole acting through the legislature. Therefore, no copyright should exist. That rationale is attractive, and authorship arguments have a lot of force, particularly in European copyright doctrine. But they tend not to carry very much water in the US today. There're lots of cases extending copyright to collectively drafted junk. Think of corporate annual reports, produced by committee, which have absolutely zero personality. Not that very many people would want to make more copies of these snooze-fests (or that their corporate authors would object), but there's not much doubt that they are copyrightable.

On the other hand, some governmental work is filled with personality. Justice Holmes's pithy paragraphs have a lot more going for them than most corporate reports do. The authorship argument would concede that Holmes wrote his opinion as an agent of the government, but it'd still end up being swayed by his stately turns of phrase. Even when it comes to model codes drafted by private bodies, sometimes you can find an individual's fingerprints all over the resulting document. Authorship theory might say that the Bipartisan Campaign Reform Act is called 'McCain-Feingold' for a reason, and that John McCain and Russ Feingold should share the copyright in it.

Thus, the authorship argument proves too much and too little. Personality is neither necessary nor sufficient for copyright. Even if we took authorship arguments seriously, many governmental works, including all sorts of stuff that constitutes 'the law', could potentially surmount whatever hurdles it set up to copyrightability.

Incentives

The main theory of copyright in the US today is based on incentives. Copyright is the solution to a public goods problem. We give out exclusive rights against copying, so that creators can make money by selling access to their works. That gives them a financial incentive to produce creative works that they wouldn't produce otherwise. Exclusive rights are a tool for creators to recover the fixed costs involved in making the first copy.

On this theory, government doesn't need to find another solution to the public goods problem of how to pay for drafting and enforcing the laws, because government is *itself* the solution to that public goods problem. You don't need exclusive rights to make legislators write the law; you just vote the bums out if they don't. You don't need to give judges copyright in their opinions; writing opinions is part of the job description.

All of this is true, as far as it goes. But it doesn't quite go far enough. The tricky part is that, as we've seen, most of the genuinely controversial copyright claims in legal materials involve claims over ancillary materials, not over the laws themselves. Think of John West's page numbering and Key Number system. These are things that the government isn't producing itself. Indeed, governments in 1880 probably *couldn't* have produced West's Key Number system. These annotations, like treatises and other material, make the law more explicable on a semantic level. They're public goods. They're useful. They're privately written. And thus, there's a perfectly good incentives-based argument that copyright is a perfectly good tool to encourage their production.

There are states in which the legislature just passes the stuff and the West publishing company adds all the annotations. If they're copyrightable in private hands, why not in government hands?

There's another move that access advocates could make. Whether or not these things are *actually* drafted by government, perhaps they're the sorts of things that *should* be drafted by government. That argument has less force than it used to. As a society, we've pretty much conceded that public-private partnerships are legitimate. We have privately-run prisons, privately-run highways, and privately-run charter schools. There's no guaranteed knock-down argument against having private entities participate in drafting laws. Take the construction industry groups that write the building codes. These are private entities doing something to help the government out, and it's a good thing, too. We have much better and safer buildings than we would if each city and county had to write its building code from scratch.

But once you've got private parties in the picture, there's also no guaranteed knock-down argument that government should pay the private party in coin, rather than with exclusive rights. We pay the people who build and maintain private highways by letting them charge tolls; why not pay the people who draft laws by letting them charge for copies? Indeed, you could even do a tax-policy analysis and argue that copyrights are fairer and more efficient than paying for the drafting with higher taxes. That way, instead of the public at large paying for the drafting costs, it's the people who actually use the results the most: the lawyers.

This is a hard theoretical problem. I don't think that exclusive rights in the law are the right way to go, not at all. I'm just saying that incentive theory doesn't provide the clear answer against legal copyrightability one might like or expect. (This happens a lot with incentive arguments in copyright; something that at first seems like it ought to yield a clear answer ends up spinning off all sorts of imponderable hypotheticals and empirical questions.)

Access

What about the arguments I gave, all the reasons why access to the law is vitally important? Well, the response to them is the oldest trick in the copyright book. Public access is important, you say? Well, the *point* of handing out copyrights is to increase access.

If we're trying to increase the supply of good works available to the public, goes the response, we should look for works that aren't being produced because potential authors don't have the incentive to produce them. Give them a copyright in their creations, and they'll actually start creating. Yes, the exclusive right means they'll cut off access to some people under some conditions (i.e. not paying). But they're still limiting access to works that wouldn't exist in the first place if there were no exclusive rights. The public is a net winner. It's a boomerang of an argument. The greater the need for access, the greater the need for copyright!

That's the argument you see used for music; there's not an immediately obvious reason to say why it doesn't work for the law. This is the argument that Henry Wheaton made; it's the argument that Oregon makes; it's the argument that everyone in our rogue's gallery of legal copyright claimants makes. They say, "It's not easy doing the work we do. We need to recover our costs, or we couldn't do it at all." The Office of Legislative Counsel will charge you[216] $390 for a complete 21-volume set of the Oregon Revised Statutes. That $390 goes to pay for the paper, for the costs of setting up the printing presses, and for the costs of compiling the laws into 21 convenient volumes. If you asked them, they'd say, "We're making Oregon's laws more accessible overall." They'd say that if there were no Office of Legislative Counsel, Oregon's laws would be in more of a shambles, not less, so they're entitled to keep Justia from undercutting them on the price.

Historically speaking, they're not completely wrong. There's a plausible argument that Henry Wheaton's high-quality reporters were sustained by his copyright and that West's reporters are good because their headnotes and Key

Numbers can be copyrighted. To refute these arguments, we'd need to go out and measure sales and costs and markets and look at things very carefully. Just like authorship and incentives, access fails to provide the unambiguous unanswerable theoretical argument that one might hope for by going to copyright theory. Access to the law is a hard, hard problem.

THE INTERNET CHANGES EVERYTHING

Or, perhaps I should say, it *was* a hard problem. There's a huge difference between the problem with previously available technology and the problem as it stands going forward. The Internet changes the game. We get trivial transmission costs to send out documents to other people. We get perfect reproduction without corruption. We get search technologies that massively reduce the logistical burden of providing comprehensive indices. Put these together, and we can get, almost as a byproduct of producing the first copy of a work for any purpose at all, copies shared all across the world at low cost and with ever-increasingly reliability. If a court uses word processing to write its opinions because the judges find it easier to draft them that way, it now has everything it needs to make digital copies for the world. And once it releases a single digital copy to the public, we've all got it. All of us.

And that's not the half of it. There's another fundamental, perhaps even more overwhelming change here. Giving people computers and networking catalyzes large-scale distributed collaboration. A network of volunteers can now do things that previously only very large entities could have tackled. Open source software and Wikipedia are classic examples of this. I'd also point out that in this environment, you only need one or a few altruistic entities to be putting things online to do the work for everyone. Once the resource exists in digital form, posting it online pretty much solves the problem. Internet distribution is something that we know how to do and we know to do well. Free web server software, running on off-the-rack boxes, using standard software formats. We know how to do this.

Similarly, we've got all the building blocks we need to solve the citation and organizational problems. We know how to design good universal citation formats (e.g. by consecutively numbering opinions as a court produces them). All we really need are unique identifiers and some reasonable sorting system—and everything has a name and a location. There are many institutions that have the capacity to make the law available in the ordinary course of their business or out of the sense that the public good demands it. So perhaps the real heirs to Henry Wheaton's legacy—his good legacy of high-quality reporting, rather than his unfortunate legacy of aggressive copyright claims—are the many institutions that are striving to do two things:

First, they're providing high-quality, cleanly organized archives of basic legal documents. Justia is doing this. So is Public. Resource.Org. The grandpappy of this tradition is Cornell's fabulous Legal Information Institute, which has been doing it since 1993. They're putting online large collections of legal documents, for free, in formats that are designed to make it easy for others to come in and do the same.

Second, services like PreCYdent, AltLaw, and v.|lex are providing advanced tools to search and analyze those basic documents. They're building better search engines for law; they're building ways to cross-reference things together. They're creating, in other words, a value-added layer on top of this public-domain foundation, to make the law easier to find and easier to understand.

The frontier of the possible is being pushed rapidly outwards. We can now get commodity publishing of the essentials for far less, proportionately speaking, than ever before. The place to compete is no longer on optimizing workflows to avoid introducing typesetting mistakes, as it was in the 19th century. The new goal for active competition is to take these basic primary documents and make them broadly usable to lawyers and the public.

This shift raises important questions. How should we ensure reliable access to primary legal materials? How should we encourage competition in providing innovative analyses of them? Where does copyright fit into this equation, if at all? What, in short, should we demand from the law when it comes to access to the law?

PRINCIPLES FOR A NEW ERA

In setting out principles for thinking about copyright in this new age of technological access to the law, I'm not going to focus here on existing copyright doctrine. Rather I'd like to look at what the essential freedoms are in relationship to law. These freedoms are the ones that everyone ideally needs to have to consult and make use of 'the law'; my argument is that computer and Internet technologies enable us to go much further in ensuring them than ever before. Think of them as guiding principles.

Once we have these principles in mind, there are a multiplicity of ways to integrate them back into copyright doctrine. They have various advantages and disadvantages; some of them would be cleaner to implement than others would be. There's a fair amount of legal scholarship on these issues, some of it quite excellent. Lyman Ray Patterson and Craig Joyce's 1989 article in the UCLA Law Review, Monopolizing the Law: The Scope of Copyright Protection for Law Reports and Statutory Compilations[217] is a good place to start. Here are some of the available routes to reform:

- We could expand Section 105 to increase the set of 'governmental' works that are uncopyrightable. It could explicitly say that state-created works are uncopyrightable, or, more narrowly, that various kinds of legal materials are uncopyrightable. This approach could be as targeted and precise as Congress is able to manage.
- We could provide a more robust and predictable fair use defense where legal materials are concerned. This approach, while flexible, suffers from the disadvantage that Larry Lessig so succinctly pointed out: "Fair use in America simply means the right to hire a lawyer ...."

- We could say that the law is always uncopyrightable idea and never copyrightable expression, and that attempts to swaddle the law in a protective layer of copyrighted materials merely result in the forfeiture of the copyright in those other materials through 'merger'. Variants of this argument are plentiful in the academic literature.
- We could find limits in the Constitution on the copyrightability of legal texts. The Copyright Clause could be read to embody a strong form of the authorship principle as to laws; the Due Process Clause limits the use of secret laws.
- We could insist that attempting to leverage your copyright into a monopoly over the law is 'copyright misuse' and makes your copyrights unenforceable. Misuse is ferocious when it shows its teeth, but can be a hard animal to coax from its den.
- We could even use copyright law itself to preempt attempts to control legal materials through contract.

Some combination of some of these approaches will be necessary. It may seem strange for a lawyer to be arguing that the specifics of the law don't matter so much as the underlying goals. But copyright has always looked to purposes when precedents are ambiguous. They are here, so it's entirely appropriate to look to our societal goals to help us deal with those ambiguities. And, of course, for legal reforms (such as expanding Section 105), the whole point is that Congress can change the law to make things better.

- *The right to access:* First and most fundamentally, people need to be able to get at the law. This puts a basic initial duty on the government not merely to publish the law but to publish it online in accessible formats with the right metadata, so that people can find it and know what it is. We shouldn't exclusively rely on the government, any more than we relied on it exclusively in the 19th century. But governmental online publication is the first step, the one that makes the rest possible.

- *The right to distribute:* Once primary legal information is online, anyone should be able to pick it up and republish it as they see fit. That could be coordinated with other materials in larger collections, it could be pushed out to mobile devices, or it could be reformatted or sliced and diced in some clever new way. Law shouldn't get in the way of people who are taking it on themselves to publish it.
- *The right to extract:* Then there's the intermingling problem. Anyone has to be free to do what Richard Peters did: to extract the public-domain legal materials and reproduce them. This is a strong principle, and needs to override any voluntary agreements to the contrary. That is, a private publisher shouldn't be able to require that you give this right up if you get the legal materials under digital rights media management with a clickwrap contract. It shouldn't matter that you click "I agree not to tell people what the law is." You should still be free to tell people what the law is.
- *The right not to extract:* The flip side of this principle is important, too. You shouldn't be able to make things hard to extract. No one should have to write a parser to strip out that green sentence from the midst of all the red that surrounds it. To the extent that copyrighted material has been so intermingled with public-domain legal material as to make it a significant challenge or to require significant work to extract the underlying material, there should be a right to redistribute the collection as a whole. Whatever the most accessible version of the law is, you have a right to use that version. One might object that this rule erases the incentive to make annotations. On the contrary, it provides an incentive to make your annotations cleanly, with a clear layer separation between the primary materials that are the law and the secondary annotations that help people understand the law.

- *The right to cite:* Finally, there's citation. Anyone, of course, is free to use the citations themselves; Oregon basically concedes this one. But to the extent that a citation system becomes a standard (and especially where government requires you to use a particular citation system), anyone should be able to reproduce the necessary citation information as part of their own materials. (West has sued companies that want to reproduce what's called "star pagination"; that is, little flags in the text or the opinion that show you whenever the West case number changes. They've won in one federal appeals court[18] and lost in another. [19]) Otherwise, a standard citation system allows its creator to assert de facto copyright control over the underlying legal materials.

These principles aren't unique to legal materials. They're not new, either. Access, arrangement, and distribution have always been important. It's just that when we look at legal materials, the case for these principles has become overwhelming. The Internet makes it possible for us to say that while previously we might have been willing to compromise and grant related copyrights in order to get legal materials before the public at all, now we can demand nothing less than full and unfettered access.

FOOTNOTES

201.Section 52(1)(q), Indian Copyright Act, 1957

202.AIR 1915 Cal 112

203.2001 PTC 57 Del

204.<judis.nic. in/supremecourt/qrydisp.aspx?filename=30019> .

205.(2006) 32 PTC 84

206.<public.resource.org/scribd/2526821. pdf>

207.<james.grimmelmann. net/essays/CopyrightTechnologyAccess> licensed under a CC 3. 0 Attribution Licence

208.<books.google.com/books?id=rYA FAAAAQAAJ & pg = PA9 & lpg= PA9&dq =% 22 cumbrous+compilation% 22 & source=web & ots=z OLbj 3K3e0 & sig=IG12lbnZ8JudL6qu92swPGckjeU & hl= en & sa= X & oi = book_ result &resnum=1&ct=result>

209.<supreme.justia.com/us/128/244/case. html>

210.<altlaw.org/v1/cases/1079356>

211.<altlaw.org/v1/cases/1081968>
212.<altlaw.org/v1/cases/131504>
213.<altlaw.org/v1/cases/1371376>
214.<altlaw.org/v1/cases/160423>
215.<supreme.justia.com/us/188/239/case.html>
216.<lc.state.or.us/orderforms/ORS.pdf>
217.36 UCLA L.Rev.719
218.<bulk.resource.org/courts. gov/c/F2/799/799. F2d. 1219.85-5399.html>
219.<bulk.resource.org/courts.gov/c/F3/158/158.F3d.674.97-7910.html>, <bulk.resource.org/courts.gov/c/F3/158/158.F3d.693.97-7430.html>

18

THE PERMISSION CULTURE

The current copyright system is heavily dependent on licensing. It's created what Nina Paley describes as 'The Permission Culture'. The way it usually operates is for almost all rights in a work to be reserved by the person who owns the copyright in the work and for that person to then allow others to do certain things which he has the exclusive right to do by granting them licences often for a hefty price.

There is of course fair use — or in India's case, fair dealing and exceptions to copyright — which allows those who do not own the copyright of a work to make use of the work in certain ways and for certain purposes: mainly for teaching, research, review and criticism. The problem with this system is that fair use is extremely limited and that when it comes down to it, whether any particular use is fair use is a debatable question dependent on the circumstances of that particular case. It means that even if the person who uses the copyrighted work thinks that his use of the work is fair use, the person who owns the copyright could quite easily either not share that opinion or choose not to share it.

There is nothing on the face of the Earth which stops a copyright owner from filing a suit for infringement in such circumstances and even if the use of work is fair use, the person accused of infringing the copyright in the work could easily wind up spending a large amount of money in legal fees defending his use of the copyrighted work. In addition to this, even the matter does not reach a court, he could still wind up losing (or spending, depending on how one looks at it) a lot of money merely hiring a lawyer to talk to the copyright owner on his behalf.

While this may not really matter if the person who has used the copyrighted work (or plans to do so) is well funded, it does matter a great deal if he is an individual, possibly an independent artist, who would like to use a work which, say, is owned by major company like EMI or Warner. Leaving aside the possibility of being accused of infringement, even if such an artist were to approach a company before using the work, that artist would in all probability have to pay lawyers an extremely large amount of money to negotiate a licensing deal with the copyright owner. Also, since the company which owned the copyright would ordinarily be far more powerful than the artist, there would be nothing to stop that company from imposing whatever terms it happened to get into its head on to the artist.

This doesn't affect the commercial art very much — commercial films, for example, are usually well-funded and are not only able to deal with such issues but also expect to have to deal with them. It does, however, make a difference to the non-commercial art world. One of the fallouts of requiring licences such as this is that even if one were to want to make an art film, step one would not be to think about what one might want to portray in the film but to make enquiries about who might be willing to foot not just production bills but also legal bills and licensing fees. The result is that independent films are not really independent and that the non-commercial art world has a distinctly commercial feel to it.

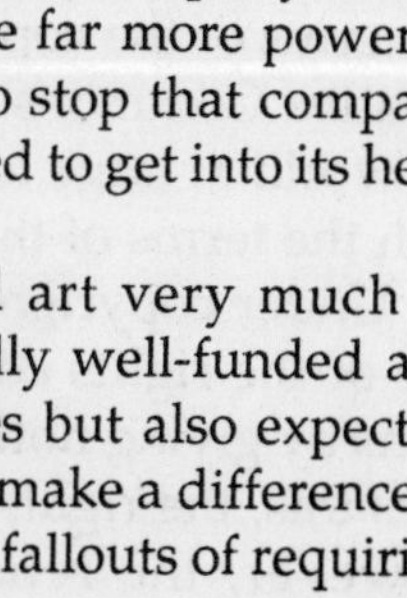

Over the years, there have been alternatives which have been proposed to avoid the ills of this particular model of licensing. They include Apple iTunes' direct licensing,[220] and NOANK Media's ISP level licensing.[221]

The copyleft licensing system which is the brainchild of Richard Stallman and which came into existence in the 1970s to license software is probably the most well known alternative though. The word 'copyleft' is a play on the term 'copyleft'. And the copyleft symbol is a mirror image of the copyright symbol. However, unlike copyright and its symbol, copyright left and its symbol have no legal significance as such.

There has been much debate in recent years about what exactly it is that copyleft means. In broad terms, copyleft too relies on licensing. The basic premise is that although copyright exists in works, the owners of that copyright can, if they so wish, instead of reserving those all the rights which copyright confers to themselves as they would ordinarily do under the copyright model, relinquish some or all of those rights under terms which they choose. The terms which they choose are the terms of the copyleft licence. Copyleft licences such as the Creative Commons licences are legal documents which allow the world at large to use the works they license in accordance with the terms of the licence.

Under copyright law, an author may relinquish his all or any of the rights comprised in the copyright of any work he owns by giving notice to the Registrar of Copyrights. Once he does this, the rights cease to exist from the date of the notice. However, the relinquishment of all or any of the rights comprised in the copyright in a work does not affect any rights which already subsist in favour of any person on the date of the notice. When the Registrar of Copyrights receives such a notice of relinquishment, he is required to cause it to be published in the Official Gazette and in any other manner he deems fit.[222]

Currently, there are a number of copyleft licences which are widely used. They do not require the owners of copyright to be paid for the use of their work and the terms of copyleft licences can be varied a great deal to suit the wants of the individual copyright owner. For example, the owner of the copyright in the work may choose whether or not to allow others to use his work for commercial purposes. He can decide whether or not to allow others to remix or adapt his work. He may choose not to allow others to use his work unless they in turn allow people to use it under the same terms which they themselves have used the work. He may also allow people to use his work without attributing him as the author; although using someone else's work without crediting them would be unethical, under the terms of such a licence, it would be legal.

One of the most important aspects of the copyleft licensing regime is that the owners of the copyright can impose share-alike terms in the licence on those who use their work. These are the terms which force those who use the work to allow others to use the work under the same terms. It is this which makes it more sensible to licence a work using share-alike terms than to simply relinquish copyright. If the owner of the copyright were to relinquish copyright, and dedicate the work to the public domain, the result would be that although anyone would be able to use the work without any legal restrictions at all, they would be allowed to convert that work into a proprietary work.

For example, if someone was to write something and relinquish his copyright in the work, a company or someone else would be able to pick it up, adapt it, copyright the adaptation and thereby effectively take the work out of the public domain. However, if the work had been licensed under share-alike terms, the company would have been forced to share the adaptation under the same terms as it had used the original work. In other words, the adaptation would be as accessible as the original work.

The result is that the work would fall into the 'intellectual commons'. This term evokes comparisons into the commons of old which exist to this day. The old commons pertain to land. The land is not common land in the sense that it belongs to everyone. Neither is it common land in the sense that it belongs to no one. The ownership of the land itself is vested in an identifiable person. However, persons other than the owner have certain rights in relation to the land. Most commonly, these are rights of pasture (to graze cattle), turbary (to take sods of turf for fuel), piscary (to fish), mast or pannage (to have pigs eat acorns in autumn) and estovers (to take small pieces of wood for domestic use usually as fuel).

Similarly, in the intellectual commons, copyright vests in certain persons although others have the right to use, adapt, share, translate, modify, and remix the work. There are, however, works in which the copyright does not vest in anyone. These are works which belong to the public domain. There are various ways in which a work can enter the public domain. Firstly, once a work ceases to be protected by copyright, it enters the public domain and anyone may then use and exploit it. Secondly, the author of a work may relinquish his copyright in the work and dedicate it to the public domain. Thirdly, things which are not protected by copyright are treated as belonging to be in the public domain. These include both things such as facts, figures and information, as well as works which cannot be protected by copyright such as court judgments.

Once a work enters the 'intellectual commons' through a copyleft licence, it ordinarily stays there. This is one 'problem' with most copyleft licences: they are irrevocable. Once they have been granted, the owner of the copyright has no control over how the work which has been licensed is used. A solution to this problem is not to relinquish any of the rights in the copyright of the work but to indicate that one, as the owner of the copyright in the work, is open to the idea of sharing rights.

One of the ways in which this can be done is to use 'Konomark'. The Konomark project is the brainchild of a project of Eric E. Johnson, a professor of intellectual property law at the University of North Dakota School of Law.

Most rights sharable.
JUST E-MAIL ME AND ASK.
LEARN MORE AT KONOMARK.ORG

Konomark is a relatively new mark which signals that persons who apply the mark to their copyrighted work are not averse to the idea of sharing it without being paid. But although it is about sharing intellectual property, unlike Creative Commons Licences or open-source software licenses such as GPL, Konomark does not grant a licence to anyone to do anything. Owners of copyrighted material to which the mark is applied do not give up any right to their material; they only signal that they are willing to be approached for permission to use their work without being paid. Also, the mark is revocable.

It is ideal in situations where owners of copyrighted material (such as text, photos, videos etc.) would like to share their work but are not comfortable with the idea of granting an irrevocable licence to the world at large.

The copyright licensing regime has created a world where no one other than the owner of the copyright in a work can do much with it without a licence. Make a film; don't use music which is copyrighted. Write a play; ensure that it doesn't infringe the copyright of some other book. The list is endless. And the effect is that many artists wind up being afraid to draw on older works simply because they might wind up infringing on someone else's copyright. They are advised not to do touch anyone else's music; they are told that they cannot do anything which might infringe the copyright of another. This is not how the art world has worked through the centuries, and it is certainly alien to the literary world. Nonetheless, as animator Nina Paley puts it: "Most of the artists I know are animators who work in studios. And some of these animators have also made their own films, being terrified to use any music they couldn't clear. And this just breaks my heart. You know, in education, all these schools are like: *'Don't use this, and don't use that, don't do this, don't do that!'* They're teaching young artists to be scared of music."[223]

If artists choose to ignore the advice not to use unlicensed music, they are likely to do so at tremendous (monetary) cost to themselves. They'll later have to pay to 'decriminalize' their work by getting licences for the use of the copyrighted work, and to get licences, they'll have to pay both licence fees and legal fees unless they find lawyers who are willing to work pro bono. Also, presumably, if they attempt to get licences after the work has already been made, presumably, their bargaining power will be much less than it would otherwise have been since the owners of the copyright would know that a licence would be essential to the artist.

Take the case of the award-winning animation film 'Sita Sings The Blues' which Nina Paley, a well-known cartoonist and animator, spent three years creating. The film tells two stories: the mythological story of Sita from the Ramayana who is separated from her husband, Lord Ram and the contemporary tale of a husband who moves to India and dumps his wife by eMail.

The film has run into trouble not only with Hindu Fundamentalists who aren't too pleased with her having interpreted the Ramayana but also with record companies. It is set to 1920s jazz vocals of Annette Hanshaw and even though the recordings are no longer protected by copyright law, the sheet music is still protected.

This effectively means that the film cannot be distributed because of licensing issues, and even if Nina wanted to delete the music from the film — which to all appearances she has never had a desire to do — it would be impossible for her to do so because the music is an integral part of the film with entire animation sequences having been created around particular songs.

Obviously, the film does not stand a chance of commercial success if it cannot even be distributed. The copyright owners initially asked for $ 220,000 as licence fees. This was later reduced to a 'bargain' price of $ 50,000 as part of a step deal i.e. they said: "Pay us $ *x*, and we'll allow you to sell *y* number of copies of your film. If you sell *y+1* copies of it, pay us more money." The good thing though is that 'promotional copies' are traditionally exempt from step deals which means that no licence fees would have to be paid in respect of them. There are also less obvious problems. For example, without a commercial run, the film is not eligible for such things as the Academy Awards: the only films which are eligible for them are films which have had a week-long commercial run. It isn't the best film which gets the Best Film award but the best *commercial* film (or what's deemed to be the best commercial film) which gets it.

Nina does, however, have an interesting plan with reference to licensing 'Sita Sings The Blues' once she (hopefully) 'decriminalizes' it. As an artist, she says that she has never benefited from copyright.

She plans to licence it under some form of share-alike copyleft licence and even though standard logic suggests that copylefting ensures that the creator is not paid, she's managed to defy this logic and come up with a model which will, in all likelihood, see her making some money. In the distribution plan[224] she's posted on her website, Nina's mentioned a number of ways in addition to fundraising screenings through which she plans to earn money despite copylefting her work. These include receiving direct donations i.e. voluntary payments of any amount, through the sale of ancillary products, by sponsorships, at DVD sales and auctions of a limited edition of official signed copies, through voluntary payments from public screenings, and by selling 35mm film prints to collectors, archives, museums, and (hopefully) distributors willing to try a non-exclusive service model instead of the existing licensing model.

Most of these plans depend on people being willing to voluntarily pay her although, with the last idea of selling 35 mm film prints, she would not only assuredly make money but also, as she has said, be able to outsource the expensive work of archiving.

She envisages ancillary products such as t-shirts, pins, toys, books, and other merchandise being open-content. There would be little incentive for competitors to invest in producing such merchandise if it were already available (and much incentive if it were not available, which is good), as she says. Relying on the fact that fans are usually enthusiastic about seeing money go directly to an artist, she suggests that companies share profits with her. This would probably be analogous to people being enthusiastic about buying green products or make-up which has not been tested on animals: people are, as a general rule, more enthusiastic about seeing their money being spent on things in which they believe than seeing it being eaten up by companies.

While it's obvious that copylefting means that artists will not make money in the same way that they do under the traditional copyright licensing model, it definitely isn't true that artists cannot make money at all if they copyleft their work.

The only thing which truly changes is that the middleman is cut out. There is no distribution in the traditional sense of the word and the artists are directly linked to those who enjoy their work: in this case, to an audience which can, if it so chooses, pay the artist directly for having created the work.

For all one knows, in the years to come, this may result in artists being paid much more than they are paid under the current business model. When it comes to books, for example, royalties are usually about 5 to 10% of the price for which each book is sold. If, however, the book was to be made available, say online, and the author was paid directly by the reader, instead of being paid $ 1 for every book sold for $ 10, he could well be paid $ 5 for a book. The reader would get the book for a 'bargain' price and the author would get five times more than a publisher would pay. Also, being available only means that distribution costs would be a sum total of zero as would costs incurred in actually printing and publishing the book.

The only persons who would make no money and become irrelevant would be the publishers and distributors which is probably why they are among the staunchest defenders of the current copyright regime.

FOOTNOTES

220.<www. apple. com/itunes>
221.<www. noankmedia. Com>
222.Section 21, Indian Copyright Act, 1957
223.Nina Paley quote from QuestionCopyright.org
224.<blog.ninapaley.com/2008/12/28/sitas-distribution-plan/>

19

NEW BUSINESS MODELS[225]

The industry's centuries-long campaign for strong copyright law is not merely a reflexive land grab. It's a natural economic response to technological circumstances. The effect of the printing press, and later of analog sound recording technology, was to make creative works inseparable from their means of distribution. Authors needed publishers the way electricity needs wires. The only economically viable method of reaching readers (or listeners) was the bulk print run: to manufacture thousands of identical copies at once, then physically ship them to various points of distribution. Before agreeing to such an investment, any publisher would naturally prefer to buy or lease the copyright from the author, and just as naturally would lobby the government for the strongest possible copyright powers, the better to protect their investment.

There is nothing inherently exploitative about this; it's just straightforward economics. From a business point of view, a print run is a daunting and risky project. It involves the high up-front costs of a physical medium (be it dead tree pulp, magnetic tape, vinyl platters, or pitted optical discs), plus complicated, expensive machinery to imprint the content onto the medium. There's also the unseen investment of vetting the master copy: because a flawed master can reduce the value of the entire run, publishers and authors go to considerable trouble to generate a polished, error-free version of the work before printing. There is little room for an incremental or evolutionary process here; the work must be brought to near-perfection before the public ever sees it. If any mistakes are overlooked, they will have to be tolerated in the finished product, at least until the process is started again for the next print run. The publisher must also negotiate prices and line up distribution paths, which is not only a matter of bookkeeping, but of physical expenses, of trucks and trains and shipping containers. Finally, as if all this weren't enough, the publisher is compelled to spend even more money on marketing and publicity, to have a better chance of at least recovering all these outlays.

When one realizes that all this must happen before the work has generated a penny of revenue, it is little wonder that publishers argue hard for copyright. The publisher's initial investment — that is, their risk — in any individual work is greater, in economic terms, than the author's. Authors by themselves might have no inherent desire to control copying, but publishers do. And in a world filled with publishers' royalty-supported marketing departments, authors, of course, need publishers all the more. The concentration of distribution revenues results, inevitably, in the familiar logic of an arms race.

The arrival of the Internet fundamentally changed this equation. It has become cliché to say that the Internet is as revolutionary a development as the printing press, and it is. But it is revolutionary in a different way. The printing press may have made it possible to turn one book into a thousand books, but those books still had to travel from the press into the hands of readers. Physical books were not only the medium in which the content was consumed; they were also the medium in which it was transported to the consumer. Thus, a publisher's total expense was proportional to the number of copies distributed. In such a situation, it is reasonable to ask that each user bear a portion of the costs of distribution. Each user is, after all, more or less responsible for her particular quantum of expense. If the book (or record) is in her hands, it must have gotten there somehow, which in turn means someone spent money to get it there. Divide those expenses by the number of copies, add in some amount for profit, and you arrive, roughly speaking, at the book's price.

But today, the medium over which content is distributed can be unrelated to the medium in which it is ultimately consumed. The data can be sent over a wire, at essentially no cost, and the user can print up a copy at her own expense, and at whatever quality she can afford, on the other end.[226] Furthermore, it is no longer important to possess the master; in fact, the concept of the master copy itself is obsolete. To make a perfect copy of a printed work is actually quite hard, although making a corrupt or abridged copy is very easy. Meanwhile, to make a perfect copy of a digital work is trivially easy — it's making an imperfect copy that requires extra effort.

Thus, the practice of charging the same fee for each copy, regardless of how many copies there are or who made them, is now unjustifiable. The cost of producing and distributing the work is now essentially fixed, no longer proportional to the number of copies. From society's point of view, every dollar spent beyond the amount needed (if any) to bring the work into existence in the first place is a waste, an impediment to the work's ability to spread on its own merits.

The Internet did something the Company of Stationers never anticipated: it made their argument a testable hypothesis. Would creators still create, without centralized publishers to distribute their works? Even minimal exposure to the Internet is enough to provide the answer: of course, they will. They already are. computer users are comfortable downloading music and making CDs at home, and, slowly but inevitably, musicians are getting comfortable releasing tracks for free downloading.[227] Many short works of both fiction and non-fiction are already available online. Printing and binding entire books on demand is rarer, but only because the equipment to do it is still somewhat expensive. That equipment is getting steadily cheaper, however, and it's only a matter of time before the copy shop down the street has it. There is no fundamental difference between music and text, from a distribution point of view. As printing and binding technology gets cheaper, authors will see more and more clearly that they have the same alternative musicians do, and the result will be the same: more and more material available without restriction, by the choice of the author.

Some might argue that authors are different, that they are more dependent on copyright than musicians are. After all, a musician expects to perform, and can therefore gain indirectly by releasing recordings for free — greater exposure leads to more performances. But authors don't perform; they reach their audience only through their works, not in person. If they now had to come up with ways to fund themselves without imposing an artificial scarcity on their works, could they do it?

Imagine the simplest scenario: you walk into the neighborhood print shop and tell the clerk the Web address of the book you want. A couple of minutes later, the clerk comes back with a freshly printed, hardbound book, straight off the Internet. He rings up the sale.

"That'll be eight dollars. Would you like to add the one dollar author's suggested donation?"

Do you say yes? Perhaps you do, perhaps not — but note that when museums charge a voluntary admission fee, people often pay it. The same sort of dynamic is at work in the copy shop. Most people are happy to pay a tiny extra bit on top of some larger amount, if they have their wallet out already and think it's for a good reason. When people fail to make small, voluntary donations to a cause they like, it's more often due to the inconvenience (writing a check, putting it in the mail, etc) than the money. But even if only half, or fewer, of all readers were to make such donations, authors would still earn more than they do under traditional royalty schemes, and furthermore would have the pleasure of finally being the readers' ally in distribution, instead of their enemy.

This is not the only possible system, and it can easily coexist with others. Those not convinced by voluntary donations should consider another method: the "Fund and Release" system (also called the "threshold pledge" system).[228] This system is designed to solve the classic problem of distributed funding, which is that each contributor wants reassurance that others are also contributing, before putting in her own money. Under fund-and-release, the hopeful creator of a new work states up front how much money will be required to produce it — this is the "threshold". An intermediary organization then collects pledges, in any amounts, from the general public. When the total amount pledged reaches the threshold (or exceeds it by some standard percentage, to account for bookkeeping and assumption of risk), the intermediary signs a contract with the creator, and the pledges are called in. Only at this stage, when there is enough money to achieve the desired result, is anyone asked to actually pay up. The intermediary holds the money in escrow, paying the creator according to whatever schedule they negotiated. The last of the money is paid when the work is completed and made publicly available, not just to the contributors, but to the entire world. If the creator doesn't produce, the intermediary returns the money to the donors.

The fund-and-release system has some interesting properties not found in the monopolistic, copyright-based marketplace. The resultant work is available to everyone in the world, free of charge. Yet the author was also paid enough to produce the work; if she needed more, she would have asked for more and seen if the market would bear it. Those who did choose to pay paid only as much as they were comfortable with, no more. And finally, there was no risk for the contributors — if the threshold is never reached, then no one pays anything.

Not all methods will be so pleasantly high-minded, of course. A couple of years ago, the established author Fay Weldon famously accepted money from Bulgari jewelry to write a novel that featured Bulgari products prominently. She did so, titling the book "The Bulgari Connection". The book was originally intended as a limited edition to be given away at a corporate function, but having written it, Weldon took it to a publisher for general release. Does this mean that in the future we'll have to scrutinize all creative works for signs of hidden corporate sponsorship? Perhaps, but this is nothing new — product placement was invented in the context of traditional copyright, and has flourished there, as it probably would anywhere. Copyright is neither the cause of corporate sponsorship nor its antidote. To look to the publishing industry as a force for decommercialization would be weirdly out of touch indeed.

These are just a few examples of ways to support creative work without copyright. There are many other methods;[229] there were many even before the Internet made convenient, direct micropayments possible. Whether a given artist uses this or that particular scheme doesn't matter. The important thing is that with little or no friction to impede the payment of tiny amounts, authors will find ways to make such payments happen on the scale they need. Those economists who are enamoured of markets as a solution to everything should be in love with the possibilities here (but, predictably, many are not, because they hate to see anything become depropertized).

To see a glimpse of the future, it may be most helpful to look not at net-savvy musicians, but at software. The flourishing Free Software movement is probably the best example we have today of a post-copyright world. Free software (some also call it "Open Source") is the brainchild of Richard Stallman, a programmer who had the idea of releasing software under a deliberately reversed copyright. Instead of prohibiting sharing, the software's license explicitly permits and encourages it. A number of others soon caught on to his idea, and because they were able to share and modify each other's programs without limit, they quickly produced a large body of working code.

Some predicted that this initial success would quickly level off as the software increased in size and complexity and required centralized, hierarchical organizations to maintain. But instead of foundering, the Free Software movement has grown so quickly that even its own participants are surprised, and it shows no signs of stopping. It now produces software whose functionality rivals that available in the proprietary market. Free software is widely used by banks, corporations, and governments, as well as individual computer users. More web sites run the free Apache web server than run all other web servers combined. Free operating systems are now the fastest-growing segment of the operating system market. Although some free software authors are paid for their work (after all, their services provide a benefit to those who use the software, and some of those users are willing to pay for it), others volunteer their time. Each software project has its own reasons for existing, and each programmer their own reasons for contributing. But the cumulative effect is a direct flaunting of copyright's entire justification: a thriving community of intellectual production now exists without enforcing copyrights, yet achieves substantially the same results as its mainstream counterpart.

According to the traditional justification of copyright, this shouldn't be happening. The software is essentially in the public domain; its copyright serves mainly to identify the original authors, and in some cases to prevent anyone else from imposing a stricter license. The authors have given up every exclusive right except the right to be identified as the authors. They have voluntarily returned to a world before copyright law: they enforce no royalties, and have no control over the distribution and modification of their works. The software's license gives everyone automatic permission both to use and to redistribute it. You can simply start handing out copies, there's no need to notify anyone or ask permission. If you want to modify it, you're free to do that too. You can even sell it, though naturally it's difficult to charge much, since you'd be competing with others handing out the same goods at no cost. A more common model is to encourage people to download the software for free, and instead sell services such as technical support, training, and customization. These models are not fantasies; they are the basis for profitable businesses that exist right now, paying real programmers competitive salaries to work on free software. But the point is not that people are paid to do it — some are, but many more are not and yet write it anyway. The real point is that a tremendous amount of free software is produced and maintained every year, at a rate that grows quickly even by the standards of the software industry.

If this phenomenon were isolated to software, it would be explainable as an aberration — software is different, programmers are overpaid, and so on. But it's not just software; if you look carefully, there are signs of it happening everywhere. Musicians are starting to release their tracks online for free downloading, and the quantity of freely available writing on the Internet — starting with reference and non-fiction works, but now including fiction and poetry — long ago passed the point of measurability. Software is not fundamentally different from these other forms of information. Like poems, songs, books, and movies, it can be transmitted digitally. It can be copied in whole or in part; it can be excerpted for use in other works; it can be modified and edited; it can even be satirized.

The abandonment of copyright is farthest along in software mainly because programmers were among the first groups to have Internet access, not because of anything special about the nature of software. Gradually, creators in other areas are realizing that they too can disseminate their works without publishers or centralized distribution chains, by simply allowing the freedom to copy. And increasingly, they are choosing to do so, because they have little to lose, and because it's the easiest way for their work to find its way to an appreciative audience. Far from being especially dependent on copyright law, creators gain the most by abandoning the copyright monopoly.

FOOTNOTES

225. This Chapter has been written by Karl Fogel.

226. When I started writing this, I assumed such developments were a few years away from commercial viability, but I was wrong: the print-on-demand service newspaperkiosk. com is already up and running.

227. See www.mp3.com, for one example. (Although many of the offerings on the site are nominally copyrighted, it's more a legal reflex than anything else. The tracks are meant to be freely downloaded, listened to, and shared — and that's exactly what people do with them.)

228. I originally called this the 'Threshold Pledge' system. However, Brandt Cannici of strayform.com, who independently invented the same system, came up with the much better name 'Fund and Release', and I now try to use that term instead.

229. For a description of one funding technique, and a survey of others, see 'The Street Performer Protocol and Digital Copyrights' by John Kelsey and Bruce Schneier, at <firstmonday. dk/issues/issue4_6/kelsey/>

20

THE REALITY AND THE RHETORIC[230]

The Internet has given us a world without distribution costs; it no longer makes any sense to restrict sharing in order to pay for centralized distribution. Abandoning copyright is now not only possible, but also desirable. Both artists and audiences would benefit, financially and aesthetically. In place of corporate gatekeepers determining what can and can't be distributed, a much finer-grained filtering process would allow works to spread based on their merit alone. We would see a return to an older and richer cosmology of creativity, one in which copying and borrowing openly from others' works is simply a normal part of the creative process, a way of acknowledging one's sources and of improving on what has come before. And the old canard that artists need copyright to earn a living would be revealed as the pretense it has always been.

None of this will happen, however, if the industry has its way. For three centuries, the publishing industry has been working very hard to obscure copyright's true origins, and to promote the myth that it was invented by writers and artists. Even today, they continue to campaign for ever stronger laws against sharing, for international treaties that compel all nations to conform to the copyright policies of the strictest, and most of all to make sure the public never asks exactly who this system is meant to help.

The reward for these efforts can be seen in the public's reaction to the file-sharing lawsuits. While most people agree that this time the industry went too far, the error is mainly treated as one of degree — as if the record companies had a valid point, but had merely resorted to excessive force in making it.

To read the true history of copyright is to understand just how completely this reaction plays into the industry's hands. The record companies don't really care whether they win or lose these lawsuits. In the long run, they don't even expect to eliminate file sharing. What they're fighting for is much bigger. They're fighting to maintain a state of mind, an attitude toward creative work that says someone ought to own products of the mind, and control who can copy them. And by positioning the issue as a contest between the Beleaguered Artist, who supposedly needs copyright to pay the rent, and The Unthinking Masses, who would rather copy a song or a story off the Internet than pay a fair price, the industry has been astonishingly successful. They have managed to substitute the loaded terms 'piracy' and 'theft' for the more accurate 'copying' — as if there were no difference between stealing your bicycle (now you have no bicycle) and copying your song (now we both have it). Most importantly, industry propaganda has made it a commonplace belief that copyright is how most creators earn a living — that without copyright, the engines of intellectual production would grind to a halt, and artists would have neither means nor motivation to produce new works.

The arrival of the Internet, with its instantaneous, costless sharing, has made that business model obsolete — not just obsolete, but an obstacle to the very benefits copyright was alleged to bring society in the first place. Prohibiting people from freely sharing information serves no one's interests but the publishers'. Although the industry would like us to believe that prohibiting sharing is somehow related to enabling artists to make a living, their claim does not stand up to even mild scrutiny. For the vast majority of artists, copyright brings no economic benefits. True, there are a few stars — some quite talented — whose works are backed by the industry; these receive the lion's share of distribution investment, and generate a correspondingly greater profit, which is shared with the artist on better than usual terms because the artist's negotiating position is stronger. Not coincidentally, these stars are whom the industry always holds up as examples of the benefits of copyright.

But to treat this small group as representative would be to confuse marketing with reality. Most artists' lives look nothing like theirs, and never will, under the current spoils system. That is why the stereotype of the impoverished artist remains alive and well after three hundred years.

The publishing industry's campaign to preserve copyright is waged out of pure self-interest, but it forces on us a clear choice. We can watch as most of our cultural heritage is stuffed into a vending machine and sold back to us dollar by dollar — or we can reexamine the copyright myth and find an alternative.

Even in their early stages, these trends raise an obvious question. If copyright is not really needed to stimulate original creation, then what purpose does it serve today? For it is quite clear that if copyright did not exist already, we wouldn't invent it now. We just finished building ourselves a gigantic copying machine (the Internet) that doubles as a communications device, and incidentally makes it convenient to transfer small amounts of money between people. Sharing is now the most natural thing in the world. The idea that artists are somehow harmed by it is demonstrated false every day, by the thousands of new works that appear online, credited and fully acknowledged by their authors, yet free for the taking. If someone were to argue that creativity would soon dry up unless we immediately institute a system of strict controls over who can copy what, we could reasonably look on them as insane. Yet, in slightly more diplomatic language, this is essentially the argument used by the copyright lobby to press for ever stronger laws.

Creativity is not what's at stake here, and in its more honest moments the publishing industry even tacitly admits this. Although for public relations purposes industry leaders make token declarations about the need for poor artists to earn a living, their most detailed and compelling statements are usually about the business effects of copyright. Larry Kenswil of Universal Music Group, the world's largest record company, was quoted in the New York Times of Jan. 5th, 2003, in an article about digital copy protection schemes, saying "You're not buying music, you're buying a key. That's what digital rights management does: it enables business models."

It's hard to imagine a more succinct statement of the industry credo. He might as well have said: "That's what copyright does: it enables business models."

Unfortunately, not all of the propaganda put out by the industry is as straightforward and honest as Kenswil's. The Recording Industry Association of America, for example, explains copyright this way on their web site at http://www.riaa.org/:

"You don't need to be a lawyer to be a musician, but you do need to know one legal term — copyright. To all creative artists — poets, painters, novelists, dancers, directors, actors, musicians, singers, and songwriters — the term matters dearly.

To all artists, "copyright" is more than a term of intellectual property law that prohibits the unauthorized duplication, performance or distribution of a creative work. To them, "copyright" means the chance to hone their craft, experiment, create, and thrive. It is a vital right, and over the centuries artists have fought to preserve that right; artists such as John Milton, William Hogarth, Mark Twain, and Charles Dickens. Twain traveled to England to protect his rights, and Dickens came to America to do the same."

Recognize that? It's a page straight out of the Stationers' playbook — an undisguised retelling of the copyright myth, complete with references to individual authors, designed to arouse our support for struggling artists valiantly fighting for their artistic integrity. Apparently, all those artists throughout history who did just fine without copyright aren't included in "all creative artists" as far as the RIAA is concerned. Professor Patterson's comments, about the Stationers' similar use of authors as a foil in front of the eighteenth century English parliament, are equally applicable today: "They [the Stationers] did so by arguments intended to elicit sympathy for the author (conveniently ignoring their role in creating the poor plight of the author that they bemoaned) and avoided sound logic and reason."[2]

The next paragraph in the RIAA's introduction to copyright is even worse. It's a brief — very brief — introduction to the origins of copyright law, heavy with the cadence of historical inevitability, but rather loose with the facts:

"Copyright law all started with the 'The Statute of Anne', the world's first copyright law passed by the British Parliament in 1709. Yet the principle of protecting the rights of artists predates this. It may sound like dry history at first blush, but since there was precedent to establish and rights to protect, much time, effort, and money has been spent in legal battles over the centuries."

This breathless summary of copyright history is the equivalent of saying "Christopher Columbus sailed to America to prove the Earth was round and make friends with the Indians". Yes, much money has indeed been spent in legal battles, but the RIAA is careful not to say who spent it, nor are any further details given about the 'principle of protecting the rights of artists' that is alleged to predate these developments.

The rest of their page continues in a similar vein, with so many omissions, mischaracterizations, and outright lies that it's hard to imagine how anyone doing even a modicum of research could have written it. It is, basically, low-grade supporting propaganda in their ongoing campaign to convince the public that copyright is as fundamental to civilization as the laws of thermodynamics.

The RIAA also indulges in one of the favorite tactics of the modern copyright lobby: equating illegal copying with the unrelated, and much more serious, offense of plagiarism. For example, Hilary Rosen, the (now former) head of the RIAA, used to speak at schools and colleges, urging the students to adopt the industry's views about information ownership. Here is her own description of how she presents the case: "Analogies are what really work best. I ask them, 'What have you done last week?' They may say they wrote a paper on this or that.

So I tell them, 'Oh, you wrote a paper, and you got an A? Would it bother you if somebody could just take that paper and get an A too? Would that bug you?' So this sense of personal investment does ring true with people."

Since people who duplicate CDs do not usually replace the artist's name with their own, let's ask the question Hilary Rosen should have asked: "Would it bother you if somebody could just show a copy of your paper around, so other people could benefit from what you wrote, and see that you got an A?" Of course, the students would have answered "No, we aren't bothered by that at all," which isn't what Rosen wanted to hear.

The RIAA is extreme only in the clumsiness of their propaganda. Their message is, in essence, the same one offered by the rest of the copyright industry, which maintains a constant drumbeat of warnings that online content swapping will deprive creators of their reputations and their ability to work, despite overwhelming evidence that copyright never provided them with much of a livelihood anyway, and that they would happily continue to create without it as long as they have a way to distribute their works. The campaign might sound harmless or silly when described as I have described it here, but because they are fighting for survival, with large budgets and skilled publicity departments, the publishers have succeeded in shaping public opinion to a surprising degree.

Consider this poor woman, from the International Herald Tribune of September 11, 2003, in an article about the RIAA file-sharing lawsuits: One woman who has received a subpoena from the recording industry association said she had struggled to explain to her 13-year-old son why file-sharing was wrong." I said, 'Suppose you wrote a song and a famous rock group sang it and you didn't get said,'" said the mother, who declined to give her name because of her legal situation." He said: 'I wouldn't care. That would be awesome.' They're still just in that young age where money doesn't matter." The mother said she had better results when she compared taking someone's song to plagiarizing a school paper.

(One can only hope the sensible 13-year-old manages to keep his head, when so many around him are apparently losing theirs.)

The combination of a still-sympathetic public and deep pockets has unfortunately allowed the copyright industry to exercise dangerous influence at the legislative level. The result is a disturbing trend: mutually reinforcing physical and legal barriers that, while ostensibly designed to combat illegal copying, have the inevitable effect of interfering with all copying. Digital copy-protection schemes are increasingly enforced by your computer's hardware itself, rather than by malleable and replaceable programs. And the same companies that own content often also manufacture the hardware that makes distribution possible. Have you bought a computer from Sony? What about a CD from Sony's music division? That's the same company, and its left hand knows what its right hand is doing. With government cooperation, this combination becomes even more powerful. In the United States we now have a law — the Digital Millennium Copyright Act — that makes it illegal to circumvent a digital protection scheme, or even to produce software that helps others circumvent a digital protection scheme. Unfortunately, since much hardware and software automatically imprints such schemes on any media it produces, the Act effectively stifles authorized copying and many other activities that would otherwise fall into the category of "fair use" under current copyright law.

It is vital to understand that these side effects are not accidents, not unexpected consequences of an otherwise well-intentioned effort to protect artists. Rather, they are an integral part of a strategy that, at bottom, has nothing to do with encouraging creativity. The purpose of this three-pronged industry effort — the publicity campaign, the legal campaign, and the hardware "protections" — is simply this: to prevent the Internet experiment from being carried out to completion. Any organization that is deeply invested in the concept of copy control cannot be pleased to see a system arise that makes copying as easy as clicking a mouse. To the extent possible, such organizations would like to see the same pay-per-cop model that we've been using for centuries continue, even though the fundamental physics of information have changed to make pay-per-copy obsolete.

Although the copyright lobby succeeds in getting new laws passed, and even in winning some court cases, these victories rest on a disintegrating foundation. How much longer will the public continue to believe in the copyright myth, the notion that copyright was invented to make creative work possible? The myth has been maintainable so far because it always had a tiny a grain of truth: although copyright was not inspired by authors, and was not enacted to protect them, it did enable the widespread distribution of many original works. Furthermore, there are still many publishers (generally the smaller or individually-owned ones) who behave with an admirable sense of cultural stewardship, subsidizing unprofitable but important works with money earned by stronger sellers, sometimes even losing money outright in order to print things they think worthwhile. But because they are all bound by the economics of large-scale printing, they are all ultimately dependent on copyright.

There won't be a dramatic battle between the publishing industry and the copying public, with a climax, a denouement, and a clear winner striding out of the dust. Instead, what we will see — are already seeing — is the emergence of two parallel streams of creative work: the proprietary stream, and the free stream. Every day, more people join the free stream, of their own volition, for all sorts of reasons. Some enjoy the fact that there are no gatekeepers, no artificial barriers. A work can succeed by its merits and word of mouth alone: although there's nothing to stop traditional marketing techniques from being used in the free stream, there's less to subsidize them, so word of mouth and peer-review networks are taking on a greater importance there. Others enter the free stream as crossovers from the proprietary, releasing a portion of their work into the free domain as an advertisement or an experiment. Some simply realize that they have no chance of success in the proprietary world anyway, and figure they might as well release what they have to the public.

As the stream of freely available material gets bigger, its stigma will slowly vanish. It used to be that the difference between a published author and an unpublished one was that you could obtain the former's books, but not the latter's. Being published meant something. It had an aura of respectability; it implied that someone had judged your work and given it an institutional stamp of approval. But now the difference between published and unpublished is narrowing. Soon, being published will mean nothing more than that an editor somewhere found your work worthy of a large-scale print run, and possibly a marketing campaign. This may affect the popularity of the work, but it won't fundamentally affect its availability; and there will be so many 'unpublished' but worthwhile works, that the lack of a publishing pedigree will no longer be considered an automatic strike against an author. Although the free stream does not use traditional copyright, it does observe, and unofficially enforce, a 'credit right'. Works are frequently copied and excerpted with attribution — but attempts to steal credit are usually detected speedily and decried publicly. The same mechanisms that make copying easy make plagiarism very difficult. It's hard to secretly use someone else's work when a Google search can quickly locate the original. For example, teachers now routinely do Google searches on representative phrases when they suspect plagiarism in student papers.

The proprietary stream cannot survive forever, in the face of such competition. The abolition of copyright law is optional; the real force here is creators freely choosing to release their works for unrestricted copying, because it's in their interests to do so. At some point, it will be obvious that all the interesting stuff is going on in the free stream, and people will simply cease dipping into the proprietary one. Copyright law may remain on the books formally, but it will fade away in practice, atrophied from disuse.

Or, we can sit back and allow this process to be halted, by permitting manufacturers to build in hardware 'protections' that interfere with our ability to copy legitimately; by allowing the copyright lobby to capture our legislatures, to the point where we are constantly looking over our shoulders for the copyright police; and by hesitating to use the free stream to its full potential, because we've been taught a false story of what copyright is all about.

We can, if we choose, have a world where concepts like 'out of print' or 'rare book' are not only obsolete, but also actually meaningless. We can live in a fertile and vibrant garden of constantly evolving works, created by people who wanted deeply to make them available, not mandated by a publisher's market research. Schools would never be forced to stay with out-of-date textbooks because of the per-copy prices set by publishers, and your computer would always let you share songs with your friends.

One way to get there is to question the copyright myth. Copying isn't theft, and it isn't piracy. It's what we did for millennia until the invention of copyright, and we can do it again, if we don't hobble ourselves with the antiquated remnants of a censorship system from the sixteenth century.

FOOTNOTES

230.This Chapter has been written by Karl Fogel.

231.'Copyright And 'The Exclusive Right' Of Authors' <lawsch.uga. edu/jipl/old/vol1/patterson.html> Journal of Intellectual Property, Vol.1, No. 1, Fall 1993, by Professor Lyman Ray Patterson, Pope Brock Professor of Law at the University of Georgia

REFERENCES

Commercial's Intellectual Property Laws; Commercial Law Publishers (India) Pvt. Ltd., 2008

Bently, Lionel; Copyright, (2005), Translations and Relations between Britain and India, 1880-1914; ATRIP, Montreal; July

Fitzgerald, P J; Salmond on Jurisprudence; Universal Law Publishing Company; 12th Edition

Kaplan, Benjamin; (1967), An Unhurried View of Copyright; Columbia University Press

Ratanlal and Dhirajlal; The Law of Evidence; Wadhwa; 21st Edition

Wadhera, B L; (2008), Law Relating to Intellectual Property; Universal Law Publishing Co., (reprint)

APPENDIX

THE INDIAN COPYRIGHT ACT, 1957

An Act to amend and consolidate the law relating to copyright. Be it enacted by Parliament in the Eighth Year of the Republic of India as follows:

CHAPTER I

Preliminary

1. Short title, extent and commencement.

(1) This Act may be called the Copyright Act, 1957.

(2) It extends to the whole of India.

(3) It shall come into force on such date as the Central Government may, by notification in the Official Gazette, appoint.

2. Interpretation.

In this Act, unless the context otherwise requires,

(a) 'adaptation' means:

(i) in relation to a dramatic work, the conversion of the work into a non-dramatic work;

(ii) in relation to a literary work or an artistic work, the conversion of the work into a dramatic work by way of performance in public or otherwise;

(iii) in relation to a literary or dramatic work, any abridgement of the work or any version of the work in which the story or action is conveyed wholly or mainly by means of pictures in a form suitable for reproduction in a book, or in a newspaper, magazine or similar periodical;

(iv) in relation to a musical work, any arrangement or transcription of the work; and

(v) in relation to any work, any use of such work involving its re-arrangement or alteration;

(b) 'work of architecture' means any building or structure having an artistic character or design, or any model for such building or structure;

(c) 'artistic work' means:

(i) a painting, a sculpture, a drawing (including a diagram, map, chart or plan), an engraving or a photograph, whether or not any such work possesses artistic quality;

(ii) work of architecture; and

(iii) any other work of artistic craftsmanship;

(d) 'author' means,

(i) in relation to a literary or dramatic work, the author of the work;

(ii) in relation to a musical work, the composer;

(iii) in relation to an artistic work other than a photograph, the artist;

(iv) in relation to a photograph, the person taking the photograph;

(v) in relation to a cinematograph or sound recording the producer; and

(vi) in relation to any literary, dramatic, musical or artistic work which is computer-generated, the person who causes the work to be created;

(dd) 'broadcast' means communication to the public:

(i) by any means of wireless diffusion, whether in any one or more of the forms of signs, sounds or visual images; or

(ii) by wire, and includes a re-broadcast;

(e) 'calendar year' means the year commencing on the 1st day of January;

(f) ' film' means any work of visual recording on any medium produced through a process from which a moving image may be produced by any means and includes a sound recording accompanying such visual recording and 'cinematograph' shall be construed as including any work produced by any process analogous to cinematography including video films;

(ff) 'communication to the public' means making any work available for being seen or heard or otherwise enjoyed by the public directly or by any means of display or diffusion other than by issuing copies of such work regardless of whether any member of the public actually sees, hears or otherwise enjoys the work so made available.

Explanation. For the purposes of this clause, communication through satellite or cable or any other means of simultaneous communication to more than one household or place of residence including residential rooms of any hotel or hostel shall be deemed to be communication to the public;

(ffa) 'composer', in relation to a musical work, means the person who composes the music regardless of whether he records it in any form of graphical notation;

(ffb) 'computer' includes any electronic or similar device having information processing capabilities;

(ffc) 'computer programme' means a set of instructions expressed in words, codes, schemes or in any other form, including a machine readable medium, capable of causing a computer to perform a particular task or achieve a particular result;

(ffd) 'copyright society' means a society registered under sub-section (3) of section 33

(g) 'delivery', in relation to a lecture, includes delivery by means of any mechanical instrument or broadcast by;

(h) 'dramatic work' includes any piece for recitation, choreographic work or entertainment in dumb show, the scenic arrangement or acting form of which is fixed in writing or otherwise but does not include a film;

(hh) 'duplicating equipment' means any mechanical contrivance or device used or intended to be used for making copies of any work;

(i) 'engravings' include etchings, lithographs, wood-cuts, prints and other similar works, not being photographs;

(j) 'exclusive licence' means a licence which confers on the licensee or on the licensee and persons authorized by him, to the exclusion of all other persons (including the owner of the copyright), any right comprised in the copyright in a work, and 'exclusive licensee' shall be construed accordingly;

(k) 'Government work' means a work which is made or published by or under the direction or control of:

(i) the Government or any department of the Government;

(ii) any Legislature in India;

(iii) any court, tribunal or other judicial authority in India;

(l) 'Indian work' means a literary, dramatic or musical work,

(i) the author of which is a citizen of India; or

(ii) which is first published in India; or

(iii) the author of which, in the case of an unpublished work, is, at the time of the making of the work, a citizen of India;

(m) 'infringing copy' means,

(i) in relation to a literary, dramatic, musical or artistic work, a reproduction thereof otherwise than in the form of a cinematographic film;

(ii) in relation to a cinematographic film, a copy of the film made on any medium by any means;

(iii) in relation to a sound recording, any other recording embodying the same sound recording, made by any means;

(iv) in relation to a programme or performance in which such a broadcast reproduction right or a performer's right subsists under the provisions of this Act, the sound recording or a cinematographic film of such programme or performance, if such reproduction, copy or sound recording is made or imported in contravention of the provisions of this Act;

(n) 'lecture' includes address, speech and sermon;

(o) 'literary work' includes computer programmes, tables and compilations including computer data bases;

(p) 'musical work' means a work consisting of music and includes any graphical notation of such work but does not include any words or any action intended to be sung, spoken or performed with the music;

(q) 'performance', in relation to performer's right, means any visual or acoustic presentation made live by one or more performers;

(qq) 'performer' includes an actor, singer, musician, dancer, acrobat, juggler, conjurer, snake charmer, a person delivering a lecture or any other person who makes a performance;

(s) 'photograph' includes photo-lithograph and any work produced by any process analogous to photography but does not include any part of a film;

(t) 'plate' includes any stereotype or other plate, stone, block, mould, matrix, transfer, negative, duplicating equipment or other device used or intended to be used for printing or reproducing copies of any work, and any matrix or other appliance by which sound recording for the acoustic presentation of the work are or are intended to be made;

(u) 'prescribed' means prescribed by rules made under this Act;

(uu) 'producer', in relation to a film or sound recording, means a person who takes the initiative and responsibility for making the work;

(x) 'reprography' means the making of copies of a work, by photo-copying or similar means;

(xx) 'sound recording' means a recording of sounds from which such sounds may be produced regardless of the medium on which such recording is made or the method by which the sounds are produced;

(y) 'work' means any of the following works, namely:

(i) a literary, dramatic, musical or artistic work;

(ii) a film;

(iii) a sound recording;

(z) 'work of joint authorship' means a work produced by the collaboration of two or more authors in which the contribution of one author is not distinct from the contribution of the other author or authors;

(za) 'work of sculpture' includes casts and models.

3. Meaning of publication.

For the purposes of this Act, 'publication' means making a work available to the public by issue of copies or by communicating the work to the public.

4. When work not deemed to be published or performed in public.

Except in relation to infringement of copyright, a work shall not be deemed to be published or performed in public, if published, or performed in public, without the licence of the owner of the copyright.

5. When work deemed to be first published in India.

For the purposes of this Act, a work published in India shall be deemed to be first published in India, notwithstanding that it has been published simultaneously in some other country, unless such other country provides a shorter term of copyright for such work; and a work shall be deemed to be published simultaneously in India and in another country if the time between the publication in India and the publication in such other country does not exceed thirty days or such other period as the Central Government may, in relation to any specified country, determine.

6. Certain disputes to be decided by Copyright Board.

If any question arises,

(a) whether a work has been published or as to the date on which a work was published for the purposes of Chapter V, or

(b) whether the term of copyright for any work is shorter in any other country than that provided in respect of that work under this Act, it shall be referred to the Copyright Board constituted under section 11 whose decision thereon shall be final:

Provided that if in the opinion of the Copyright Board, the issue of copies or communication to the public referred to in section 3 was of an insignificant nature it shall not be deemed to be publication for the purposes of that section.

7. Nationality of author where the making of unpublished work is extended over considerable period.

Where, in the case of an unpublished work, the making of the work is extended over a considerable period, the author of the work shall, for the purposes of this Act, be deemed to be a citizen of, or domiciled in, that country of which he was a citizen or wherein he was domiciled during any substantial part of that period.

8. Domicile of corporations.

For the purposes of this Act, a body corporate shall be deemed to be domiciled in India if it is incorporated under any law in force in India.

CHAPTER II

Copyright Office and Copyright Board

9. Copyright Office.

(1) There shall be established for the purposes of this Act an office to be called the Copyright Office.

(2) The Copyright Office shall be under the immediate control of the Registrar of Copyrights who shall act under the superintendence and direction of the Central Government.

(3) There shall be a seal for the Copyright Office.

10. Registrar and Deputy Registrars of Copyrights.

(1) The Central Government shall appoint a Registrar of Copyrights and may appoint one or more Deputy Registrars of Copyrights.

(2) A Deputy Registrar of Copyrights shall discharge under the superintendence and direction of the Registrar of Copyrights such functions of the Registrar under this Act as the Registrar may, from time to time, assign to him; and any reference in this Act to the Registrar of Copyrights shall include a reference to a Deputy Registrar of Copyrights when so discharging any such functions.

11. Copyright Board.

(1) As soon as may be after the commencement of this Act, the Central Government shall constitute a Board to be called the

Copyright Board which shall consist of a Chairman and not less than two or more than fourteen other members.

(2) The Chairman and other members of the Copyright Board shall hold office for such period and on such terms and conditions as may be prescribed.

(3) The Chairman of the Copyright Board shall be a person who is, or has been, a Judge of a High Court or is qualified for appointment as a Judge of a High Court.

(4) The Registrar of Copyrights shall be the Secretary of the Copyright Board and shall perform such functions as may be prescribed.

12. Powers and procedure of Copyright Board.

(1) The Copyright Board shall, subject to any rules that may be made under this Act, have power to regulate its own procedure, including the fixing of places and times of its sittings:

Provided that the Copyright Board shall ordinarily hear any proceeding instituted before it under this Act within the zone in which, at the time of the institution of the proceeding, the person instituting the proceeding actually and voluntarily resides or carries on business or personally works for gain.

Explanation. In this sub-section 'zone' means a zone specified in section 15 of the States Reorganization Act, 1956.

(2) The Copyright Board may exercise and discharge its powers and functions through Benches constituted by the Chairman of the Copyright Board from amongst its members, each Bench consisting of not less than three members.

'Provided that, if the Chairman is of opinion that any matter of importance is required to be heard by a larger bench, he may refer the matter to a special bench consisting of five members.';

(3) If there is a difference of opinion among the members of the Copyright Board or any Bench thereof in respect of any matter coming before it for decision under this Act, the opinion of the majority shall prevail:

Provided that where there is no such majority, the opinion of the Chairman shall prevail.

(4) The Chairman may authorize any of its members to exercise any of the powers conferred on it by section 74 and any order made or act done in exercise of those powers by the member so authorized shall be deemed to be the order or act, as the case may be, of the Board.

(5) No member of the Copyright Board shall take part in any proceedings before the Board in respect of any matter in which he has a personal interest.

(6) No act done or proceeding taken by the Copyright Board under this Act shall be questioned on the ground merely of the existence of any vacancy in, or defect in the constitution of, the Board.

(7) The Copyright Board shall be deemed to be a civil court for the purposes of sections 345 and 346 of the Code of Criminal Procedure, 1973, and all proceedings before the Board shall be deemed to be judicial proceedings within the meaning of sections 193 and 228 of the Indian Penal Code.

CHAPTER III
Copyright

13. Works in which copyright subsists.

(1) Subject to the provisions of this section and the other provisions of this Act, copyright shall subsist throughout India in the following classes of works, that is to say,

(a) original literary, dramatic, musical and artistic works;

(b) films; and

(c) sound recordings;

(2) Copyright shall not subsist in any work specified in sub-section (1), other than a work to which the provisions of section 40 or section 41 apply, unless,

(i) in the case of a published work, the work is first published in India, or where the work is first published outside India, the author is at the date of such publication, or in a case where the author was dead at that date, was at the time of his death, a citizen of India;

(ii) in the case of an unpublished work other than a work of architecture the author is at the date of the making of the work a citizen of India or domiciled in India; and

(iii) in the case of work of architecture the work is located in India.

Explanation. in the case of a work of joint authorship, the conditions conferring copyright specified in this sub-section shall be satisfied by all the authors of the work.

(3) Copyright shall not subsist:

(a) in any film if a substantial part of the film is an infringement of the copyright in any other work;

(b) in any sound recording made in respect of a literary, dramatic or musical work, if in making the sound recording, copyright in such work has been infringed.

(4) The copyright in a film or a sound recording shall not affect the separate copyright in any work in respect of which or a substantial part of which, the film, or as the case may be, the sound recording is made.

(5) In the case of a work of architecture, copyright shall subsist only in the artistic character and design and shall not extent to processes or methods of construction.

14. Meaning of copyright.

For the purposes of this Act, 'copyright' means the exclusive right subject to the provisions of this Act, to do or authorize the doing of any of the following acts in respect of a work or any substantial part thereof, namely:

(a) in the case of a literary, dramatic or musical work, not being a computer programme,

(i) to reproduce the work in any material form including the storing of it in any medium by electronic means;

(ii) to issue copies of the work to the public not being copies already in circulation;

(iii) to perform the work in public, or communicate it to the public;

(iv) to make any film or sound recording in respect of the work;

(v) to make any translation of the work;

(vi) to make any adaptation of the work;

(vii) to do, in relation to a translation or an adaptation of the work, any of the acts specified in relation to the work in sub-clauses (i) to (vi);

(b) in the case of a computer programme,

(i) to do any of the acts specified in clause (a);

(ii) to sell or give on commercial rental or offer for sale or for commercial rental any copy of the computer programme:

Provided that such commercial rental does not apply in respect of computer programmes where the programme itself is not the essential object of the rental.

(c) in the case of an artistic work,

(i) to reproduce the work in any material form including depiction in three dimensions of a two dimensional work or in two dimensions of a three dimensional work;

(ii) to communicate the work to the public;

(iii) to issue copies of the work to the public not being copies already in circulation;

(iv) to include the work in any film;

(v) to make any adaptation of the work;

(vi) to do in relation to an adaptation of the work any of the acts specified in relation to the work in sub-clauses (i) to (iv);

(d) In the case of film,

(i) to make a copy of the film, including a photograph of any image forming part thereof;

(ii) to sell or give on hire, or offer for sale or hire, any copy of the film, regardless of whether such copy has been sold or given on hire on earlier occasions;

(iii) to communicate the film to the public;

(e) In the case of sound recording,

(i) to make any other sound recording embodying it;

(ii) to sell or give on hire, or offer for sale or hire, any copy of the sound recording regardless of whether such copy has been sold or given on hire on earlier occasions;

(iii) to communicate the sound recording to the public.

Explanation: For the purposes of this section, a copy which has been sold once shall be deemed to be a copy already in circulation.

15. Special provision regarding copyright in designs registered or capable of being registered under the Designs Act, 1911.

(1) Copyright shall not subsist under this Act in any design which is registered under the Designs Act, 1911.

(2) Copyright in any design, which is capable of being registered under the Designs Act, 1911, but which has not been so registered, shall cease as soon as any article to which the design has been applied has been reproduced more than fifty times by an industrial process by the owner of the copyright or, with his license, by any other person.

16. No copyright except as provided in this Act.

No person shall be entitled to copyright or any similar right in any work, whether published or unpublished, otherwise than under and in accordance with the provisions of this Act or any other law for the time being in force, but nothing in this section shall be constructed as abrogating any right or jurisdiction to restrain a breach of trust or confidence.

CHAPTER IV

Ownership of Copyright and the Rights of the Owner

17. First owner of copyright.

Subject to the provisions of this Act, the author of a work shall be the first owner of the copyright therein Provided that:

(a) in the case of a literary, dramatic or artistic work made by the author in the course of his employment by the proprietor of a newspaper, magazine or similar periodical under a contract of service or apprenticeship, for the purpose of publication in a newspaper, magazine or similar periodical, the said proprietor shall, in the absence of any agreement to the contrary, be the first owner of the copyright in the work in so far as the copyright relates to the publication of the work in any newspaper, magazine or similar periodical, or to the reproduction of the work for the purpose of its being so published, but in all other respects the author shall be the first owner of the copyright in the work;

(b) subject to the provisions of clause (a), in the case of a photograph taken, or a painting or portrait drawn, or an engraving or a film made, for valuable consideration at the instance of any person, such person shall, in the absence of any agreement to the contrary, be the first owner of the copyright therein;

(c) in the case of a work made in the course of the author s employment under a contract of service or apprenticeship, to which clause (a) or clause (b) does not apply, the employer shall, in the absence of any agreement to the contrary, be the first owner of the copyright therein;

(cc) in the case of any address or speech delivered in public, the person who has delivered such address or speech or if such person has delivered such address or speech on behalf of any other person, such other person shall be the first owner of the copyright therein notwithstanding that the person who delivers such address or speech, or, as the case may be, the person on whose behalf such address or speech is delivered, is employed by any other person who arranges such address or speech or on whose behalf or premises such address or speech is delivered;

(d) in the case of a Government work, Government shall, in the absence of any agreement to the contrary, be the first owner of the copyright therein;

(dd) in the case of a work made or first published by or under the direction or control of any public undertaking, such public undertaking shall, in the absence of any agreement to the contrary, be the first owner of the copyright therein.

Explanation. For the purposes of this clause and section 28A, 'public undertaking' means:

(i) an undertaking owned or controlled by Government; or

(ii) a Government company as defined in section 617 of the Companies Act, 1956; or

(iii) a body corporate established by or under any Central, Provincial or State Act;

(e) in the case of a work to which the provisions of section 41 apply, the international organization concerned shall be the first owner of the copyright therein.

18. Assignment of copyright.

(1) The owner of the copyright in an existing work or the prospective owner of the copyright in a future work may assign to any person the copyright either wholly or partially and either generally or subject to limitations and either for the whole term of the copyright or any part thereof:

Provided that in the case of the assignment of copyright in any future work, the assignment shall take effect only when the work comes into existence.

(2) Where the assignee of a copyright becomes entitled to any right comprised in the copyright, the assignee as respects the rights so assigned, and the assignor as respects the rights not assigned, shall be treated for the purposes of this Act as the owner of copyright and the provisions of this Act shall have effect accordingly.

(3) In this section, the expression 'assignee' as respects the assignment of the copyright in any future work includes the legal representatives of the assignee, if the assignee dies before the work comes into existence.

19. Mode of assignment.

(1) No assignment of the copyright in any work shall be valid unless it is in writing signed by the assignor or by his duly authorized agent.

(2) The assignment of copyright in any work shall identify such work, and shall specify the rights assigned and the duration and territorial extent of such assignment.

(3) The assignment of copyright in any work shall also specify the amount of royalty payable, if any, to the author or his legal heirs during the currency of the assignment and the assignment shall be subject to revision, extension or termination on terms mutually agreed upon by the parties.

(4) Where the assignee does not exercise the rights assigned to him under any of the other sub-sections of this section within

a period of one year from the date of assignment, the assignment in respect of such rights shall be deemed to have lapsed after the expiry of the said period unless otherwise specified in the assignment.

(5) If the period of assignment is not stated, it shall be deemed to be five years from the date of assignment.

(6) If the territorial extent of assignment of the rights is not specified, it shall be presumed to extend within India.

(7) Nothing in sub-section (2) or sub-section (3) or sub-section (4) or sub-section (5) or sub-section (6) shall be applicable to assignments made before the coming into force of the Copyright (Amendment) Act, 1994.

19A. Disputes with respect to assignment of copyright.

(1) If an assignee fails to make sufficient exercise of the rights assigned to him, and such failure is not attributable to any act or omission of the assignor, then, the Copyright Board may, on receipt of a complaint from the assignor and after holding such inquiry as it may deem necessary, revoke such assignment.

(2) If any dispute arises with respect to the assignment of any copyright the Copyright Board may, on receipt of a complaint from the aggrieved party and after holding such inquiry as it considers necessary, pass such order as it may deem fit including an order for the recovery of any royalty payable:

Provided that the Copyright Board shall not pass any order under this sub-section to revoke the assignment unless it is satisfied that the terms of assignment are harsh to the assignor in case the assignor is also the author:

Provided further that no order of revocation of assignment under this sub-section, be made within a period of five years from the date of such assignment.

20. Transmission of copyright in manuscript by testamentary disposition.

Where under a bequest a person is entitled to the manuscript of a literary, dramatic or musical work, or to an artistic work, and the work was not published before the death of the testator, the bequest shall, unless the contrary intention is indicated in the testator's will or any codicil thereto, be construed as including the copyright in the work in so far as the testator was the owner of the copyright immediately before his death.

Explanation. In this section, the expression 'manuscript' means the original document embodying the work, whether written by hand or not.

21. Right of author to relinquish copyright.

(1) The author of a work may relinquish all or any of the rights comprised in the copyright in the work by giving notice in the prescribed form to the Registrar of Copyrights and thereupon such rights shall, subject to the provisions of sub-section (3), cease to exist from the date of the notice.

(2) On receipt of a notice under sub-section (1), the Registrar of Copyrights shall cause it to be published in the Official Gazette and in such other manner as he may deem fit.

(3) The relinquishment of all or any of the rights comprised in the copyright in a work shall not affect any rights subsisting in favour of any person on the date of the notice referred to in sub-section (1).

CHAPTER V

Term of Copyright

22. Term of copyright in published literary, dramatic, musical and artistic works.

Except as otherwise hereinafter provided, copyright shall subsist in any literary, dramatic, musical or artistic work (other than a photograph) published within the lifetime of the author until sixty years from the beginning of the calendar year next following the year in which the author dies.

Explanation. In this section the reference to the author shall, in the case of a work of joint authorship, be construed as a reference to the author who dies last.

23. Term of copyright in anonymous and pseudonymous works.

(1) In the case of a literary, dramatic, musical or artistic work (other than a photograph), which is published anonymously

or pseudonymously, copyright shall subsist until sixty years from the beginning of the calendar year next following the year in which the work is first published:

Provided that where the identity of the author is disclosed before the expiry of the said period, copyright shall subsist until sixty years from the beginning of the calendar year next following the year in which the author dies.

(2) In sub-section (1), references to the author shall, in the case of an anonymous work of joint authorship, be construed,

(a) where the identity of one of the authors is disclosed, as references to that author;

(b) where the identity of more authors than one is disclosed, as references to the author who dies last from amongst such authors.

(3) In sub-section (1) references to the author shall, in the case of a pseudonymous work of joint authorship, be construed,

(a) where the names of one or more (but not all) of the authors are pseudonymous and his or their identity is not disclosed, as references to the author whose name is not a pseudonym, or, if the names of two or more of the authors are not pseudonyms, as references to such of those authors who dies last;

(b) where the names of one or more (but not all) of the authors are pseudonyms and the identity of one or more of them is disclosed, as references to the author who dies last from amongst the authors whose names are not pseudonyms and the authors whose names are pseudonyms and are disclosed; and

(c) where the names of all the authors are pseudonyms and the identity of one of them is disclosed, as references to the author whose identity is disclosed or if the identity of two or more of such authors is disclosed, as references to such of those authors who dies last.

Explanation. For the purposes of this section, the identity of an author shall be deemed to have been disclosed, if either identity of the author is disclosed publicly by both the author and the publisher or is otherwise established to the satisfaction of the Copyright Board by that author.

24. Term of copyright in the posthumous work.

(1) In the case of a literary, dramatic or musical work or an engraving, in which copyright subsists at the date of the death of the author or, in the case of any such work of joint authorship, at or immediately before the date of the death of the author who dies last, but which, or any adaptation of which, has not been published before that date, copyright shall subsist until sixty years from the beginning of the calendar year next following the year in which the work is first published or, where an adaptation of the work is published in any earlier year, from the beginning of the calendar year next following that year.

(2) For the purposes of this section a literary, dramatic or musical work or an adaptation of any such work shall be deemed to have been published, if it has been performed in public or if any records made in respect of the work have been sold to the public or have been offered for sale to the public.

25. Term of copyright in photographs.

In the case of a photograph, copyright shall subsist until sixty years from the beginning of the calendar year next following the year in which the photograph is published.

26. Term of copyright in films.

In the case of a film, copyright shall subsist until sixty years from the beginning of the calendar year next following the year in which the film is published.

27. Term of copyright in records.

In the case of a sound recording, copyright shall subsist until sixty years from the beginning of the calendar year next following the year in which the sound recording is published.

28. Term of copyright in Government work.

In the case of Government work, where Government is the first owner of the copyright therein, copyright shall subsist until sixty years from the beginning of the calendar year next following the year in which the work is first published.

28A. Term of copyright in works of public undertakings.

In the case of a work, where a public undertaking is the first owner of the copyright therein, copyright shall until sixty years from the beginning of the calendar year next following the year in which the work is first published.

29. Term of copyright in works of international organizations.

In the case of a work of an international organization to which the provisions of section 41 apply, copyright shall subsist until sixty years from the beginning of the calendar year next following the year in which the work is first published.

CHAPTER VI

Licences

30. Licences by owners of copyright.

The owner of the copyright in any existing work or the prospective owner of the copyright in any future work may grant any interest in the right by licence in writing signed by him or by his duly authorized agent:

Provided that in the case of a licence relating to copyright in any future work, the licence shall take effect only when the work comes into existence.

Explanation. Where a person to whom a licence relating to copyright in any future work is granted under this section dies before the work comes into existence, his legal representatives shall, in the absence of any provision to the contrary in the licence, be entitled to the benefit of the licence.

30A. Application of sections 19and 19A.

The provisions of sections 19 and 19A shall, with any necessary adaptations and modifications, apply in relation to a licence under section 30 as they apply in relation to assignment of copyright in a work.

31. Compulsory licence in works withheld from public.

(1) If at any time during the term of copyright in any Indian work which has been published or performed in public, a complaint is made to the Copyright Board that the owner of copyright in the work:

(a) has refused to republish or allow the republication of the work or has refused to allow the performance in public of the work, and by reason of such refusal the work is withheld from the public; or

(b) has refused to allow communication to the public by broadcast, of such work or in the case of sound recording the work recorded in such sound recording, on terms which the complainant considers reasonable; the Copyright Board, after giving to the owner of the copyright in the work a reasonable opportunity of being heard and after holding such inquiry as it may deem necessary, may, if it is satisfied that the grounds for such refusal are not reasonable, direct the Registrar of Copyrights to grant to the complainant a licence to republish the work, perform the work in public or communicate the work to the public by broadcast, as the case may be, subject to payment to the owner of the copyright of such compensation and subject to such other terms and conditions as the Copyright Board may determine; and thereupon the Registrar of Copyrights shall grant the licence to the complainant in accordance with the directions of the Copyright Board, on payment of such fee as may be prescribed.

Explanation. In this sub-section, the expression 'Indian work' includes:

(i) an artistic work, the author of which is a citizen of India; and

(ii) a film or a record made or manufactured in India.

(2) Where two or more persons have made a complaint under sub-section (1), the licence shall be granted to the complainant who in the opinion of the Copyright Board would best serve the interests of the general public.

31A. Compulsory licence in unpublished Indian works.

(1) Where, in the case of an Indian work referred to in sub-clause (iii) of clause (a) of section 2, the author is dead or unknown or cannot be traced, or the owner of the copyright in such work cannot be found, any person may

apply to the Copyright Board for a licence to publish such work or a translation thereof in any language.

(2) Before making an application under sub-section (1), the applicant shall publish his proposal in one issue of a daily newspaper in the English language having circulation in the major part of the country and where the application is for the publication of a translation in any language, also in one issue of any daily newspaper in that language.

(3) Every such application shall be made in such form as may be prescribed and shall be accompanied with a copy of the advertisement issued under sub-section (2) and such fee as may be prescribed.

(4) Where an application is made to the Copyright Board under this section, it may, after holding such inquiry as may be prescribed, direct the Registrar of Copyrights to grant to the applicant a licence to publish the work or a translation thereof in the language mentioned in the application subject to the payment of such royalty and subject to such other terms and conditions as the Copyright Board may determine, and thereupon the Registrar of Copyrights shall grant the licence to the applicant in accordance with the direction of the Copyright Board.

(5) Where a licence is granted under this section, the Registrar of Copyrights may, by order, direct the applicant to deposit the amount of the royalty determined by the Copyright Board in the public account of India or in any other account specified by the Copyright Board so as to enable the owner of the copyright or, as the case may be, his heirs, executors or the legal representatives to claim such royalty at any time.

(6) Without prejudice to the foregoing provisions of this section, in the case of a work referred to in sub-section (1), if the original author is dead, the Central Government may, if it considers that the publication of the work is desirable in the national interest, require the heirs, executors or legal representatives of the author to publish such work within such period as may be specified by it.

(7) Where any work is not published within the period specified by the Central Government under sub-section (6), the Copyright Board may, on an application made by any person for permission to publish the work and after hearing the parties concerned, permit such publication on payment of such royalty as the Copyright Board may, in the circumstances of such case, determine in the prescribed manner.

32. Licence to produce and publish translations.

(1) Any person may apply to the Copyright Board for a licence to produce and publish a translation of a literary or dramatic work in any language after a period of seven years from the first publication of the work. (1A) Notwithstanding anything contained in sub-section (1), any person may apply to the Copyright Board for a licence to produce and publish a translation, in printed or analogous forms of reproduction, of a literary or dramatic work, other than an Indian work, in any language in general use in India after a period of three years from the publication of such work, if such translation is required for the purposes of teaching, scholarship or research: Provided that where such translation is in a language not in general use in any developed country, such application may be made after a period of one year from such publications.

(2) Every application under this section shall be made in such form as may be prescribed and shall state the proposed retail price of a copy of the translation of the work.

(3) Every applicant for a licence under this section shall, along with his application, deposit with the Registrar of Copyrights such fee as may be prescribed.

(4) Where an application is made to the Copyright Board under this section, it may, after holding such inquiry as may be prescribed, grant to the applicant a licence, not being an exclusive licence, to produce and publish a translation of the work in the language mentioned in the application:

(i) subject to the condition that the applicant shall pay to the owner of the copyright in the work royalties in respect of copies of the translation of the work sold to the public, calculated at such rate as the Copyright Board may, in the circumstances of each case, determine in the prescribed manner; and

(ii) where such licence is granted on an application under sub-section (1A), subject also to the condition that the licence shall not extend to the export of copies of the translation of the work outside India and every copy of such translation shall contain a notice in the language of such translation that the copy is available for distribution only in India:

Provided that nothing in clause (ii) shall apply to the export by Government or any authority under the Government of copies of such translation in a language other than English, French or Spanish to any country if:

(1) such copies are sent to citizens of India residing outside India or to any association of such citizens outside India; or

(2) such copies are meant to be used for purposes of teaching, scholarship or research and not for any commercial purpose; and

(3) in either case, the permission for such export has been given by the Government of that country provided further that no licence under this section shall be granted, unless:

(a) a translation of the work in the language mentioned in the application has not been published by the owner of the copyright in the work or any person authorized by him, within seven years or three years or one year, as the case may be, of the first publication of the work, or if a translation has been so published, it has been out of print;

(b) the applicant has proved to the satisfaction of the Copyright Board that he had requested and had been denied authorisation by the owner of the copyright to produce and publish such translation, or that he was, after due diligence on his part, unable to find the owner of the copyright;

(c) where the applicant was unable to find the owner of the copyright, he had sent a copy of his request for such authorisation by registered air mail post to the publisher whose name appears from the work, and in the case of an application for a licence under sub-section (1), not less than two months before such application;

(cc) a period of six months in the case of an application under sub-section (1A) (not being an application under the proviso thereto), or nine months in the case of an application under the proviso to that sub-section, has elapsed from the date of making the request under clause (b) of this proviso, or where a copy of the request has been sent under clause (c) of this proviso, from the date of sending of such copy, and the translation of the work in the language mentioned in the application has not been published by the owner of the copyright in the work or any person authorized by him within the said period of six months or nine months, as the case may be;

(ccc) in the case of any application made under sub-section (1A),

(i) the name of the author and the title of the particular edition of the work proposed to be translated are printed on all the copies of the translation;

(ii) if the work is composed mainly of illustrations, the provisions of section 32A are also complied with;

(d) the Copyright Board is satisfied that the applicant is competent to produce and publish a correct translation of the work and possesses the means to pay to the owner of the copyright the royalties payable to him under this section;

(e) the author has not withdrawn from circulation copies of the work; and

(f) an opportunity of being heard is given, wherever practicable, to the owner of the copyright in the work.

(5) Any broadcasting authority may apply to the Copyright Board for a licence to produce and publish the translation of:

(a) a work referred to in sub-section (1A) and published in printed or analogous forms of reproduction; or

(b) any text incorporated in audio-visual fixations prepared and published solely for the purpose of systematic instructional activities, for broadcasting such translation for the purposes of teaching or for the dissemination of the results of specialized, technical or scientific research to the experts in any particular field.

(6) The provisions of sub-sections (2) to (4) in so far as they are relatable to an application under sub-section (1A), shall, with the necessary modifications, apply to the grant of a licence under sub-section (5) and such licence shall not also be granted unless:

(a) the translation is made from a work lawfully acquired;

(b) the broadcast is made through the medium of sound and visual recordings;

(c) such recording has been lawfully and exclusively made for the purpose of broadcasting in India by the applicant or by any other broadcasting agency; and

(d) the translation and the broadcasting of such translation are not used for any commercial purposes.

Explanation. For the purposes of this section,

(a) 'developed country' means a country which is not a developing country;

(b) 'developing country' means a country which is for the time being regarded as such in conformity with the practice of the General Assembly of the United Nations;

(c) 'purposes of research' does not include purposes of industrial research, or purposes of research by bodies corporate (not being bodies corporate owned or controlled by Government) or other associations or body of persons for commercial purposes;

(d) 'purposes of teaching, research or scholarship' includes:

(i) purposes of instructional activity at all levels in educational institutions, including Schools, Colleges, Universities and tutorial institutions; and

(ii) purposes of all other types of organized educational activity.

32A. Licence to reproduce and publish works for certain purposes.

(1) Where, after the expiration of the relevant period from the date of the first publication of an edition of a literary, scientific or artistic work,

(a) the copies of such edition are not made available in India; or

(b) such copies have not been put on sale in India for a period of six months to the general public, or in connection with systematic instructional activities at a price reasonably related to that normally charged in India for comparable works by the owner of the right of reproduction or by any person authorized by him in this behalf, any person may apply to the Copyright Board for a licence to reproduce and publish such work in printed or analogous forms of reproduction at the price at which such edition is sold or a lower price for the purposes of systematic instructional activities.

(2) Every such application shall be made in such form as may be prescribed and shall state the proposed retail price of a copy of the work to be reproduced.

(3) Every applicant for a licence under this section shall, along with his application, deposit with the Registrar of Copyrights such fee as may be prescribed.

(4) Where an application is made to the Copyright Board under this section, it may, after holding such inquiry as may be prescribed, grant to the applicant a licence, not being an exclusive licence, to produce and publish a reproduction of the work mentioned in the application subject to the conditions that,

(i) the applicant shall pay to the owner of the copyright in the work royalties in respect of copies of the reproduction of the work sold to the public, calculated at such rate as the Copyright Board may, in the circumstances of each case, determine in the prescribed manner;

(ii) a licence granted under this section shall not extend to the export of copies of the reproduction of the work outside India and every copy of such reproduction shall contain a notice that the copy is available for distribution only in India:

Provided that no such licence shall be granted unless:

(a) the applicant has proved to the satisfaction of the Copyright Board that he had requested and had been denied authorisation by the owner of the copyright in the work to reproduce and publish such work or that he was, after due diligence on his part, unable to find such owner;

(b) where the applicant was unable to find the owner of the copyright, he had sent a copy of his request for such authorisation by registered airmail post to the publisher whose name appears from the work not less than three months before the application for the licence;

(c) the Copyright Board is satisfied that the applicant is competent to reproduce and publish an accurate reproduction of the work and possesses the means to pay to the owner of the copyright the royalties payable to him under this section;

(d) the applicant undertakes to reproduce and publish the work at such price as may be fixed by the Copyright Board, being a price reasonably related to the price normally charged in India for works of the same standard on the same or similar subjects;

(e) a period of six months in the case of application for the reproduction and publication of any work of natural science, physical science, mathematics or technology, or a period of three months in the case of an application for the reproduction and publication of any other work, has elapsed from the date of making the request under clause (a), or where a copy of the request has been sent under clause (b), from the date of sending of a copy, and a reproduction of the work has not been published by the owner of the copyright in the work or any person authorized by him within the said period of six months or, three months, as the case may be;

(f) the name of the author and the title of the particular edition of the work proposed to be reproduced are printed on all the copies of the reproduction;

(g) the author has not withdrawn from circulation copies of the work; and

(h) an opportunity of being heard is given, wherever practicable, to the owner of the copyright in the work.

(5) No licence to reproduce and publish the translation of a work shall be granted under this section unless such translation has been published by the owner of the right of translation or any person authorized by him and the translation is not in a language in general use in India.

(6) The provisions of this section shall also apply to the reproduction and publication, or translation into a language in general use in India, of any text incorporated in audio-visual fixations prepared and published solely for the purpose of systematic instructional activities.

Explanation. For the purposes of this section, 'relevant period', in relation to any work, means a period of:

(a) seven years from the date of the first publication of that work, where the application is for the reproduction and publication of any work of, or relating to, fiction, poetry, drama, music or art;

(b) three years from the date of the first publication of that work, where the application is for the reproduction and publication of any work of, or relating to, natural science, physical science, mathematics or technology; and

(c) five years from the date of the first publication of that work, in any other case.

32B. *Termination of licences issued under this chapter.*

(1) If, at any time after the granting of a licence to produce and publish the translation of a work in any language under sub-section (1A) of section 32 (hereafter in this sub-section referred to as the licensed work), the owner of the copyright in the work or any person authorized by him publishes a translation of such work in the same language and which is substantially the same in content at a price reasonably related to the price normally charged in India for the translation of works of the same standard on the same or similar subject, the licence so granted shall be terminated:

Provided that no such termination shall take effect until after the expiry of a period of three months from the date of service of a notice in the prescribed manner on the person holding such licence by the owner of the right of translation intimating the publication of the translation as aforesaid:

Provided further that copies of the licensed work produced and published by the person holding such licence before the termination of the licence takes effect may continue to be sold or distributed until the copies already produced and published are exhausted.

(2) If, at any time after the granting of a licence to produce and publish the reproduction or translation of any work under section 32A, the owner of the right of reproduction or any person authorized by him sells or distributes copies of such work or a translation thereof, as the case may be, in the same language and which is substantially the same in content at a price reasonably related to the price normally charged in India for work of the same standard on the same or similar subject, the licence so granted shall be terminated:

Provided that no such termination shall take effect until after the expiry of a period of three months from the date of service of a notice in the prescribed manner on the person holding the licence by the owner of the right of reproduction intimating the sale or distribution of the copies of the editions of work as aforesaid:

Provided further that any copies already reproduced by the licensee before such termination takes effect may continue to be sold or distributed until the copies already produced are exhausted.

CHAPTER VII
Copyright Societies

33. Registration of Copyright Society.

(1) No person or association of persons shall, after coming into force of the Copyright (Amendment) Act, 1994 commence or, carry on the business of issuing or granting licences in respect of any work in which copyright subsists on respect or in

respect of any other rights conferred by this Act except under or in accordance with the registration granted under sub-section (3):

Provided that owner of copyright shall, in his individual capacity, continue to have the right to grant licences in respect of his own works consistent with his obligations as a member of the registered copyright society:

Provided further that the performing rights society functioning in accordance with the provisions of section 33 on the date immediately before the coming into force of the Copyright (Amendment) Act, 1994 shall be deemed to be a copyright society for the purposes of this Chapter and every such society shall get itself registered within a period of one year from the date of commencement of the Copyright (Amendment) Act, 1994.

(2) Any association of persons who fulfils such conditions as may be prescribed may apply for permission to do the business specified in sub-section (1) to the Registrar of Copyrights who shall submit the application to the Central Government.

(3) The Central Government may, having regard to the interests of the authors and other owners of rights under this Act, the interest and convenience of the public and in particular of the groups of persons who are most likely to seek licences in respect of the relevant rights and the ability and professional competence of the applicants, register such association of persons as a copyright society subject to such conditions as may be prescribed:

Provided that the Central Government shall not ordinarily register more than one copyright society to do business in respect of the same class of works.

(4) The Central Government may, if it is satisfied that a copyright society is being managed in a manner detrimental to the interests of the owners of rights concerned, cancel the registration of such society after such inquiry as may be prescribed.

(5) If the Central Government is of the opinion that in the interest of the owners of rights concerned, it is necessary so to do, it may, by order, suspend the registration of such society pending inquiry for such period not exceeding one year as

may be specified in such order under sub-section (4) and that Government shall appoint an administrator to discharge the functions of the copyright society.

34. Administration of rights of owner by copyright society.

(1) Subject to such conditions as may be prescribed,

(a) a copyright society may accept from an owner of rights exclusive authorisation to administer any right in any work by issue of licences or collection of licence fees or both; and

(b) an owner of rights shall have the right to withdraw such authorisation without prejudice to the rights of the copyright society under any contract.

(2) It shall be competent for a copyright society to enter into agreement with any foreign society or organization administering rights corresponding to rights under this Act, to entrust to such foreign society or organization the administration in any foreign country of rights administered by the said copyright society in India, or for administering in India the rights administered in a foreign country by such foreign society or organization:

Provided that no such society or organization shall permit any discrimination in regard to the terms of licence or the distribution of fees collected between rights in Indian and other works.

(3) Subject to such conditions as may be prescribed, a copyright society may:

(i) issue licences under section 30 in respect of any rights under this Act;

(ii) collect fees in pursuance of such licences;

(iii) distribute such fees among owners of rights after making deductions for its own expenses;

(iv) perform any other functions consistent which the provisions of section 35.

34A. Payment of remuneration by copyright society.

(1) If the Central Government is of the opinion that a copyright society for a class of work is generally

administering the rights of the owners of rights in such work throughout India, it shall appoint that society for the purpose of this section.

(2) The copyright society shall, subject to such rules as may be made in this behalf, frame a scheme for determining the quantum of remuneration payable to individual copyright owners having regard to the number of copies of the work in circulation:

Provided that such scheme shall restrict payment to the owners of rights whose works have attained a level of circulation which the copyright society considers reasonable.

35. Control over the copyright society by the owner of rights.

(1) Every copyright society shall be subject to the collective control of the owners of rights under this Act whose rights it administers (not being owners of rights under this Act administered by a foreign society or organization referred to in sub-section (2) of section (34) and shall, in such manner as may be prescribed,

(a) obtain the approval of such owners of rights for its procedures of collection and distribution of fees;

(b) obtain their approval for the utilization of any amounts collected as fees for any purpose other than distribution to the owner of rights; and

(c) provide to such owners regular, full and detailed information concerning all its activities, in relation to the administration of their rights.

(2) All fees distributed among the owners of rights shall, as far as may be, be distributed in proportion to the actual use of their works.

36. Submission of returns and reports.

(1) Every copyright society shall submit to the Registrar of Copyrights such returns as may be prescribed.

(2) Any officer duly authorized by the Central Government in this behalf may call for any report and also call for any records of any copyright society for the purpose of satisfying himself that the fees collected by the society in respect of rights

administered by it are being utilized or distributed in accordance with the provisions of this Act.

36A. Rights and liabilities of performing rights societies.

Nothing in this Chapter shall affect any rights or liabilities in any work in connection with a performing rights society which had accrued or were incurred on or before the day prior to the commencement of the Copyright (Amendment) Act, 1994, or any legal proceedings in respect of any such rights or liabilities pending on that day.'

CHAPTER VIII

Rights of Broadcasting Organization and of Performers

37. Broadcast reproduction right.

(1) Every broadcasting organization shall have a special right to be known as 'broadcast reproduction right' in respect of its broadcasts.

(2) The broadcast reproduction right shall subsist until twenty-five years from the beginning of the calendar year next following the year in which the broadcast is made.

(3) During the continuance of a broadcast reproduction right in relation to any broadcast, any person who, without the licence of the owner of the right does any of the following acts of the broadcast or any substantial part thereof,

- (a) re-broadcasts the broadcast; or
- (b) causes the broadcast to be heard or seen by the public on payment of any charges; or
- (c) makes any sound recording or visual recording of the broadcast; or
- (d) makes any reproduction of such sound recording or visual recording where such initial recording was done without licence or, where it was licensed, for any purpose not envisaged by such licence; or
- (e) sells or hires to the public or offers for such sale or hire, any such sound recording or visual recording referred to in clause (c) or clause (d) shall, subject to the provisions of section 39, be deemed to have infringed the broadcast reproduction right.

38. Performer's right.

(1) Where any performer appears or engages in any performance, he shall have a special right to be known as the 'performer's right' in relation to such performance.

(2) The performer's right shall subsist until fifty years from the beginning of the calendar year next following the year in which the performance is made.

(3) During the continuance of a performer's right in relation to any performance, any person who, without the consent of the performer, does any of the following acts in respect of the performance or any substantial part thereof, namely:

(a) makes a sound recording or visual recording of the performance; or

(b) reproduces a sound recording or visual recording of the performance, which sound recording or visual recording was:

(i) made without the performer's consent; or

(ii) made for purposes different from those for which the performer gave his consent; or

(iii) made for purposes different from those referred to in section 39 from a sound recording or visual recording which was made in accordance with section 39; or

(c) broadcasts the performance except where the broadcast is made from a sound recording or visual recording other than one made in accordance with section 39, or is a re-broadcast by the same broadcasting organization of an earlier broadcast which did not infringe the performer's right; or

(d) communicates the performance to the public otherwise than by broadcast, except where such communication to the public is made from a sound recording or a visual recording or a broadcast, shall, subject to the provision of section 39, be deemed to have infringed the performer's right.

(4) Once a performer has consented to the incorporation of his performance in a film, the provisions of sub-sections (1), (2) and (3) shall have no further application to such performance.

39. Acts not infringing broadcast reproduction right or performer's right.

No broadcast reproduction right or performer's right shall be deemed to be infringed by:

(a) the making of any sound recording or visual recording for the private use of the person making such recording, or solely for purposes of *bona fide* teaching or research; or

(b) the use, consistent with fair dealing, of excerpts of a performance or of a broadcast in the reporting of current events or for *bona fide* review, teaching or research; or

(c) such order acts, with any necessary adaptations and modifications, which do not constitute infringement of copyright under section 52.

39A. Other provisions applying to broadcast reproduction right and performer's right.

Sections 18, 19, 30, 53, 55, 58, 64, 65, and 66 shall, with any necessary adaptations and modifications, apply in relation to the broadcast reproduction right in any broadcast and the performers' right in any performance as they apply in relation to copyright in a work:

Provided that where copyright or performer's right subsists in respect of any work or performance that has been broadcast, no licence to reproduce such broadcast shall take effect without the consent of the owner of rights or performer, as the case maybe, or both of them.

CHAPTER IX
International Copyright

40. Power to extend copyright to foreign works.

The Central Government may, by order published in the Official Gazette, direct that all or any provisions of this Act shall apply:

(a) to work first published in any class territory outside India to which the order relates in like manner as if they were first published within India;

(b) to unpublished works, or any class thereof, the authors whereof were at the time of the making of the work, subjects or citizens of a foreign country to which the order relates, in like manner as if the authors were citizens of India;

(c) in respect of domicile in any territory outside India to which the order relates in like manner as if such domicile were in India;

(d) to any work of which the author was at the date of the first publication thereof, or, in a case where the author was dead at that date, was at the time of his death, a subject or citizen of a foreign country to which the order relates in like manner as if the author was a citizen of India at that date or time; and thereupon, subject to the provisions of this Chapter and of the order, this Act shall apply accordingly:

Provided that:

(i) before making an order under this section in respect of any foreign country (other than a country with which India has entered into a treaty or which is a party to a convention relating to copyright to which India is also a party), the Central Government shall be satisfied that that foreign country has made, or has undertaken to make, such provisions if any, as it appears to the Central Government expedient to require for the protection in that country of works entitled to copyright under the provisions of this Act;

(ii) the order may provide that the provisions of this Act shall apply either generally or in relation to such classes of works or such classes of cases as may be specified in the order;

(iii) the order may provide that the term of copyright in India shall not exceed that conferred by the law of the country to which the order relates;

(iv) the order may provide that the enjoyment of the rights conferred by this Act shall be subject to the accomplishment of such conditions and formalities, if any, as may be prescribed by the order;

(v) in applying the provisions of this Act as to ownership of copyright, the order may make such exceptions and modifications as appear necessary, having regard to the law of the foreign country;

(vi) the order may provide that this Act or any part thereof shall not apply to works made before the commencement of the order or that this Act or any part thereof small not apply to works first published before the commencement of the order.

40A. (1) If the Central Government is satisfied that a foreign country (other than a country with which India has entered into a treaty or which is a party to a convention relating to rights of broadcasting organizations and performers to which India is also a party) has made or has undertaken to make such provisions, if any, as it appears to the Central Government expedient to require, for the protection in that foreign country, of the rights of broadcasting organizations and performers as is available under this Act, it may, by order published in the Official Gazette, direct that the provisions of Chapter VIII shall apply:

(a) to broadcasting organizations whose headquarters is situated in a country to which the order relates or, the broadcast was transmitted from a transmitter situated in a country to which the order relates as if the headquarters of such organization were situated in India or such broadcast were made from India;

(b) to performances that took place outside India to which the order relates in like manner as if they took place in India;

(c) to performances that are incorporated in a sound recording published in a country to which the order relates as if it was published in India;

(d) to performances not fixed on a sound recording broadcast by a broadcasting organization the headquarters of which is located in a country to which the order relates or where the broadcast is transmitted from a transmitter which is situated in a country to which the order relates as if the headquarters of such organization were situated in India or such broadcast were made from India.

(2) Every order made under sub-section (1) may provide that:

(i) the provisions of Chapter VIII shall apply either generally or in relation to such class or classes of broadcasts or performances or such other class or classes of cases as may be specified in the order;

(ii) the term of the rights of broadcasting organizations and performers in India shall not exceed such term as is conferred by the law of the country to which the order relates;

(iii) the enjoyment of the rights conferred by Chapter VIII shall be subject to the accomplishment of such conditions and formalities, if any, as may be specified in that order;

(iv) Chapter VIII or any part thereof shall not apply to broadcast and performances made before the commencement of the order or that Chapter VIII or any part thereof shall not apply to broadcasts and performances broadcast or performed before the commencement of the order;

(v) in case of ownership of rights of broadcasting organizations and performers, the provisions of Chapter VIII shall apply with such exceptions and modifications as the Central Government may, having regard to the law of the foreign country, consider necessary.

41. Provisions as to works of certain international organizations.

(1) Where:

(a) any work is made or first published by or under the direction or control of any organization to which this section applies, and

(b) there would, apart from this section, be no copyright in the work in India at the time of the making or, as the case may be, of the first publication thereof, and

(c) either:

(i) the work is published as aforesaid in pursuance of an agreement in that behalf with the author, being an agreement which does not reserve to the author the copyright, if any, in the work, or

(ii) under section 17 any copyright in the work would belong to the organization; there shall, by virtue of this section, be copyright in the work throughout India.

(2) Any organization to which this section applies which at the material time had not the legal capacity of a body corporate shall have and be deemed at all material times to have had the legal capacity of a body corporate for the purpose of holding, dealing with, and enforcing copyright and in connection with all legal proceedings relating to copyright.

(3) The organization to which this section applies are such organizations as the Central Government may, by order published in the Official Gazette, declare to be organizations of which one or more sovereign powers or the Government or Governments thereof are members to which it is expedient that this section shall apply.

42. Power to restrict rights in works of foreign authors first published in India.

If it appears to the Central Government that a foreign country does not give or has not undertaken to give adequate protection to the works of Indian authors, the Central Government may, by order published in the Official Gazette, direct that such of the provisions of this Act as confer copyright on works first published in India shall not apply to works, published after the date specified in the order, the authors whereof are subjects or citizens of such foreign country and are not domiciled in India, and thereupon those provisions shall not apply to such works.

42A. Power to restrict rights in works of foreign broadcasting organizations and performers.

If it appears to the Central Government that a foreign country does not give or has not undertaken to give adequate protection to rights of broadcasting organizations or performers, the Central Government may, by order published in the Official Gazette, direct that such of the provisions of this Act as confer right to broadcasting organizations or performers, as the case may be, shall not apply to broadcasting organizations or performers whereof are based or incorporated in such foreign country or are subjects or citizens of such foreign country and are not incorporated or domiciled in India, and thereupon those provisions shall not apply to such broadcasting organizations or performers.

43. Orders under this Chapter to be laid before Parliament.

Every order made by the Central Government under this Chapter shall, as soon as may be after it is made, be laid before both Houses of Parliament and shall be subject to such modifications as Parliament may make during the session in which it is so laid or the session immediately following.

CHAPTER X

Registration of Copyright

44. Register of Copyrights.

There shall be kept at the Copyright Office a register in the prescribed form to be called the Register of Copyrights in which may be entered the names or titles of works and the names and addresses of authors, publishers and owners of copyright and such other particulars as may be prescribed.

45. Entries in register of Copyrights.

(1) The author or publisher of, or the owner of or other person interested in the copyright in, any work may make an application in the prescribed form accompanied by the prescribed fee to the Registrar of Copyrights for entering particulars of the work in the Register of Copyrights:

Provided that in respect of an artistic work which is used or is capable of being used in relation to any goods, the application shall include a statement to that effect and shall be accompanied by a certificate from the Registrar of Trade Marks referred to in section 4 of the Trade and Merchandise Marks Act, 1958, to the effect that no trade mark identical with or deceptively similar to such artistic work has been registered under that Act in the name of, or that no application has been made under that Act for such registration by, any person other than the applicant.

(2) On receipt of an application in respect of any work under sub-section (1), the Registrar of Copyrights may, after holding such inquiry as he may deem fit, enter the particulars of the work in the Register of Copyrights.

46. Indexes.

There shall be also kept at the Copyright Office such indexes of the Register of Copyrights as may be prescribed.

47. Forms and inspection of register.

The Register of Copyrights and indexes thereof kept under this Act shall at all reasonable times be open to inspection, and any person shall be entitled to take copies of, or make extracts from, such register or indexes on payment of such fee and subject to such conditions as may be prescribed.

48. Register of Copyrights to be *prima facie* evidence of partriculars entered therein.

The Register of Copyrights shall be prima facie evidence of the particulars entered therein and documents purporting to be copies of any entries therein, or extracts therefrom certified by the Registrar of Copyrights and sealed with the seal of the Copyright Office shall be admissible in evidence in all courts without further proof or production of the original.

49. Correction of entries in the Register of Copyrights.

The Registrar of Copyrights may, in the prescribed cases and subject to the prescribed conditions, amend or alter the Register of Copyrights by:

(a) correcting any error in any name, address or particulars; or

(b) correcting any other error which may have arisen therein by accidental slip or omission.

50. Rectification of Register by Copyright Board.

The Copyright Board, on application of the Registrar of Copyrights or of any person aggrieved, shall order the rectification of the Register of Copyrights by:

(a) the making of any entry wrongly omitted to be made in the register, or

(b) the expunging of any entry wrongly made in, or remaining on, the register, or

(c) the correction of any error or defect in the register.

50A. Entries in the Register of Copyrights, etc., to be published.

Every entry made in the Register of Copyrights or the particulars of any work entered under section 45, the correction of every entry made in such register under section 49, and every rectification ordered under section 50, shall be published by the Registrar of Copyrights in the Official Gazette or in such other manner as he may deem fit.

CHAPTER XI

Infringement of Copyright

51. When copyright infringed.

Copyright in a work shall be deemed to be infringed:

(a) when any person, without a licence granted by the owner of the copyright or the Registrar of Copyrights under this Act or in contravention of the conditions of a licence so granted or of any condition imposed by a competent authority under this Act:

   (i) does anything, the exclusive right to do which is by this Act conferred upon the owner of the copyright, or

   (ii) permits for profit any place to be used for the communication of the work to the public where such communication constitutes an infringement of the copyright in the work, unless he was not aware and had no reasonable ground for believing that such communication to the public would be an infringement of copyright; or

(b) when any person:

   (i) makes for sale or hire, or sells or lets for hire, or by way of trade displays or offers fór sale or hire, or

   (ii) distributes either for the purpose of trade or to such an extent as to affect prejudicially the owner of the copyright, or

   (iii) by way of trade exhibits in public, or

   (iv) imports into India, any infringing copies of the work

Provided that nothing in sub-clause (iv) shall apply to the import of one copy of any work for the private and domestic use of the importer.

Explanation. For the purposes of this section, the reproduction of a literary, dramatic, musical or artistic work in the form of a film shall be deemed to be an 'infringing copy'.

52. Certain acts not to be infringement of copyright.

(1) The following acts shall not constitute an infringement of copyright, namely:

(a) a fair dealing with a literary, dramatic, musical or artistic work not being a computer programme for the purposes of: (i) private use, including research; (ii) criticism or review, whether of that work or of any other work;

(aa) the making of copies or adaptation of a computer programme by the lawful possessor of a copy of such computer programme, from such copy: (i) in order to utilize the computer programme for the purposes for which it was supplied; or (ii) to make back-up copies purely as a temporary protection against loss, destruction or damage in order only to utilize the computer programme for the purpose for which it was supplied;

(ab) the doing of any act necessary to obtain information essential for operating inter-operability of an independently created computer programme with other programmes by a lawful possessor of a computer programme provided that such information is not otherwise readily available;

(ac) the observation, study or test of functioning of the computer programme in order to determine the ideas and principles which underline any elements of the programme while performing such acts necessary for the functions for which the computer programme was supplied;

(ad) the making of copies or adaptation of the computer programme from a personally legally obtained copy for non-commercial personal use;

(b) a fair dealing with a literary, dramatic, musical or artistic work for the purpose of reporting current events: (i) in a newspaper, magazine or similar periodical, or (ii) by broadcast or in a film or by means of photographs.

Explanation. The publication of a compilation of addresses or speeches delivered in public is not a fair dealing of such work within the meaning of this clause;

(c) the reproduction of a literary, dramatic, musical or artistic work for the purpose of a judicial proceeding or for the purpose of a report of a judicial proceeding;

(d) the reproduction or publication of a literary, dramatic, musical or artistic work in any work prepared by the Secretariat of a Legislature or, where the Legislature consists of two Houses, by the Secretariat of either House of the Legislature, exclusively for the use of the members of that Legislature;

(e) the reproduction of any literary, dramatic or musical work in a certified copy made or supplied in accordance with any law for the time being in force;

(f) the reading or recitation in public of any reasonable extract from a published literary or dramatic work;

(g) the publication in a collection, mainly composed of non-copyright matter, *bona fide* intended for the use of educational institutions, and so described in the title and in any advertisement issued by or on behalf of the publisher, of short passages from published literary or dramatic works, not themselves published for the use of educational institutions, in which copyright subsists: Provided that not more than two such passages from works by the same author are published by the same publisher during any period of five years. Explanation. In the case of a work of joint authorship, references in this clause to passages from works shall include references to passages from works by any one or more of the authors of those passages or by any one or more of those authors in collaboration with any other person;

(h) the reproduction of a literary, dramatic, musical or artistic work: (i) by a teacher or a pupil in the course of instruction; or (ii) as part of the questions to be answered in an examination; or (iii) in answers to such questions;

(i) the performance, in the course of the activities of an educational institution, of a literary, dramatic or musical work by the staff and students of the institution, or of a film or a sound recordings if the audience is limited to such staff and students, the parents and guardians of the students and persons directly connected with the activities of the institution or the communication to such an audience of a film or sound recording.

(j) the making of sound recordings in respect of any literary, dramatic or musical work, if: (i) sound recordings of that work have been made by or with the licence or consent of the owner of the right in the work; (ii) the person making the sound recordings has given a notice of his intention to make the sound recordings, has provided copies of all covers or labels with which the sound recordings are to be sold, and has paid in the prescribed manner to the owner of rights in the work royalties in respect of all such sound recordings to be made by him, at the rate fixed by the Copyright Board in this behalf: Provided that: (i) no alterations shall be made which have not been made previously by or with the consent of the owner of rights, or which are not reasonably necessary for the adaptation of the work for the purpose of making the sound recordings; (ii) the sound recordings shall not be issued in any form of packaging or with any label which is likely to mislead or confuse the public as to their identity; (iii) no such sound recording shall be made until the expiration of two calendar years after the end of the year in which the first sound recording of the work was made; and (iv) the person making such sound recordings shall allow the owner of rights or his duly authorized agent or representative to inspect all records and books of account relating to such sound recording: Provided further that if on a complaint brought before the Copyright Board to the effect that the owner of rights has not been paid in full for any sound recordings purporting to be made in pursuance of this clause, the Copyright Board is, *prima facie*, satisfied that the complaint is genuine, it may pass an order *ex parte* directing the person making the sound recording to cease from making further copies and, after holding such inquiry as it considers necessary, make such further order as it may deem fit, including an order for payment of royalty;

(k) the causing of a recording to be heard in public by utilizing it: (i) in an enclosed room or hall meant for the common use of residents in any residential premises (not being a hotel or similar commercial establishment) as part of the amenities provided exclusively or mainly for residents therein; or (ii) as part of the activities of a club or similar organization which is not established or conducted for profit; (iii) as part of the activities of a club, society or other organization which is not established or conducted for profit;

(l) the performance of a literary, dramatic or musical work by an amateur club or society, if the performance is given to a non-paying audience, or for the benefit of a religious institution;

(m) the reproduction in a newspaper, magazine or other periodical of an article on current economic, political, social or religious topics, unless the author of such article has expressly reserved to himself the right of such reproduction;

(n) the publication in a newspaper, magazine or other periodical of a report of a lecture delivered in public;

(o) the making of not more than three copies of a book (including a pamphlet, sheet of music, map, chart or plan) by or under the direction of the person in charge of a public library for the use of the library if such book is not available for sale in India;

(p) the reproduction, for the purpose of research or private study or with a view to publication, of an unpublished literary, dramatic or musical work kept in a library, museum or other institution to which the public has access: Provided that where the identity of the author of any such work or, in the case of a work of joint authorship, of any of the authors is known to the library, museum or other institution, as the case may be, the provisions of this clause shall apply only if such reproduction is made at a time more than sixty years from the date of the death of the author or, in the case of a work of joint authorship, from the death of the author whose identity is known or, if the identity of more authors than one is known from the death of such of those authors who dies last;

(q) the reproduction or publication of: (i) any matter which has been published in any Official Gazette except an Act of a Legislature; (ii) any Act of a Legislature subject to the condition that such Act is reproduced or published together with any commentary thereon or any other original matter; (iii) the report of any committee, commission, council, board or other like body appointed by the Government if such report has been laid on the Table of the Legislature, unless the reproduction or publication of such report is prohibited by the Government; (iv) any judgment or order of a court, tribunal or other judicial authority, unless the reproduction or publication of such judgment or order is prohibited by the court, the tribunal or other judicial authority, as the case may be;

(r) the production or publication of a translation in any Indian language of an Act of a Legislature and of any rules or orders made thereunder: (i) if no translation of such Act or rules or orders in that language has previously been produced or published by the Government; or (ii) where a translation of such Act or rules or orders in that language has been produced or published by the Government, if the translation is not available for sale to the public: Provided that such translation contains a statement at a prominent place to the effect that the translation has not been authorized or accepted as authentic by the Government;

(s) the making or publishing of a painting, drawing, engraving or photograph of a work of architecture or the display of a work of architecture;

(t) the making or publishing of a painting, drawing, engraving or photograph of a sculpture, or other artistic work failing under sub-clause (iii) of clause (c) of section 2, if such work is permanently situate in a public place or any premises to which the public has access;

(u) the inclusion in a film of: (i) any artistic work permanently situate in a public place or any premises to which the public has access; or (ii) any other artistic work, if such inclusion is only by way of background or is otherwise incidental to the principal matters represented in the film;

(v) the use by the author of an artistic work, where the author of such work is not the owner of the copyright therein, of any mould, cast, sketch, plan, model or study made by him for the purpose of the work: Provided that he does not thereby repeat or imitate the main design of the work;

(x) the reconstruction of a building or structure in accordance with the architectural drawings or plans by reference to which the building or structure was originally constructed: Provided that the original construction was made with the consent or licence of the owner of the copyright in such drawings and plans;

(y) in relation to a literary, dramatic or musical work recorded or reproduced in any film the exhibition of such film after the expiration of the term of copyright therein: Provided that the provisions of sub-clause (ii) of clause (a), sub-clause (a) of clause (b) and clauses (d), (f), (g), (m) and (p) shall not apply as respects any act unless that act is accompanied by an acknowledgment: (i) identifying the work by its title or other description; and (ii) unless the work is anonymous or the author of the work has previously agreed or required that no acknowledgement of his name should be made, also identifying the author.

(z) the making of an ephemeral recording, by a broadcasting organization using its own facilities for its own broadcast by a broadcasting organization of a work which it has the right to broadcast; and the retention of such recording for archival purposes on the ground of its exceptional documentary character;

(za) the performance of a literary, dramatic or musical work or the communication to the public of such work or of a sound recording in the course of any *bona fide* religious ceremony or an official ceremony held by the Central Government or the State Government or any local authority. Explanation. For the purpose of this clause, religious ceremony including a marriage procession and other social festivities associated with a marriage.

(2) The provisions of sub-section (1) shall apply to the doing of any act in relation to the translation of a literary, dramatic or musical work or the adaptation of a literary, dramatic, musical or artistic work as they apply in relation to the work itself.

52A. *Particulars to be included in records and video films.*

(1) No person shall publish a sound recording in respect of any work unless the following particulars are displayed on the sound recording and on any container thereof, namely:

(a) the name and address of the person who has made the sound recording;

(b) the name and address of the owner of the copyright in such work; and

(c) the year of its first publication.

(2) No person shall publish a video film in respect of any work unless the following particulars are displayed in the video film, when exhibited, and on the video cassette or other container thereof, namely:

(a) if such work is a film required to be certified for exhibition under the provisions of the Cinematograph Act, 1952, a copy of the certificate granted by the Broad of Film Certification under section 5A of that Act in respect of such work;

(b) the name and address of the person who has made the video film and a declaration by him that he has obtained the necessary licence or consent from the owner of the copyright in such work for making such video film; and

(c) the name and address of the owner of the copyright in such work.

52B. *Accounts and Audit.*

(1) Every copyright society appointed under section 34A shall maintain proper accounts and other relevant records and prepare an annual statement of accounts, in such

form and in such manner as may be prescribed by the Central Government in consultation with the Comptroller and Auditor-General of India.

(2) The accounts of each of the copyright societies in relation to the payments received from the Central Government shall be audited by the Comptroller and Auditor-General of India at such intervals as may be specified by him and any expenditure incurred in connection with such audit shall be payable by the copyright society to the Comptroller and Auditor-General.

(3) The Comptroller and Auditor-General of India or any other person appointed by him in connection with the audit of the accounts of the copyright society referred to in sub-section (2) shall have the same rights and privileges and authority in connection with such audit as the Comptroller and Auditor-General has in connection with the audit of the Government accounts and, in particular, shall have the right to demand the production of books, accounts and other documents and papers and to inspect any of the offices of the copyright society for the purpose only of such audit.

(4) The accounts of each of the copyright societies as certified by the Comptroller and Auditor-General of India or any other person appointed by him in this behalf together with the audit report thereon shall be forwarded annually to the Central Government and that Government shall cause the same to be laid before each House of Parliament.

53. Importation of infringing copies.

(1) The Registrar of Copyrights, on application by the owner of the copyright in any work or by his duly authorized agent and on payment of the prescribed fee, may, after making such inquiry as he deems fit, order that copies made out of India of the work which if made in India would infringe copyright shall not be imported.

(2) Subject to any rules made under this Act, the Registrar of Copyrights or any person authorized by him in this behalf may enter any ship, dock or premises where any such copies as are referred to in sub-section (1) may be found and may examine such copies.

(3) All copies to which any order made under sub-section (1) applies shall be deemed to be goods of which the import has been prohibited or restricted under section 11 of the Customs Act, 1962, and all the provisions of that Act shall have effect accordingly:

Provided that all such copies confiscated under the provisions of the said Act shall not vest in the Government but shall be delivered to the owner of the copyright in the work.

53A. Resale share right in original copies.

(1) In the case of resale for a price exceeding ten thousand rupees, of the original copy of a painting, sculpture or drawing, or of the original manuscript of a literary or dramatic work or musical work, the author of such work if he was the first owner of rights under section 17 or his legal heirs shall, notwithstanding any assignment of copyright in such work, have a right to share in the resale-price of such original copy or manuscript in accordance with the provisions of this section:

Provided that such right shall cease to exist on the expiration of the term of copyright in the work.

(2) The share referred to in sub-section (1) shall be such as the Copyright Board may fix and the decision of the Copyright Board in this behalf shall be final:

Provided that the Copyright Board may fix different shares for different classes of work:

Provided further that in no case shall the share exceed ten per cent of the resale price.

(3) If any dispute arises regarding the right conferred by this section, it shall be referred to the Copyright Board whose decision shall be final.

CHAPTER XII

Civil Remedies

54. Definition.

For the purposes of this Chapter, unless the context otherwise requires, the expression 'owner of copyright' shall include:

(a) an exclusive licensee;

(b) in the case of an anonymous or pseudonymous literary, dramatic, musical or artistic work, the publisher of the work, until the identity of the author or, in the case of an anonymous work of joint authorship, or a work of joint authorship published under names all of which are pseudonyms, the identity of any of the authors, is disclosed publicly by the author and the publisher or is otherwise established to the satisfaction of the Copyright Board by that author or his legal representatives.

55. Civil remedies for infringement of copyright.

(1) Where copyright in any work has been infringed, the owner of the copyright shall, except as otherwise provided by this Act, be entitled to all such remedies by way of injunction, damages, accounts and otherwise as are or may be conferred by law for the infringement of a right:

Provided that if the defendant proves that at the date of the infringement he was not aware and had no reasonable ground for believing that copyright subsisted in the work, the plaintiff shall not be entitled to any remedy other than an injunction in respect of the infringement and a decree for the whole or part of the profits made by the defendant by the sale of the infringing copies as the court may in the circumstances deem reasonable.

(2) Where, in the case of a literary, dramatic, musical or artistic work, a name purporting to be that of the author or the publisher, as the case may be, appears on copies of the work as published, or, in the case of an artistic work, appeared on the work when it was made, the person whose name so appears or appeared shall, in any proceeding in respect of infringement of copyright in such work, be presumed, unless the contrary is proved, to be the author or the publisher of the work, as the case may be.

(3) The costs of all parties in any proceedings in respect of the infringement of copyright shall be in the discretion of the court.

56. Protection of separate rights.

Subject to the provisions of this Act, where the several rights comprising the copyright in any work are owned by different persons, the owner of any such right shall, to the extent of that right be entitled to the remedies provided by this Act and may individually enforce such right by means of any suit, action or other proceeding without making the owner of any other right a party to such suit, action or proceeding.

57. Author's special rights.

(1) Independently of the author's copyright and even after the assignment either wholly or partially of the said copyright, the author of a work shall have the right:

(a) to claim authorship of the work; and

(b) to restrain or claim damages in respect of any distortion, mutilation, modification or other act in relation to the said work which is done before the expiration of the term of copyright if such distortion, mutilation, modification or other act would be prejudicial to his honour or reputation:

Provided that the author shall not have any right to restrain or claim damages in respect of any adaptation of a computer programme to which clause (aa) of sub-section (1) of section 52 applies.

Explanation. Failure to display a work or to display it to the satisfaction of the author shall not be deemed to be an infringement of the rights conferred by this section.

(2) The right conferred upon an author of a work by sub-section (1), other than the right to claim authorship of the work, may be exercised by the legal representatives of the author.

58. Rights of owner against persons possessing or dealing with infringing copies.

All infringing copies of any work in which copyright subsists, and all plates used or intended to be used for the production of such infringing copies, shall be deemed to be the property of the owner of the copyright, who accordingly may take proceedings for the recovery of possession thereof or in respect of the conversion thereof:

Provided that the owner of the copyright shall not be entitled to any remedy in respect of the conversion of any infringing copies, if the opponent proves:

(a) that he was not aware and had no reasonable ground to believe that copyright subsisted in the work of which such copies are alleged to be infringing copies; or

(b) that he had reasonable grounds for believing that such copies or plates do not involve infringement of the copyright in any work.

59. Restriction on remedies in the case of works of architecture.

(1) Notwithstanding anything contained in the Specific Relief Act, 1963, where the construction of a building or other structure which infringes or which, if completed, would infringe the copyright in some other work has been commenced, the owner of the copyright shall not be entitled to obtain an injunction to restrain the construction of such building or structure or to order its demolition.

(2) Nothing in section 58 shall apply in respect of the construction of a building or other structure which infringes or which, if completed, would infringe the copyright in some other work.

60. Remedy in the case of groundless threat of legal proceedings.

Where any person claiming to be the owner of copyright in any work, by circulars, advertisements or otherwise, threatens any other person with any legal proceedings or liability in respect of an alleged infringement of the copyright, any person aggrieved thereby may, notwithstanding anything contained in section 34 of the Specific Relief Act, 1963 institute a declaratory suit that the alleged infringement to which the threats related was not in fact an infringement of any legal rights of the person making such threats and may in any such suit:

(a) obtain an injunction against the continuance of such threats; and

(b) recover such damages, if any, as he has sustained by reason of such threats.

Provided that this section shall not apply if the person making such threats, with due diligence, commences and prosecutes an action for infringement of the copyright claimed by him.

61. Owners of copyright to be party to the proceeding.

(1) In every civil suit or other proceeding regarding infringement of copyright instituted by an exclusive licensee, the owner of

the copyright shall, unless the court otherwise directs, be made a defendant and where such owner is made a defendant, he shall have the right to dispute the claim of the exclusive licensee.

(2) Where any civil suit or other proceeding regarding infringement of copyright instituted by an exclusive licensee is successful, no fresh suit or other proceeding in respect of the same cause of action shall lie at the instance of the owner of the copyright.

62. Jurisdiction of court over matters arising under this Chapter.

(1) Every suit or other civil proceeding arising under this Chapter in respect of the infringement of copyright in any work or the infringement of any other right conferred by this Act shall be instituted in the district court having jurisdiction.

(2) For the purpose of sub-section (1), and 'district court having jurisdiction' shall, notwithstanding anything contained in the Code of Civil Procedure, 1908, or any other law for the time being in force, include a district court within the local limits of whose jurisdiction, at the time of the institution of the suit or other proceeding, the person instituting the suit or other proceeding or, where there are more than one such persons, any of them actually and voluntarily resides or carries on business or personally works for gain.

CHAPTER XIII

Offences

63. Offence of infringement of copyright or other rights conferred by this Act.

Any person who knowingly infringes or abets the infringement of:

(a) the copyright in a work, or

(b) any other right conferred by this Act, except the right conferred by section 53A shall be punishable with imprisonment for a term which shall not be less than six months but which may extend to three years and with fine which shall not be less than fifty thousand rupees but which may extend to two lakh rupees:

Provided that where the infringement has not been made for gain in the course of trade or business the court may, for adequate and special reasons to be mentioned in the judgment, impose a sentence of imprisonment for a term of less than six months or a fine of less than fifty thousand rupees.

Explanation. Construction of a building or other structure which infringes or which, if completed, would infringe the copyright in some other work shall not be an offence under this section.

63A. Enhanced penalty on second and subsequent convictions.

Whoever having already been convicted of an offence under section 63 is again convicted of any such offence shall be punishable for the second and for every subsequent offence, with imprisonment for a term which shall not be less than one year but which may extend to three years and with fine which shall not be less than one lakh rupees but which may extend to two lakh rupees:

Provided that where the infringement has not been made for gain in the course of trade or business the court may, for adequate and special reasons to be mentioned in the judgment impose a sentence of imprisonment for a term of less than one year or a fine of less than one lakh rupees:

Provided further that for the purposes of this section, no cognizance shall be taken of any conviction made before the commencement of the Copyright (Amendment) Act, 1984.

63B. Knowing use of infringing copy of computer programme to be an offence.

Any person who knowingly makes use on a computer of an infringing copy of a computer programme shall be punishable with imprisonment for a term which shall not be less than seven days but which may extend to three years and with fine which shall not be less than fifty thousand rupees but which may extend to two lakh rupees:

Provided that where the computer programme has not been used for gain or in the course of trade or business, the court may, for adequate and special reasons to be mentioned in the judgment, not impose any sentence of imprisonment and may impose a fine which may extend to fifty thousand rupees.

64. Power of police to seize infringing copies.

(1) Any police officer, not below the rank of a sub-inspector, may, if he is satisfied that an offence under section 63 in respect of the infringement of copyright in any work has been, is being, or is likely to be, committed, seize without warrant, all copies of the work, and all plates used for the purpose of making infringing copies of the work, wherever found, and all copies and plates so seized shall, as soon as practicable, be produced before a Magistrate.

(2) Any person having an interest in any copies of a work or plates seized under sub-section (1) may, within fifteen days of such seizure, make an application to the Magistrate for such copies. or plates being restored to him and the Magistrate, after hearing the applicant and the complainant and making such further inquiry as may be necessary, shall make such order on the application as he may deem fit.

65. Possession of plates for purpose of making infringing copies.

Any person who knowingly makes, or has in his possession, any plate for the purpose of making infringing copies of any work in which copyright subsists shall be punishable with imprisonment which may extend to two years and shall also be liable to fine.

66. Disposal of infringing copies or plates for purpose of making infringing copies.

The court trying any offence under this Act may, whether alleged offender is convicted or not, order that all copies of the work or all plates in the possession of the alleged offender, which appear to it to be infringing copies, or plates for the purpose of making infringing copies, be delivered up to the owner of the copyright.

67. Penalty for making false entries in register, etc., for producing or tendering false entries.

Any person who,

(a) makes or causes to be made a false entry in the Register of Copyrights kept under this Act, or

(b) makes or causes to be made a writing falsely purporting to be a copy of any entry in such register, or

(c) produces or tenders or causes to be produced or tendered as evidence any such entry or writing, knowing the same to be false, shall be punishable with imprisonment which may extend to one year, or with fine, or with both.

68. Penalty for making false statements for the purpose of deceiving or influencing any authority or officer.

Any person who,

(a) with a view to deceiving any authority or officer in the execution provisions of this Act, or

(b) with a view to procuring or influencing the doing or omission of anything relation to this Act or any matter thereunder, makes a false statement or representation knowing the same to be false, shall be punishable with imprisonment which may extend to one year, or with fine, or with both.

68A. Penalty for contravention of section 52A.

Any person who publishes a sound recording or a video film in contravention of the provisions of section 52A shall be punishable with imprisonment which may extend to three years and shall also be liable to fine.

69. Offences by companies.

(1) Where any offence under this Act has been committed by a company, every person who at the time the offence was committed was in charge of, and was responsible to the company for, the conduct of the business of the company, as well as the company shall be deemed to be guilty of such offence and shall be liable to be proceeded against and punished accordingly:

Provided that nothing contained in this sub-section shall render any person liable to any punishment, if he proves that the offence was committed without his knowledge or that he exercised all due diligence to prevent the commission of such offence.

(2) Notwithstanding anything contained in sub-section (1), where an offence under this Act has been committed by a company, and it is proved that the offence was committed with the

consent or connivance of, or is attributable to any negligence on the part of, any director, manager, secretary or other officer of the company, such director, manager, secretary or other officer shall also be deemed to be guilty of that offence and shall be liable to be proceeded against and punished accordingly.

Explanation. For the purposes of this section:

(a) 'company' means any body corporate and includes a firm or other association of persons; and

(b) 'director' in relation to a firm means a partner in the firm.

70. Cognizance of offences.

No court inferior to that of a Metropolitan Magistrate or a Judicial Magistrate of the first class shall try any offence under this Act.

CHAPTER XIV

Appeals

71. Appeals against certain orders of Magistrate.

Any person aggrieved by an order made under sub-section (2) of section 64 or section 66 may, within thirty days of the date of such order, appeal to the court to which appeals from the court making the order ordinarily lie, and such appellate court may direct that execution of the order be stayed pending disposal of the appeal.

72. Appeals against orders of Registrar of Copyrights and Copyright Board.

(1) Any person aggrieved by any final decision or order of the Registrar of Copyrights may, within three months from the date of the order or decision, appeal to the Copyright Board.

(2) Any person aggrieved by any final decision or order of the Copyright Board, not being a decision or order made in an appeal under sub-section (1), may, within three months from the date of such decision or order, appeal to the High Court within whose jurisdiction the appellant actually and voluntarily resides or carries on business or personally works for gain;

Provided that no such appeal shall lie against a decision of the Copyright Board under section 6.

(3) In calculating the period of three months provided for an appeal under this section, the time taken in granting a certified copy of the order or record of the decision appealed against shall be excluded.

73. Procedure for appeals.

The High Court may make rules consistent with this Act as to the procedure to be followed in respect of appeals made to it under section 72.

CHAPTER XV
Miscellaneous

74. Registrar of Copyrights and Copyright Board to possess certain powers of civil courts.

The Registrar of Copyrights and the Copyright Board shall have the powers of a civil court when trying a suit under the Code of Civil Procedure, 1908, in respect of the following matters, namely:

(a) summoning and enforcing the attendance of any person and examining him on oath;

(b) requiring the discovery and production of any document;

(c) receiving evidence on affidavits;

(d) issuing commissions for the examination of witnesses or documents;

(e) requisitioning any public record or copy thereof from any court or office;

(f) any other matter which may be prescribed.

Explanation. For the purpose of enforcing the attendance of witnesses, the local limits of the jurisdiction of the Registrar of Copyrights or the Copyright Board, as the case may be, shall be limits of the territory of India.

75. Orders for payment of money passed by Registrar of Copyrights and Copyright Board to be executable as a decree.

Every order made by the Registrar of Copyrights or the Copyright Board under this Act for the payment of any money or by the High Court in any appeal against any such order of the Copyright Board shall, on a certificate issued by the Registrar of Copyrights, the

Copyright Board or the Registrar of the High Court, as the case may be, be deemed to be a decree of a civil court and shall be executable in the same manner as a decree of such court.

76. Protection of action taken in good faith.

No suit or other legal proceeding shall lie against any person in respect of anything which is in good faith done or intended to be done in pursuance of this Act.

77. Certain persons to be public servants.

Every officer appointed under this Act and every member of the Copyright Board shall be deemed to be a public servant within the meaning of section 21 of the Indian Penal Code.

78. Power to make rules.

(1) The Central Government may, by notification in the Official Gazette, make rules for carrying out the purposes of this Act.

(2) In particular, and without prejudice to the generality of the foregoing power, the Central Government may make rules to provide for all or any of the following matters, namely:

- (a) the term of office and conditions of service of the Chairman and other members of the Copyright Board;
- (b) the form of complaints and applications to be made, and the licences to be granted, under this Act;
- (c) the procedure to be followed in connection with any proceeding before the Registrar of Copyrights;
  - (ca) the conditions for submission of application under sub-section (2) of section 33;
  - (cb) the conditions subject to which a copyright society may be registered under sub-section (3) of section 33;
  - (cc) the inquiry for cancellation of registration under sub-section (4) of section 33;
  - (cd) the conditions subject to which the copyright society may accept authorisation under clause (a) of sub-section (1) of section 34 and the conditions subject to which owners of rights have right to withdraw such authorisation under clause (b) of that sub-section;

(ce) the conditions subject to which a copyright society may issue licences, collect fees and distribute such fees amongst owners of rights under sub-section (3) of section 34;

(cf) the manner in which the approval of the owners of rights regarding collection and distribution of fees, approval for utilisation of any amount collected as fees and to provide to such owners information concerning activities in relation to the administration of their rights under sub-section (1) of section 35;

(cg) the returns to be filed by copyright societies to the Registrar of Copyrights under sub-section (1) of section 36;

(d) the manner of determining any royalties payable under this Act, and the security to be taken for the payment of such royalties;

(da) the manner of payment of royalty under clause (j) of sub-section (1) of section 52;

(db) the form and the manner in which the copyright society shall maintain accounts and other relevant records and prepare annual statements of accounts and the manner in which the quantum of remuneration is to be paid to individual owner of rights under sub-section (1) of section 52B;

(e) the form of Register of Copyrights to be kept under this Act and the particulars to be entered therein;

(f) the matter in respect of which the Registrar of Copyrights and the Copyright Board shall have powers of a civil court;

(g) the fees which may be payable under this Act;

(h) the regulation of business of the Copyright Office and of all things by this Act placed under the direction or control of the Registrar of Copyrights.

(3) Every rule made under this section shall be laid, as soon as may be after it is made, before each House of Parliament, while it is in session, for a total period of thirty days which may be comprised in one session or in two or more successive sessions,

and if, before the expiry of the session immediately following the session or the successive sessions aforesaid, both Houses agree in making any modification in the rule or both Houses agree that the rule should not be made, the rule shall thereafter have effect only in such modified form or be of no effect, as the case may be; so, however, that any such modification or annulment shall be without prejudice to the validity of anything previously done under that rule.

79. Repeals, savings and transitional provisions.

(1) The Indian Copyright Act, 1914, and the Copyright Act of 1911 passed by the Parliament of the United Kingdom as modified in its application to India by the Indian Copyright Act, 1914, are hereby repealed.

(2) Where any person has, before the commencement of this Act, taken any action whereby he has incurred any expenditure or liabilities in connection with the reproduction or performance of any work in a manner which at the time was lawful or for the purpose of or with a view to the reproduction or performance of a work at a time when such reproduction or performance would, but for the coming into force of this Act, have been lawful, nothing in this section shall diminish or prejudice any rights or interests arising from or in connection with such action which are subsisting and valuable at the said date, unless the person who, by virtue of this Act, becomes entitled to restrain such reproduction or performance agrees to pay such compensation as, failing agreement, may be determined by the Copyright Board.

(3) Copyright shall not subsist by virtue of this Act in any work in which copyright did not subsist immediately before the commencement of this Act under any Act repealed by sub-section (1).

(4) Where copyright subsisted in any work immediately before the commencement of this Act, the rights comprising such copyright shall, as from the date of such commencement, be the rights specified in section 14 in relation to the class of works to which such work belongs, and where any new rights are conferred by that section, the owner of such rights shall be:

(a) in any case where copyright in the work was wholly assigned before the commencement of this Act, the assignee or his successor-in-interest;

(b) in any other case, the person who was the first owner of the copyright in the work under any Act repealed by sub-section (1) or his legal representatives.

(5) Except as otherwise provided in this Act, where any person is entitled immediately before the commencement of this Act to copyright in any work or any right in such copyright or to an interest in any such right, he shall continue to be entitled to such right or interest for the period for which he would have been entitled thereto if this Act had not come into force.

(6) Nothing contained in this Act shall be deemed to render any act done before its commencement an infringement of copyright if that act would not otherwise have constituted such an infringement.

(7) Save as otherwise provided in this section, nothing in this section shall be deemed to affect the application of the General Clauses Act, 1897, with respect to the effect of repeals.

THE OPINIONS OF EXPERTS AND OTHERS AS EVIDENCE

Generally, people who have no connection to a dispute in Court cannot give evidence regarding it. However, there are some exceptions to this. Sections 45 to 51 of the Evidence Act, 1872 deal with the opinions of third persons including experts.

Section	*Question before the Court*	*Whose opinion is relevant*	*Remarks*
45	As to a point of: foreign law, science, art, or the identity of handwriting or finger impressions	An expert or person specially skilled	
46	Facts, not otherwise relevant, are relevant if they support or are inconsistent with the opinions of experts, when such opinions are relevant.		
47	If a document has been written or signed by the person by whom it is supposed to have been written or	Any person acquainted with the handwriting of the person by whom it is supposed to be written or signed because of	If it is/is not the handwriting of the person by whom it is supposed to be written or signed

Contd.

Section	*Question before the Court*	*Whose opinion is relevant*	*Remarks*
	signed	having seen that person write, receiving a reply from him or a document habitually submitted in the course of business.	
47 A	As to a digital signature	Certifying Authority which has issued it	
48	As to a general custom or right including that of any considerable class of persons	Person likely to be aware of its existence	
49	The usages and tenets of any body of men or family, the constitution and government of any religious or charitable foundation, or the meaning of words or terms used in particular districts or by particular or by particular classes of people	Person who has special means of knowledge thereon	
50	The relationship of one person to another	The opinion expressed by conduct, as to the existence of such relationship, of any person who, as a member of the family or otherwise, has special means of knowledge on the subject	Such opinion shall not be sufficient to prove a marriage in proceedings under the India Divorce Act, 1869 or in prosecutions under Sections 494, 495, 497 or 498 of the IPC
51	Whenever the opinion of any living person is relevant, the grounds on which such opinion is based are also relevant.		

However, when it comes to experts, there are a number of other provisions in the Evidence Act which also deal with them. These provisions mention:

1. The opinions expressed in any treatise commonly offered for sale (Section 60)
2. Expert opinion as to the general result of a number of documents Section 65(g)
3. An expert refreshing his memory Section 159

It is also worth noting that unlike other witnesses, witnesses who are called to give expert testimony may be asked hypothetical questions.

THE EXCLUSION OF ORAL BY DOCUMENTARY EVIDENCE

While signing a contract, it is important to ensure that the whole agreement is in writing. The reason for this lies in the depths of the Indian Evidence Act of 1872.

The best evidence must always be produced in court, and the acceptance of the fact that no matter how good a person's memory may be, the best evidence of the content of a document is the document itself means that oral evidence of a document is excluded. The principle does not demand the largest amount of evidence — it simply requires the best evidence and since this is documentary evidence, oral evidence is excluded. However, it was held in Javarasetty v. Ningamma, 1992, that oral evidence is not excluded when the writing in question is not evidence of the matter reduced to writing; there is no reason for the Court to prefer either documentary or oral evidence to the other.

The general rule excluding oral evidence in the presence of documentary evidence is laid down in Sections 91 and 92. This general rule is subject to the 'exceptions' contained in Sections 93 to 100 which speak of how oral evidence may be used to interpret documents.

Section 91 of the Indian Evidence Act deals with the evidence of terms of contracts, grants and other dispositions of property reduced to form of document. When the terms of a contract, or of a grant, or of any other disposition of property, have been reduced to the form of a document, and in all cases in which any matter is required by law to be reduced to the form of a document, no evidence can be given in proof of the terms of such contract, grant or other disposition of property, or of such matter, except the document itself, or secondary evidence of its contents in cases in which secondary evidence is admissible under the provisions of the Act.

However, when a public officer is required by law to be appointed in writing, and when it is shown that any particular person has acted as such officer, the writing by which he is appointed need not be proved. This exception is partly a reflection of the maxim '*Omnia praesumuntur rite esse acta*' which means that all acts are presumed to be rightly done (and is also seen in Section 79 of the Indian Evidence Act).

Wills admitted to probate in India may be proved by the probate. Thus, probate is admissible (even though it is secondary evidence).

This Section should be read along with (a) Section 364 of the Code of Criminal Procedure, (b) O XVIII R 5 of the Code of Civil Procedure and (c) the proviso to Section 49 of the Indian Registration Act which respectively say that (a) evidence may be taken to show that a recorded statement of an accused person was duly made if a Criminal Court finds that the statement was not recorded in the proper manner, (b) the deposition of a witness must be read over to him (and if this is not done, oral evidence of its contents is inadmissible) and (c) an unregistered document which is required to be registered is admissible as evidence of collateral facts or any collateral transaction which need not be effected by a registered document.

Explanation 1. This Section applies equally to cases in which the contracts grants or dispositions of property referred to are contained in one document and to cases in which they are contained in more documents than one.

Explanation 2. Where there are more originals than one, one original only need be proved.

Explanation 3. The statement, in any document whatever, of a fact other then the facts referred to in this Section, shall, not preclude the admission of oral evidence as to the same fact.

Under this Section, no oral evidence can be given of the terms of a written contract, grant or other disposition of property. However, oral evidence may be given to show:

- There was no agreement between the parties and as such, no contract (Tyagaraja Mudialiar v. Vadethanni, 1935)
- A condition precedent to the formation of the contract (P B Bhatt v. V R Thakkar, 1971)

Thus, the only oral evidence excluded by this Section is oral evidence regarding the terms written in a document. If there is no document, this Section does not apply.

For example, under Hindu law, a partition may be oral. If it is oral, Section 91 has no application. But if it is in writing, the Section applies (and if it involves immovable property, the document must be registered).

92. Exclusion of evidence of oral agreement

When the terms of any such contract, grant or other disposition of property, or any matter required by law to be reduced to the form of a document have been proved according to Section 91, no evidence of any oral agreement of statement can be admitted, as between the parties to any such instrument or their representatives in interest, for purpose of contradicting, varying, adding to, or subtracting from, its terms.

Proviso (1) — Any fact may be proved which would invalidate any document, or which would entitle any person to any decree or order relating thereto; such as fraud, intimidation, illegality, want of due execution, want of capacity in any contracting party, want or failure of consideration, or mistake in fact or law. This proviso deals with agreements whose validity has been impeached and should be read with Section 31 of the Specific Relief Act.

Proviso (2) — The existence of any separate oral agreement as to any matter on which a document is silent, and which is not inconsistent with its terms, may be proved. In considering whether or not this proviso applies, the Court shall have regard to the degree of formality of the document. It is under this proviso that oral evidence is admissible on matters which the document does not speak of although the evidence given cannot be inconsistent with the written terms of the agreement. Also, the Court considers the formality of the document which deciding whether or not the proviso applies i.e. a Court may permit the missing links in a document drafted by a layman to be filled in by oral evidence but may not do so if the document in question has been drafted by a team of lawyers: in such a case, the Court may conclude that what has been left blank has been deliberately left blank.

Proviso (3) — The existence of any separate oral agreement, constituting a condition precedent to the attaching of any obligation under any such contract, grant or disposition of property, may be proved. Thus, Proviso 3 deals with conditions precedent to obligation. For example, Section 144 of the Contract Act which deals with guarantees says 'where a person gives a guarantee upon a contract that a creditor shall not act upon it till another person has joined in it as co-surety, the guarantee is not valid if that other person does not join'. Here, the agreement that the person would be under no obligation until a co-surety joined in the guarantee may be proved.

Proviso (4) — The existence of any distinct subsequent oral agreement to rescind or modify any such contract, grant or disposition of property, may be proved, except in cases in which such contract grant or disposition of property is by law required to be in writing, or has been registered according to the law in force for the time being as to the registration of documents.

Proviso (5) — Any usage or custom by which incidents not expressly mentioned in any contract are usually annexed to contracts of that description, may be proved provided that the annexing of such incident would not be repugnant to, or inconsistent with the express terms of the contract.

Proviso (6) — Any fact may be proved which shows in what manner the language of a document is related to existing facts.

This Section supplements Section 91 as it would be pointless to make evidence of a document (other than the document itself) inadmissible if it contradicting, varying, adding to, or subtracting from its terms was permitted.

Sections 91 and 92 are, as the Supreme Court pointed out in Roop Kumar v. Mohan Thedani, 2003, different in some material particulars. It was held that 'Section 91 applies to all documents, whether they purport to dispose of rights or not whereas Section 92 applies to documents which can be described as dispositive. Section 91 applies to documents which are both bilateral and unilateral, unlike Section 92 whose application is confined to bilateral agreements'.

Section 92 applies only when there is no infirmity in the document; facts which invalidate a document can be proved by oral evidence.

PROOF OF A DOCUMENT BY SECONDARY EVIDENCE

The contents of documents may be proved in Court either by primary or by secondary evidence. [232] Primary evidence[233] means that the document itself is produced for the inspection of the Court while secondary evidence[234] of a document basically means and includes:

(1) certified copies given under the provisions hereinafter contained;

(2) Copies made from the original by mechanical processes which in themselves ensure the accuracy of the copy, and copies compared with such copies.

(3) copies made from or compared with the original;

(4) counterparts of documents as against the parties who did not execute them;

(5) oral accounts of the contents of a documents given by some person who has himself seen it.

As a general rule, documents must be proved by primary evidence.[235] However, there are some exceptions to this rule. Section 65 of the Indian Evidence Act deals with cases in which secondary evidence relating to documents may be given.

Section	*Status of the Original Document*	*Circumstances*	*Admissible Secondary Evidence*
65 (a)	It is shown or appears to be in the possession or power— 1. of the person against whom the document is sought to be proved, or 2. of any person out of reach of, or not subject to, the process of the Court or 3. of any person legally bound to produce it, 4. and when, after the notice mentioned in Section 66, such person does not produce it;	After the notice mentioned in Section 66, the person in whose possession or power it is does not produce it.	The contents of the document
65 (b)		The existence, condition or contents of the original have been proved to be admitted in writing by the person against whom it is proved or by his representative in interest.	The written admission
65 (c)	1. The original has been destroyed or lost, or 2. the party offering evidence of its contents cannot, for any other reason not arising from his own default or neglect, produce it in reasonable time		The contents of the document

Contd.

Section	Status of the Original Document	Circumstances	Admissible Secondary Evidence
65 (d)	The original is of such a nature as not to be easily movable		The contents of the document
65 (e)	The original is public document within the meaning of Section 74		Only a certified copy of the document
65 (f)	The original is a document of which a certified copy is permitted by this Act, or by any other law in force in India to be given in evidence		Only a certified copy of the document
65 (g)	The originals consist of numerous accounts or other documents which cannot conveniently be examined in Court	The fact to be proved it the general result of the whole collection	The general result of the documents by a person who has examined them, and who is skilled in the examination of such documents

Secondary evidence of a document cannot be given unless:

1. The non-production of the original is accounted for so as to bring it under one of the exceptions of Section 65. (Krishna Kishori Chowdhrani v. Kirshori Lal Roy, 1887)
2. The original document is admissible.

A conjoint reading of Section 65 (b) and Section 22 of the Indian Evidence Act shows that the admission of a document amounts to the admission of its contents but not of its truth. (Section 22 speaks of when oral admissions regarding the contents of documents are admissible.)

If secondary evidence is sought to be given under Section 65 (c) because of the loss of the original, it must first be proved that the original has been lost. (Illustration (b) to Section 104)

A party who is in custody of the original document cannot give secondary evidence of its contents. (Hira Lal v. Ganesh Prasad, 1882)

Section 65 (d) applies to such things as tombstones, writing on a wall etc. which would be impractical to bring into a Court. It has been held in a number of cases though that this rule applies to 'written documents' in the strict sense of the term. It does not extend to films, tapes, etc. And, in Mertimer v. M Challan, 1840, it was held that the rule applied to books of the Bank of England as removing the originals would cause a great deal of public inconvenience.

Section 65 (e) is mainly to protect public documents from possibly damage that they may sustain from being continually produced in evidence.

Section 65 (f) can be read along with Sections 76, 78 and 86 which deal with certified copies of public documents, proof of other official documents and presumptions regarding certified copies of foreign judicial records respectively.

The object of Section 65 (g) is simply to expedite Court proceedings by saving time.

FOOTNOTES

232.Section 61, Indian Evidence Act, 1972
233.Section 62, Indian Evidence Act, 1972
234.Section 63, Indian Evidence Act, 1972
235.Section 64, Indian Evidence Act, 1972